MW01639773

35 Years of Painting with Light

The RIT Big Shot: Photographs & History 1987–2022

Edited by Michael Peres
Rochester Institute of Technology
School of Photographic Arts & Sciences
Published by Booksmart Studio

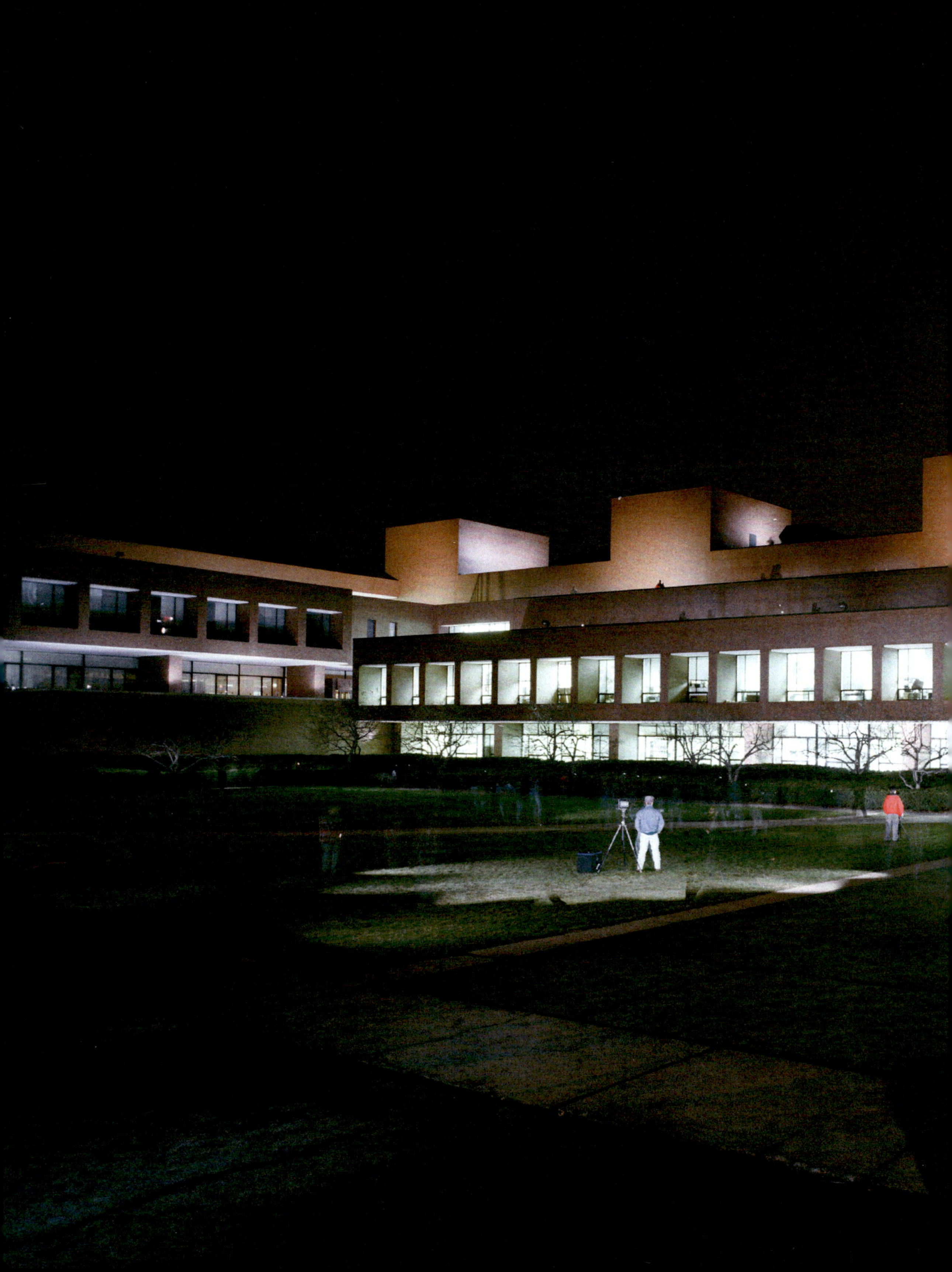

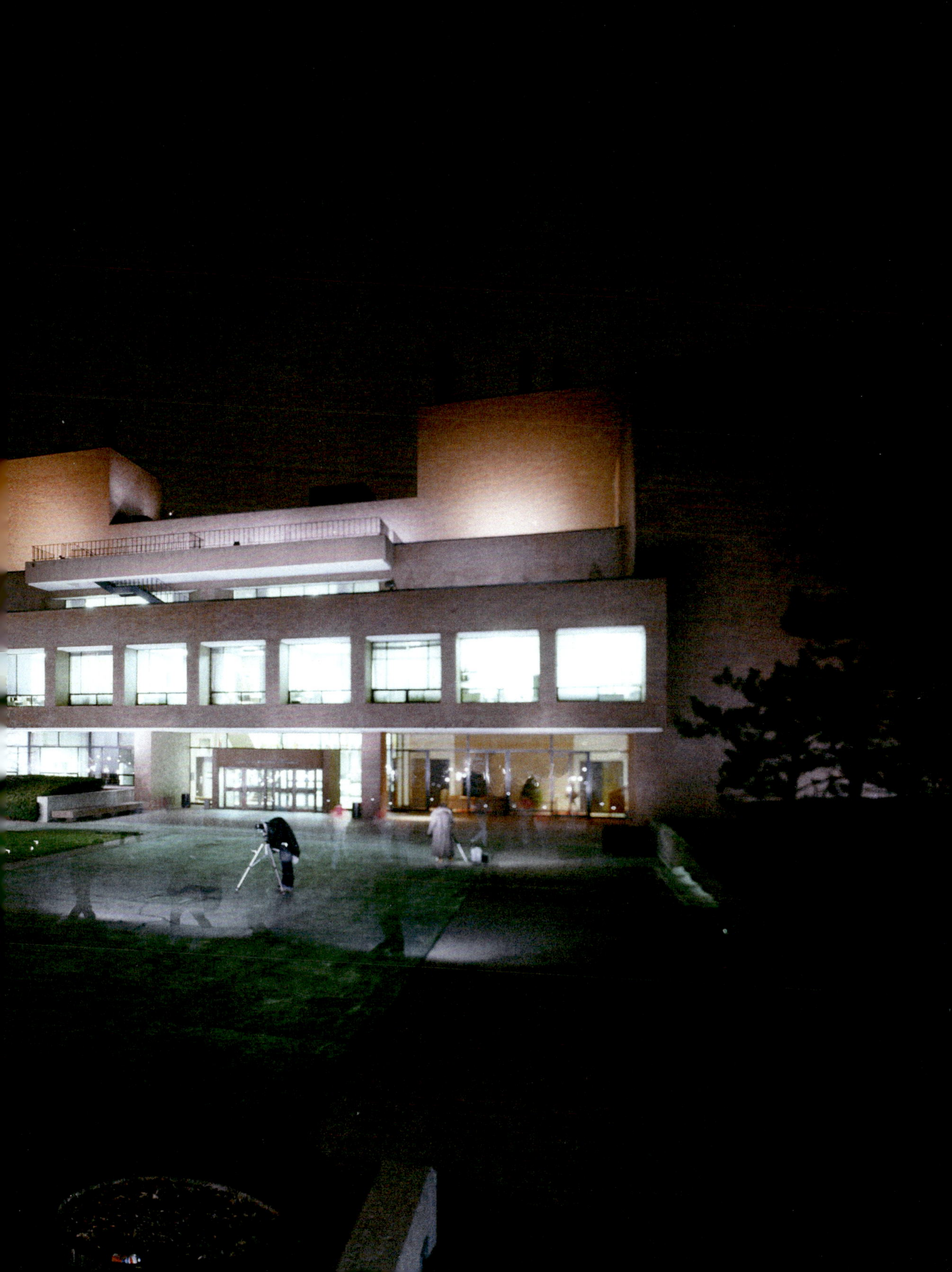

This catalog was published in conjunction with the exhibition *RIT Big Shot: Thirty-Five Years of Painting with Light*, on view at the University Gallery at Rochester Institute of Technology from August 11–October 16, 2022. The exhibition was organized by Director Wendy Marks.

Started in 1987, RIT Big Shot is a nighttime community photography project produced by the School of Photographic Arts & Sciences at Rochester Institute of Technology, Rochester, New York.

Library of Congress Control Number: 2021951469
ISBN: 978-1-939026-21-7

Printed and bound in the United States of America
National Technical Institute for the Deaf
RIT Visual Communications Studies Department
First printing August 2022

Published by Booksmart Studio, Inc.
12 Walnut Street, Rochester, NY 14611 USA
www.booksmartstudio.com

Exhibition Graphics: Avalon Peyton, PHMS '22
Catalog Design: Samantha Haedrich
Typography: Gibson, 2011 & Orpheus Pro, 2011

http://bigshot.cad.rit.edu

BIG SHOT

Thirty-Five Years of Painting with Light

The Big Shot is a nighttime community photographic project that relies on students and volunteers to solve lighting challenges using simple hand-held lighting equipment and an extended camera exposure of a pre-determined view.

The Big Shot is a signature RIT event, traveling to significant national and international locations.

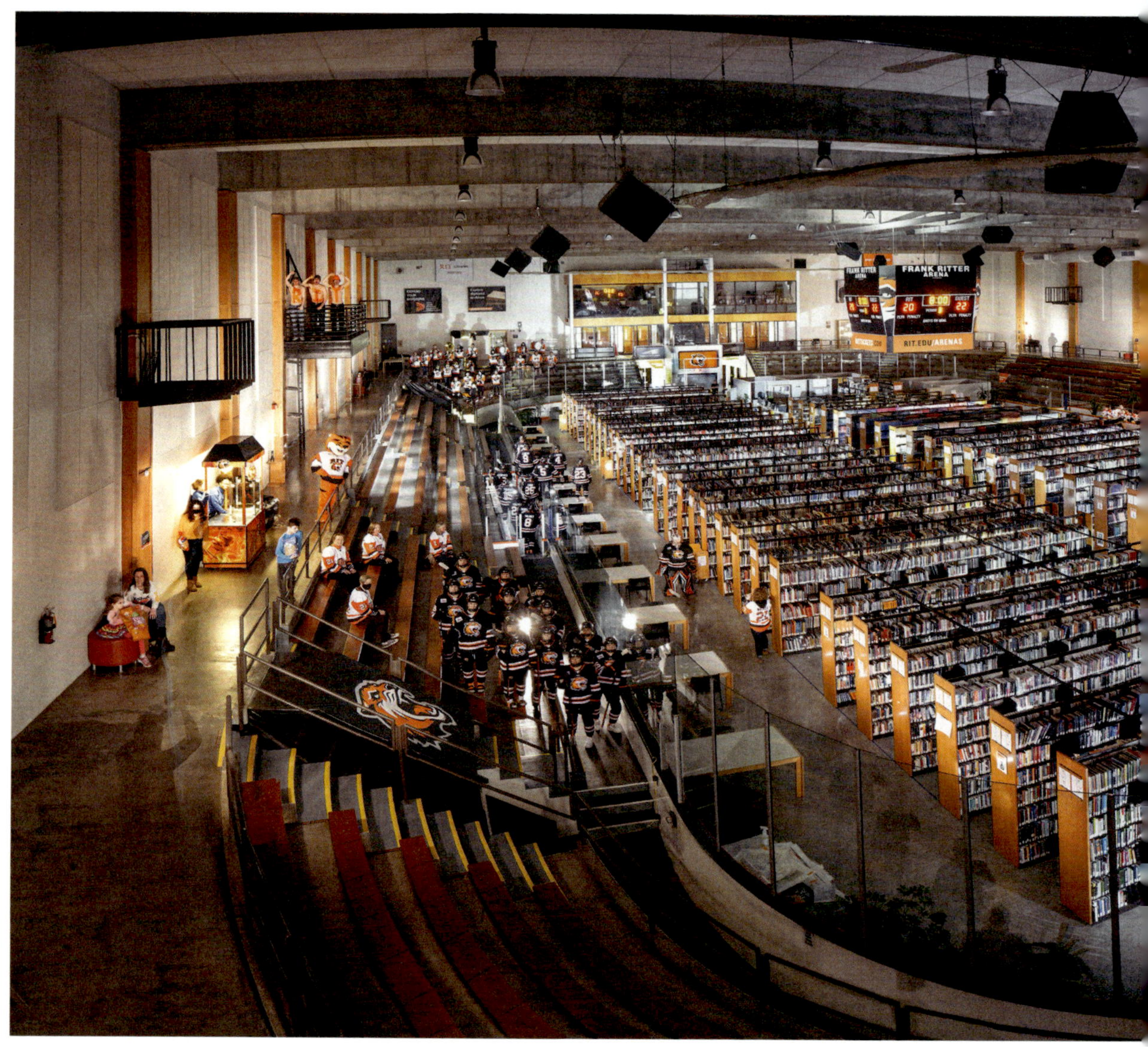
FRANK RITTER ARENA
RIT.EDU/ARENAS

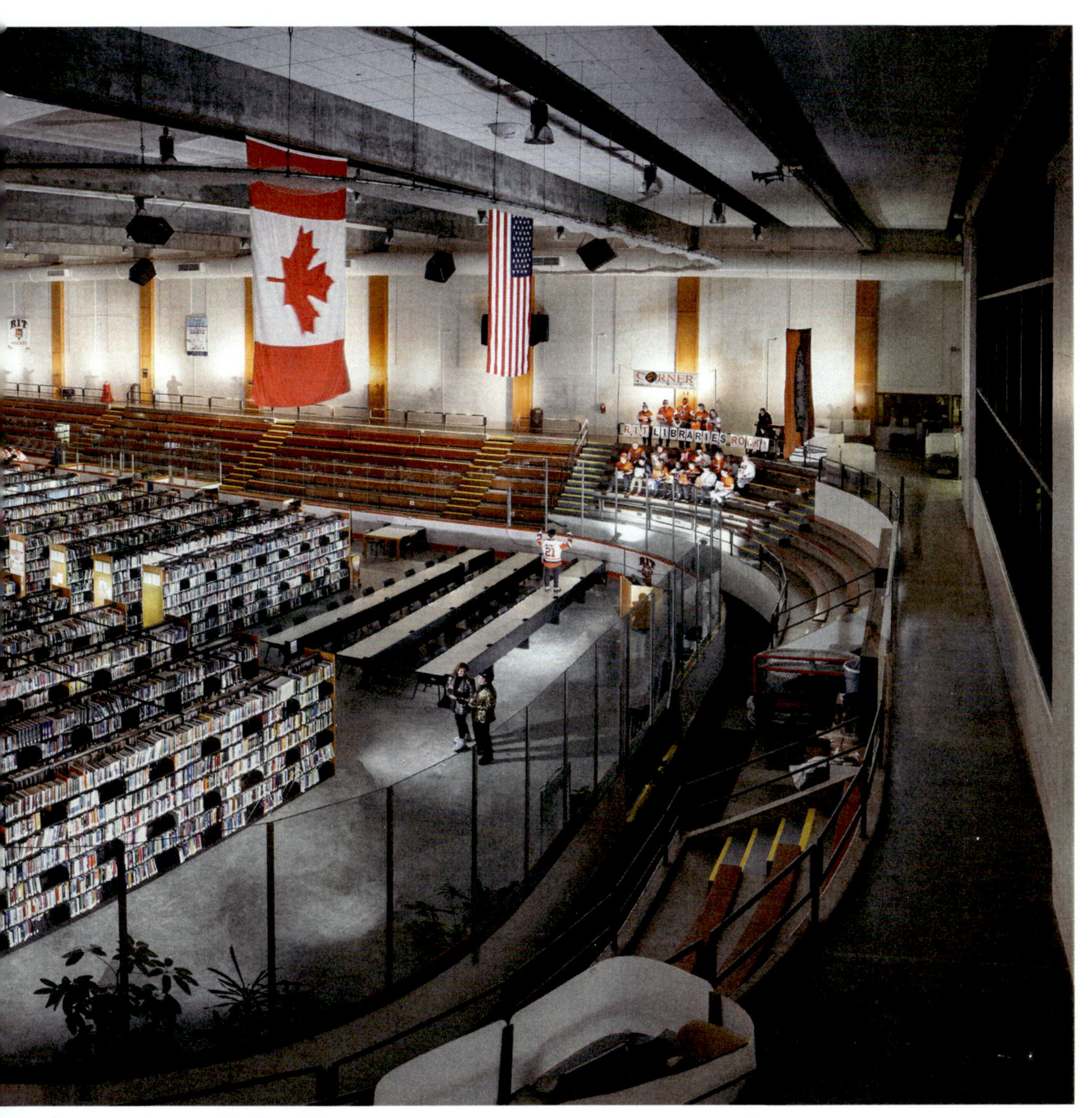

Wallace on Ice, RIT Campus, Rochester, NY

2022

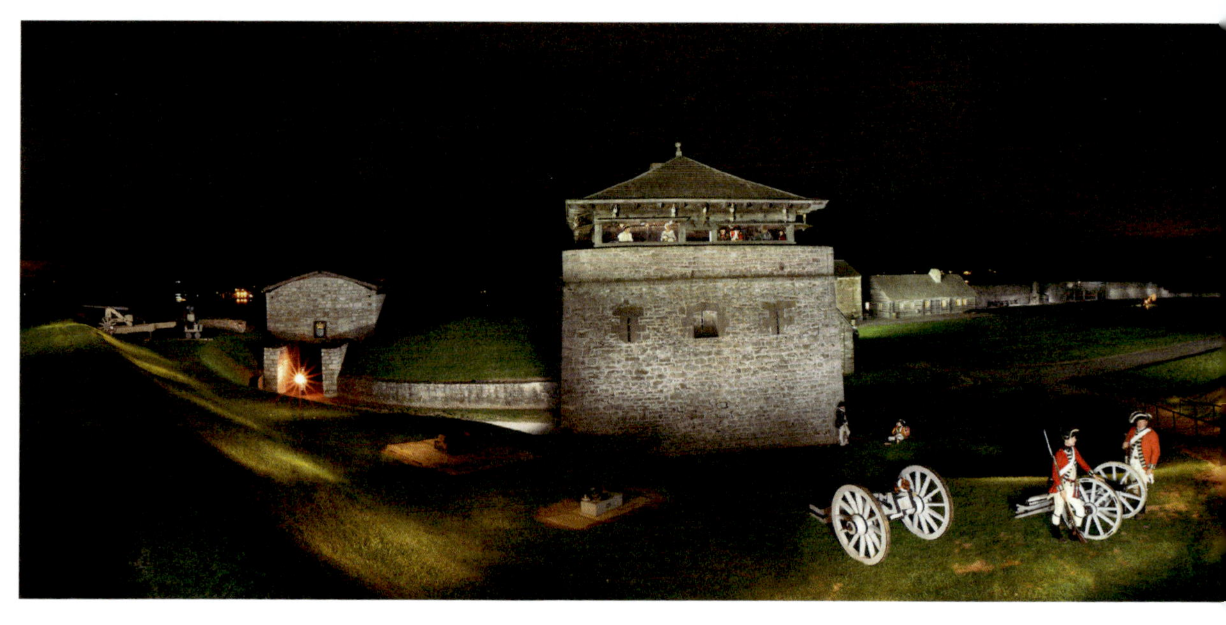

BIG SHOT NO. 33

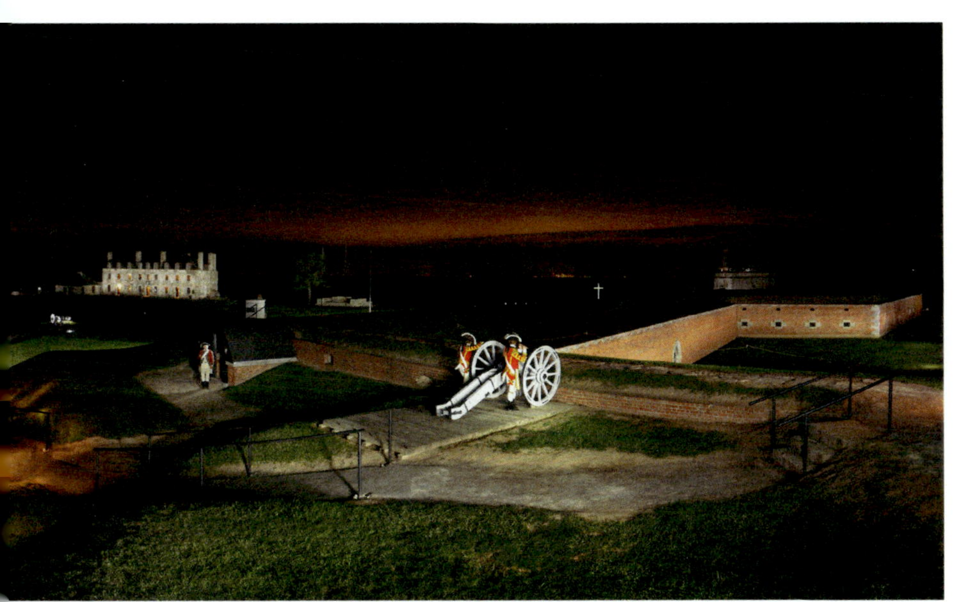

Old Fort Niagara, Niagara State Park, Porter, NY

2018

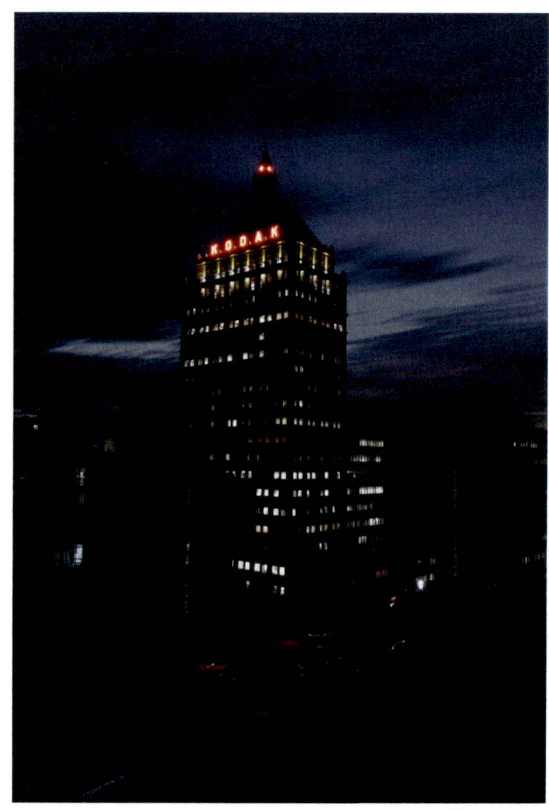

Above: before painting with light. Right: Big Shot No. 32 which took place September 18, 2016 at 8:18pm. Exposure: 60 sec. at *f*/14 ISO 50

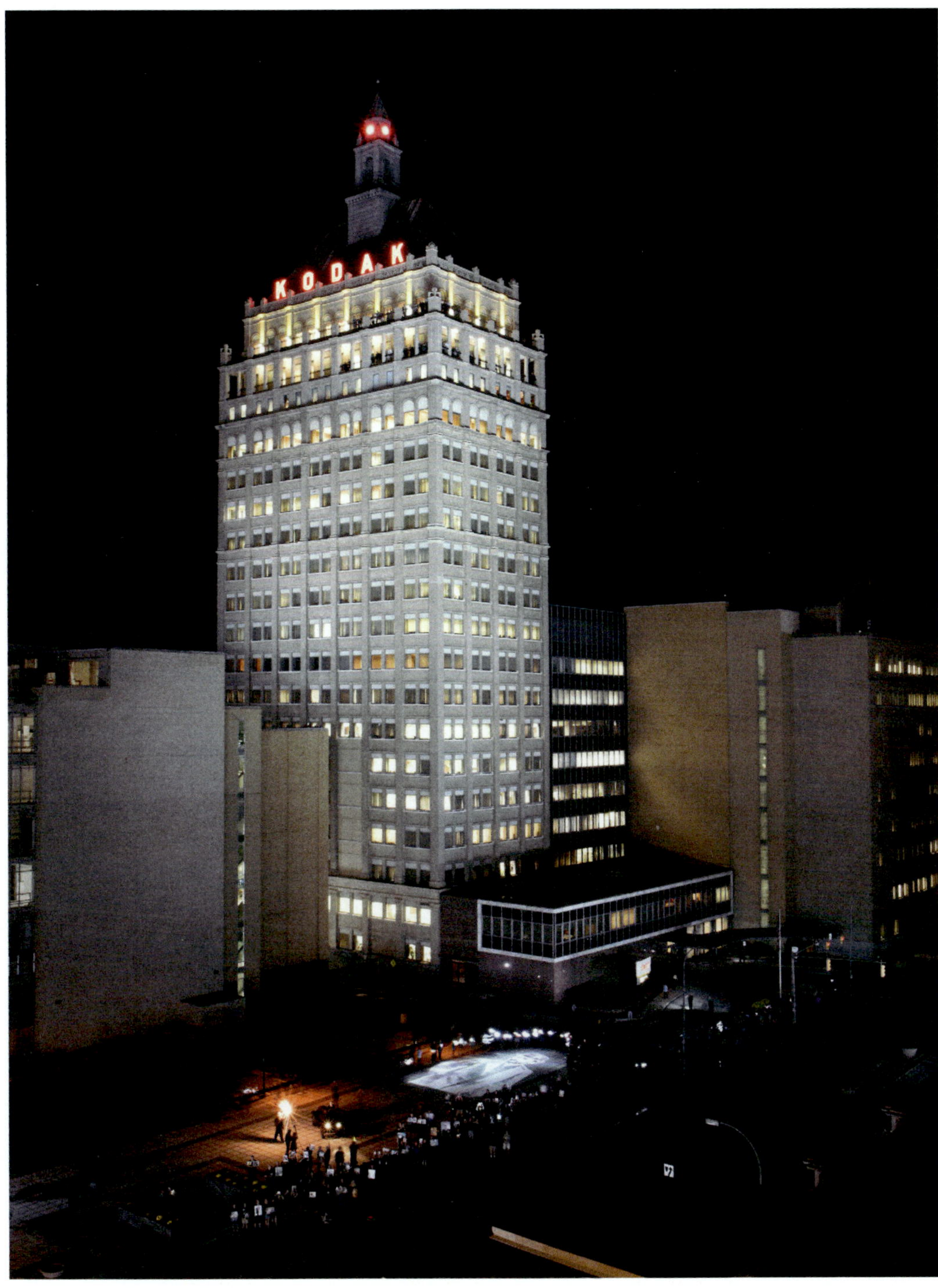
KODAK

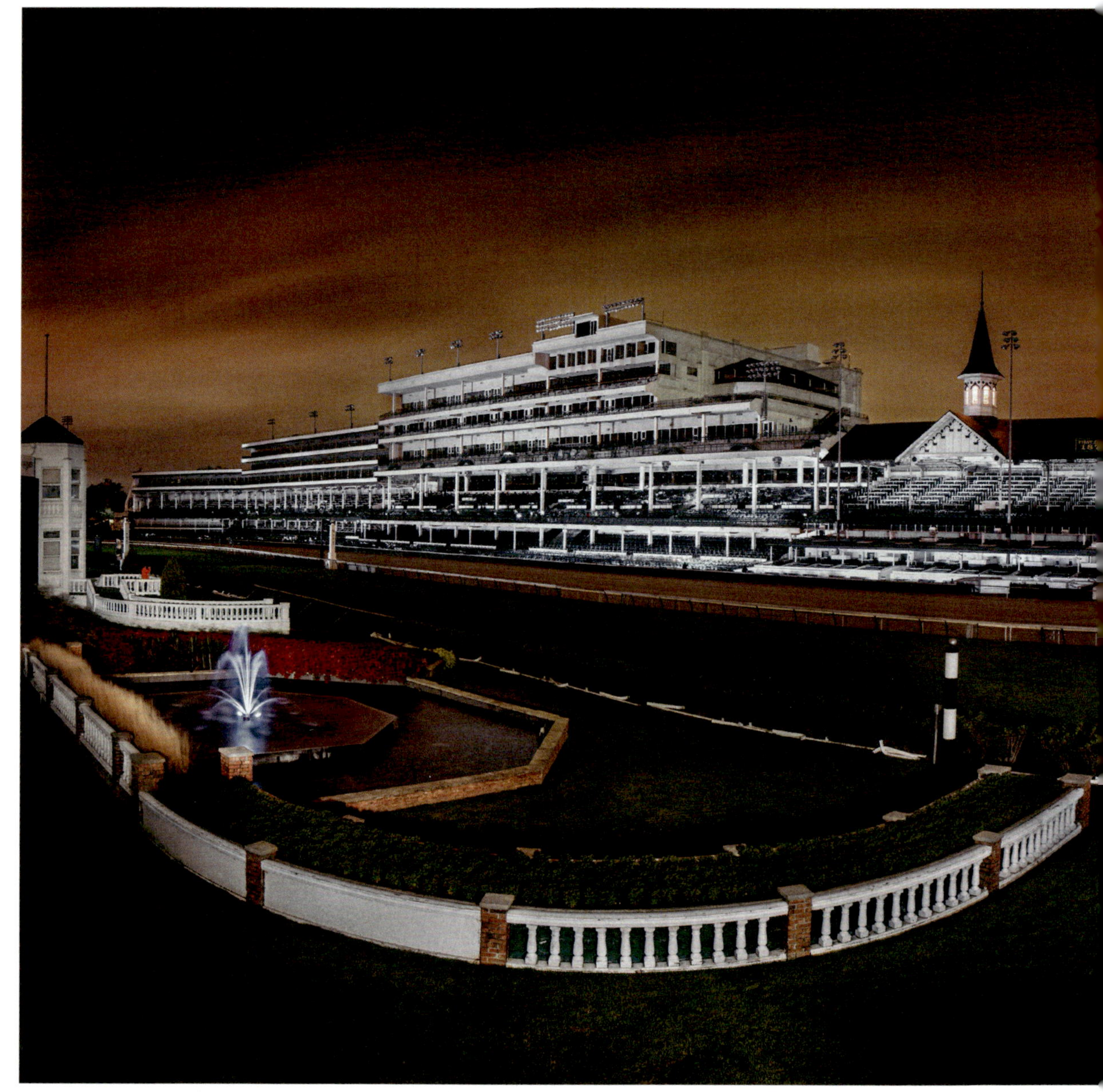

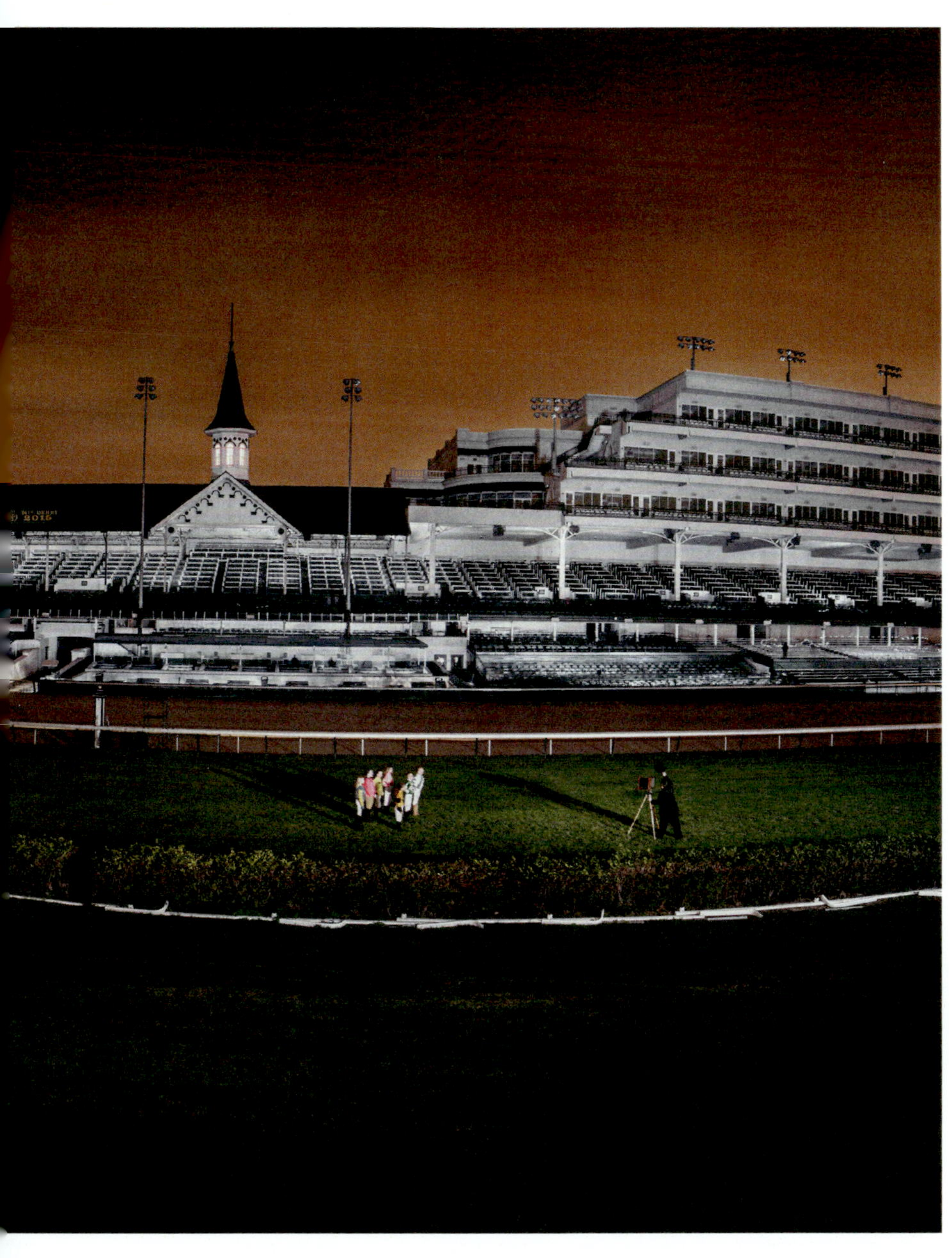

Churchill Downs, Louisville, KY

2015

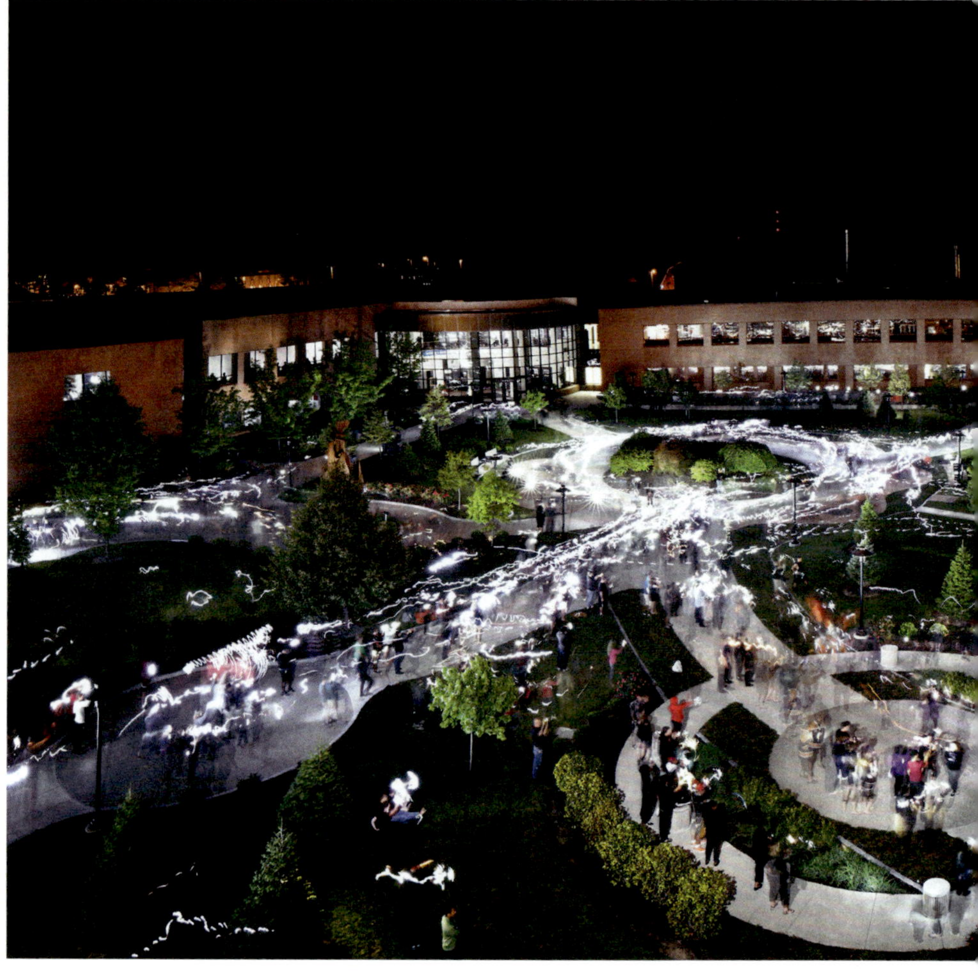

Golisano Institute for Sustainability, Louise M. Slaughter Building and Quad, RIT Campus, Rochester, NY

2014

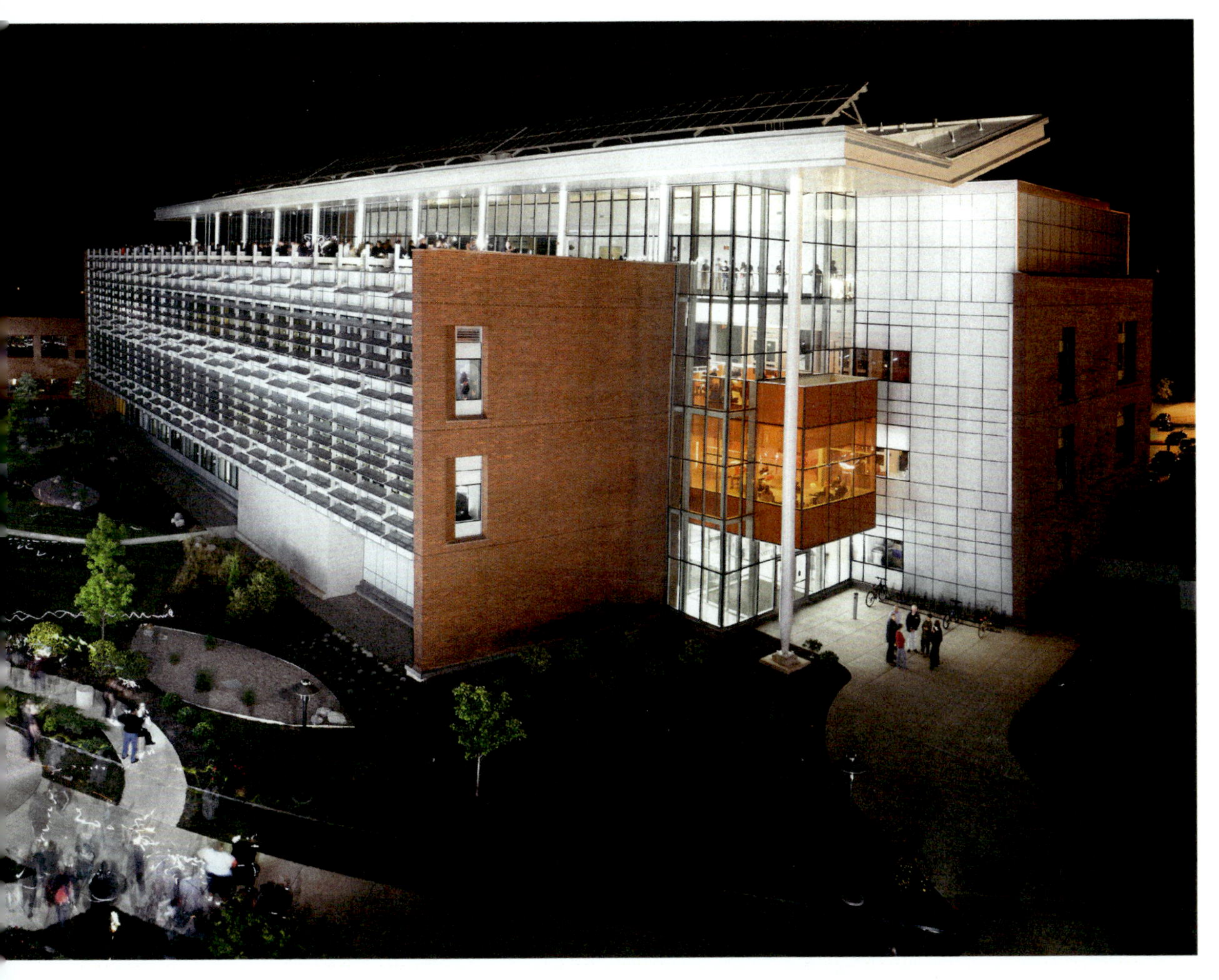

BIG SHOT NO. 30

BIG SHOT NO. 29

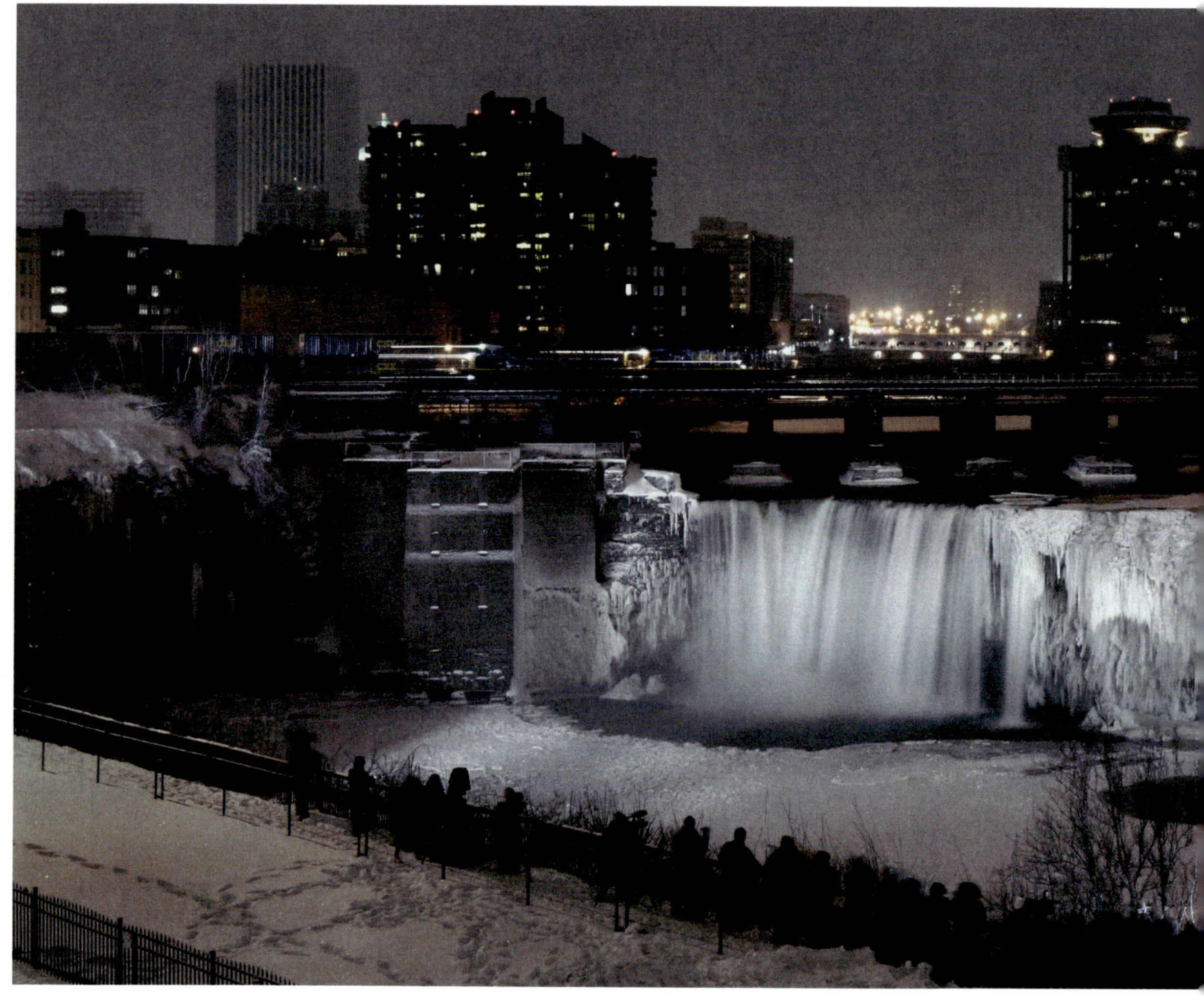

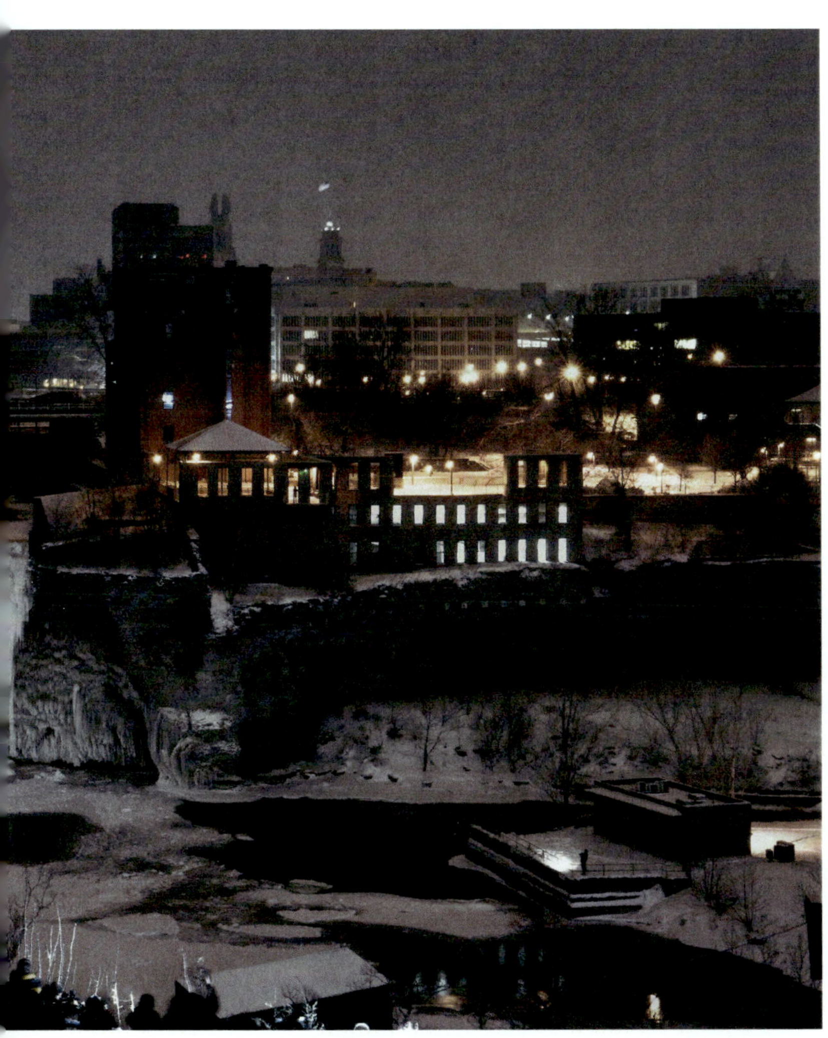

High Falls, Rochester, NY

2014

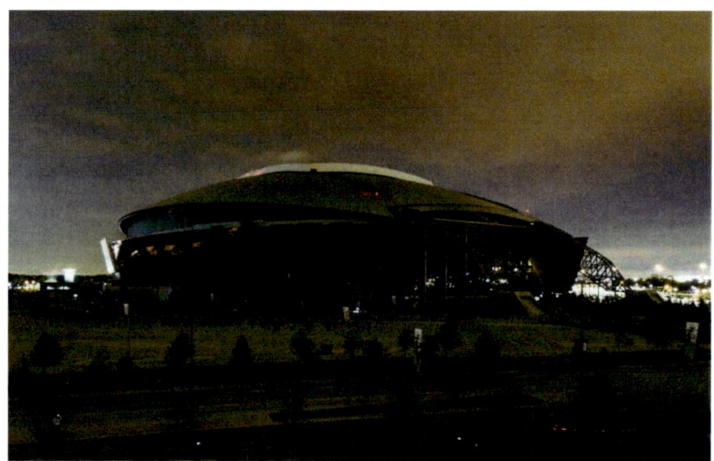

Above: before painting with light. Right: Big Shot No. 28 which took place March 23, 2013 at 9:05pm. Exposure: 30 sec. at *f*/16

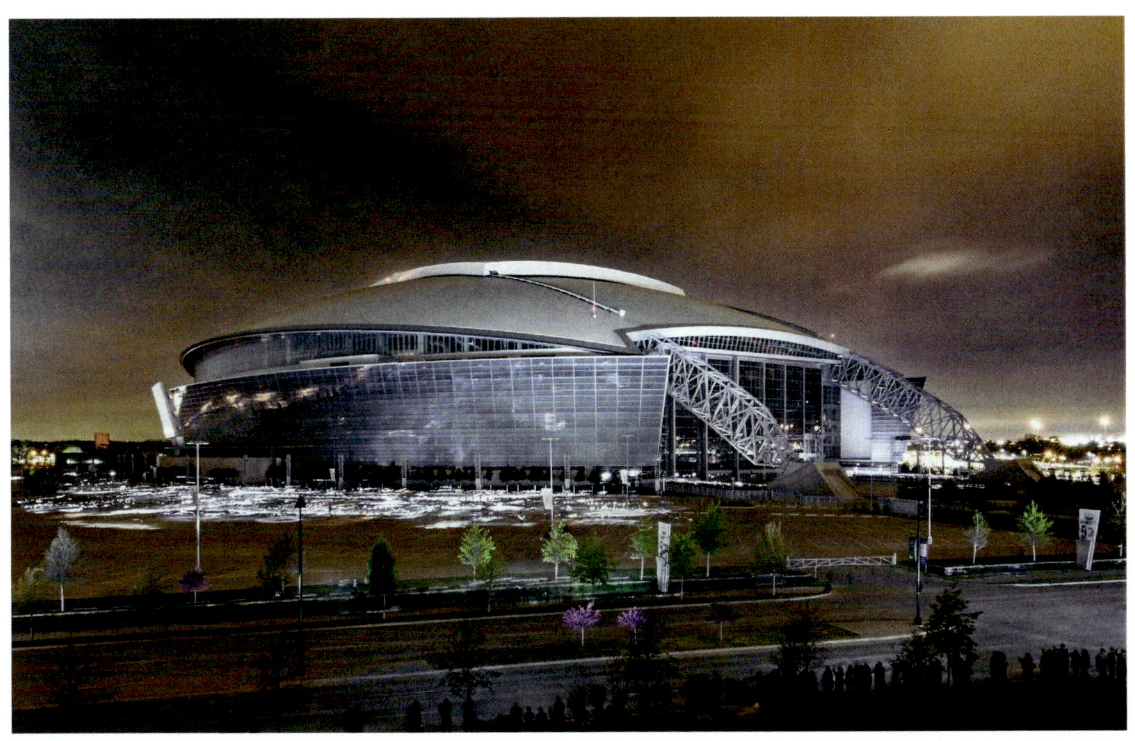

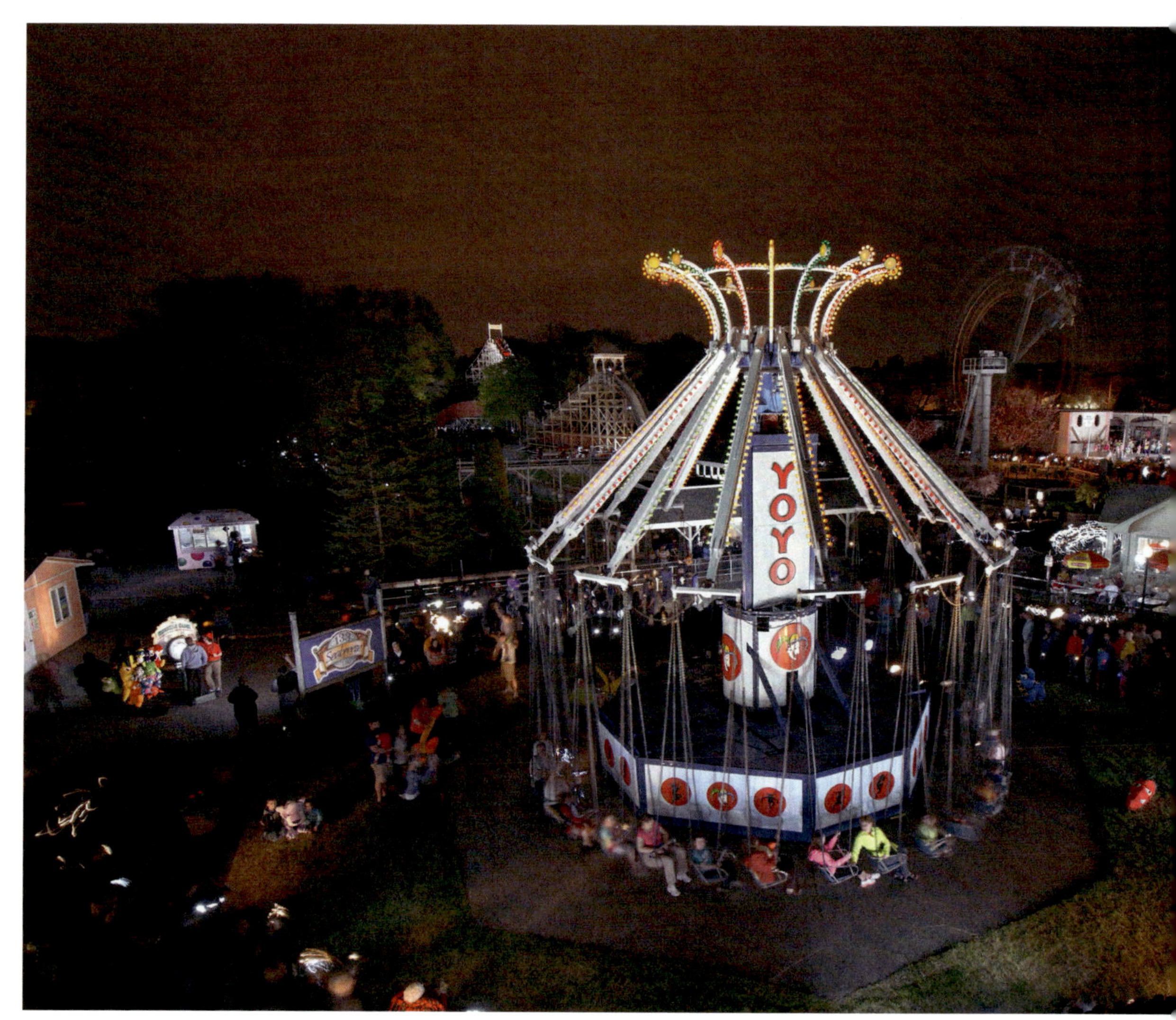
YOYO

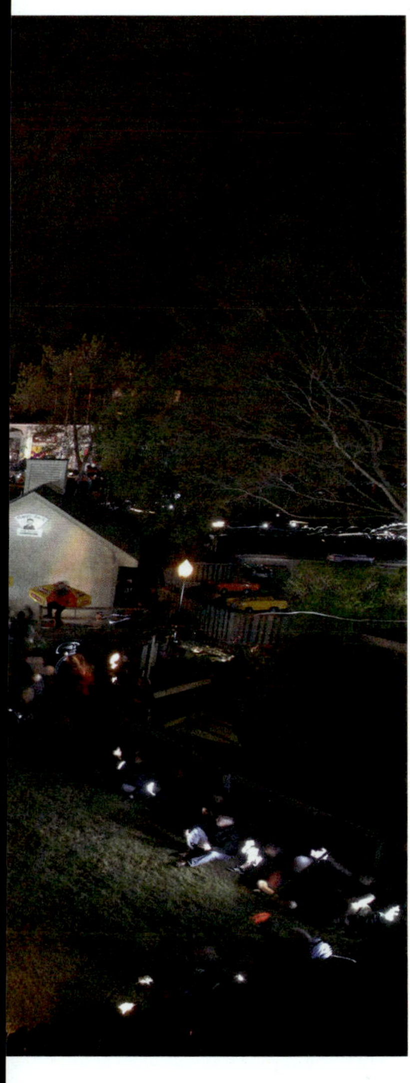

BIG SHOT NO. 27

Seabreeze Amusement Park, Rochester, NY

2012

The Strong National Museum of Play, Rochester, NY

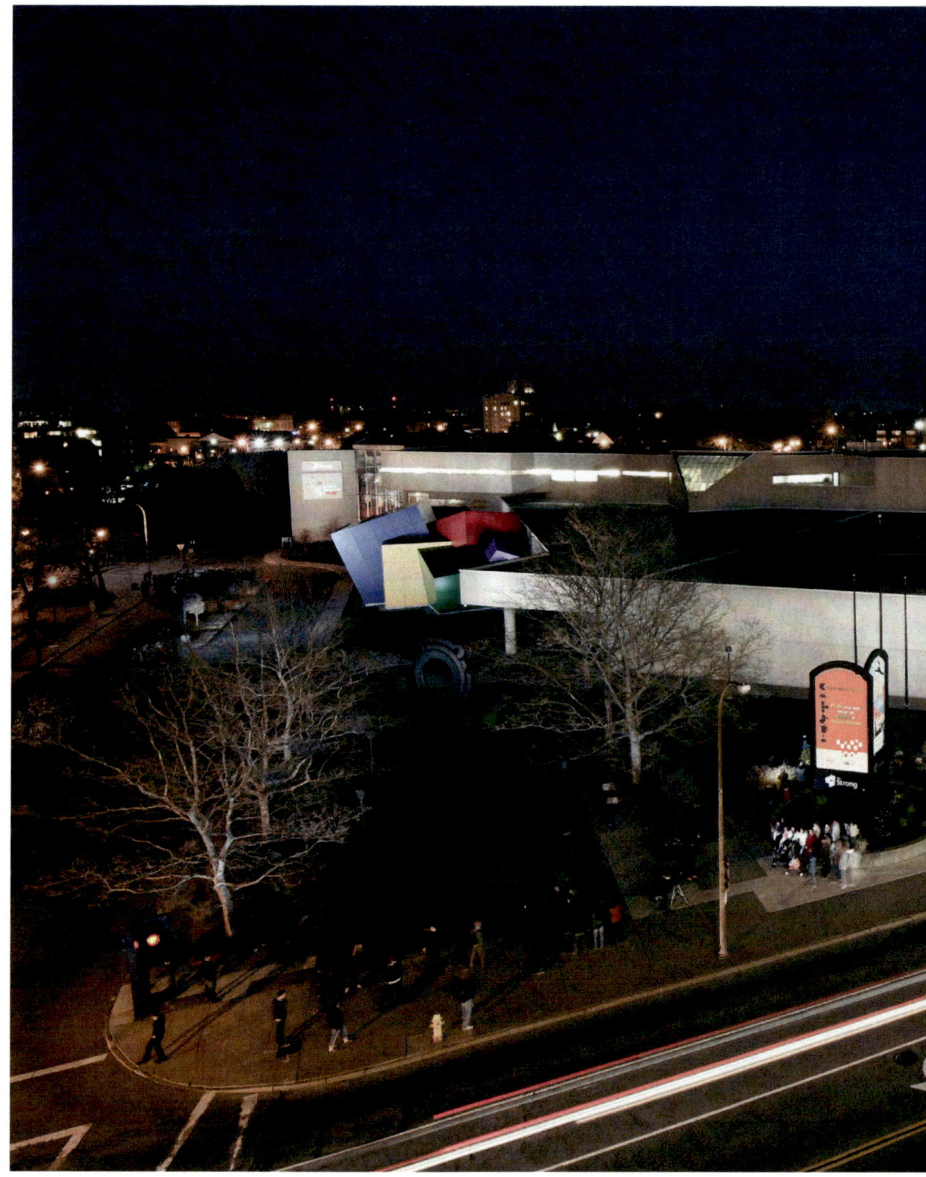

2011

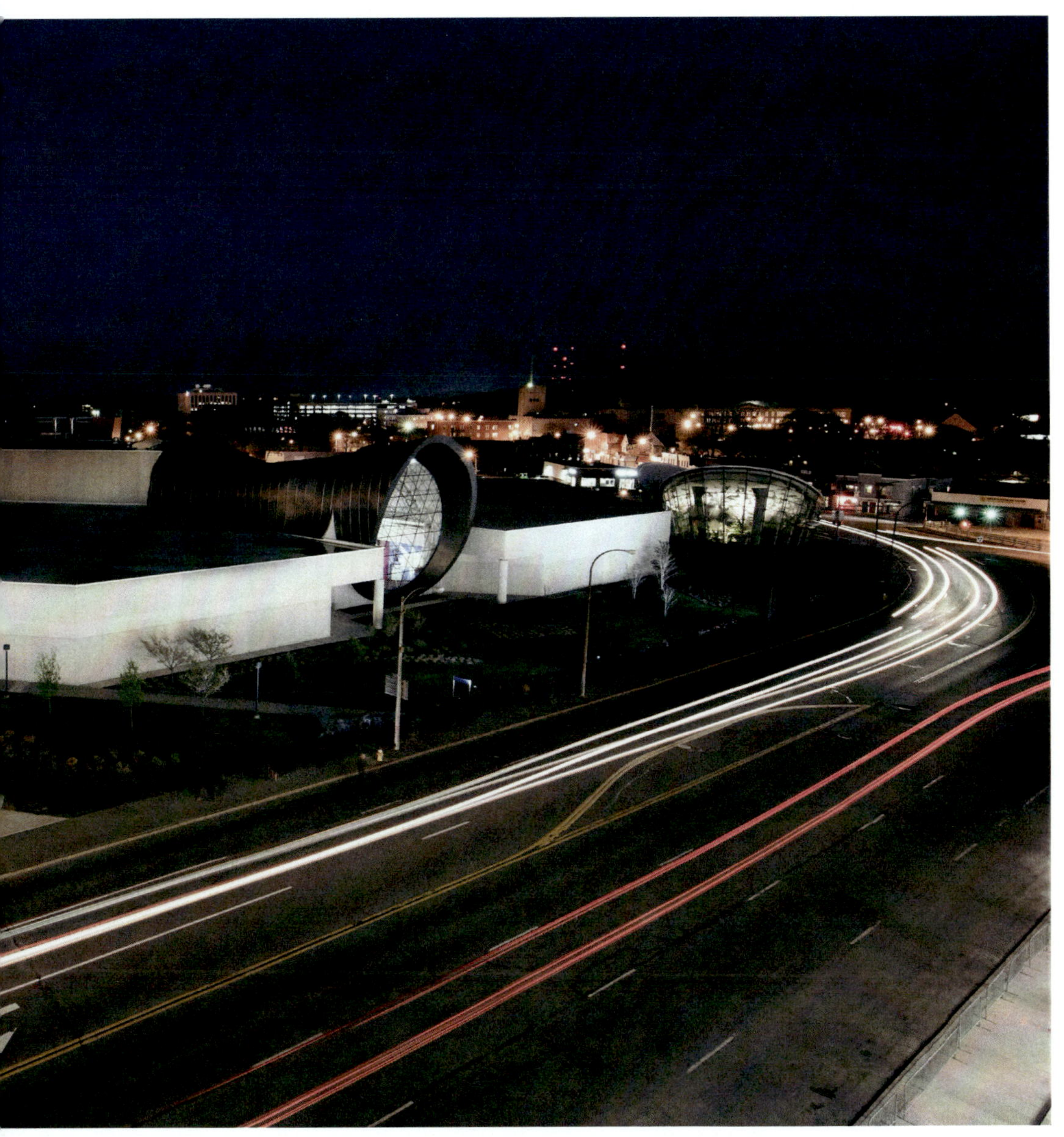

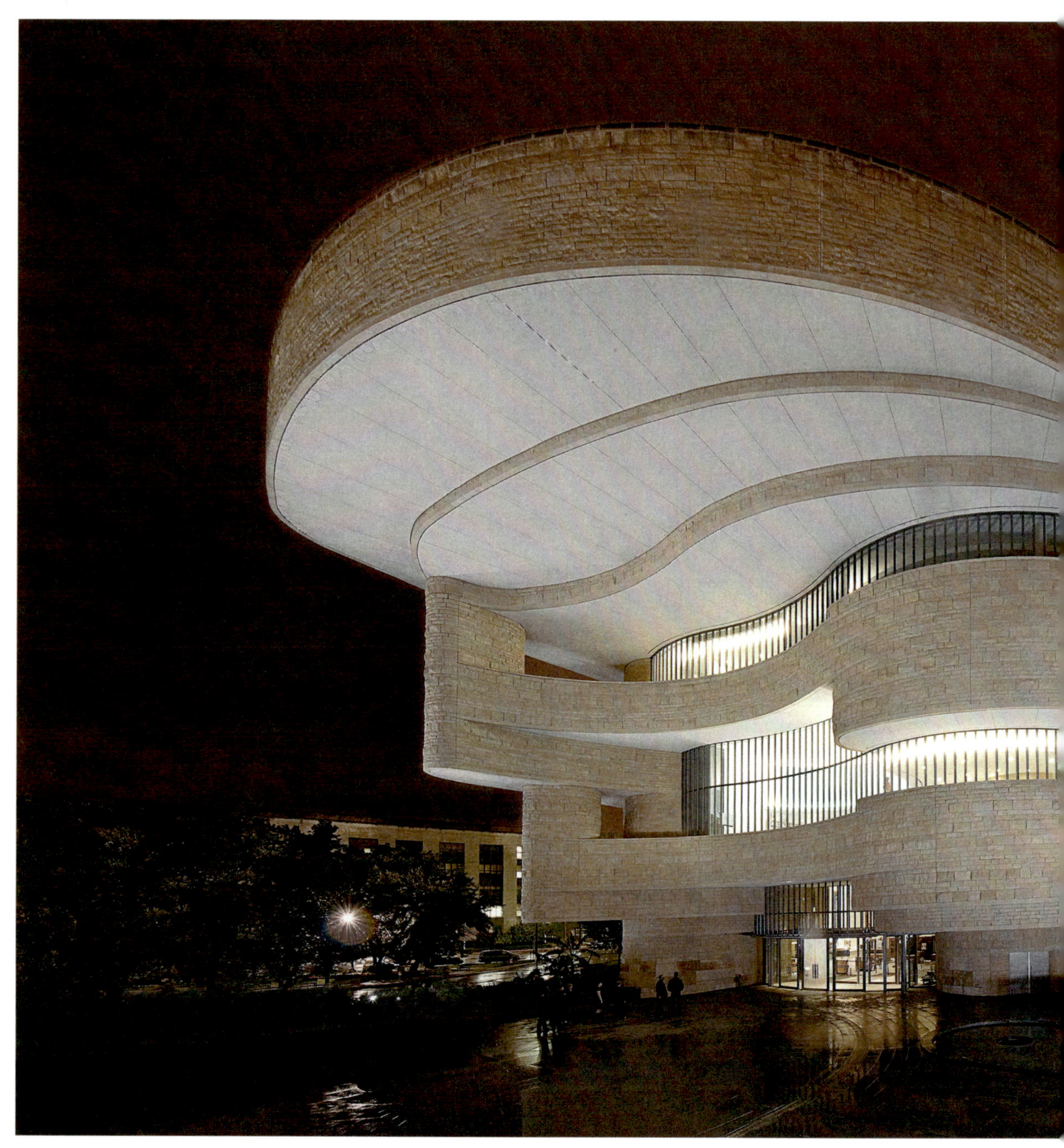

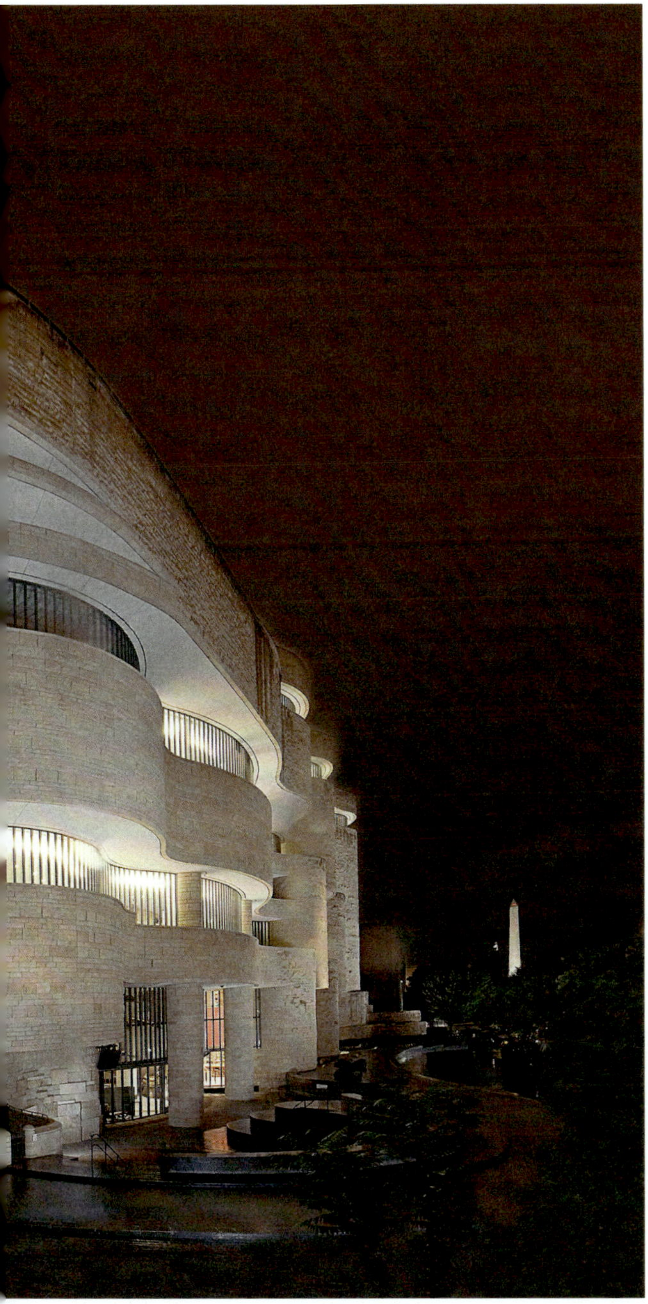

BIG SHOT NO. 25

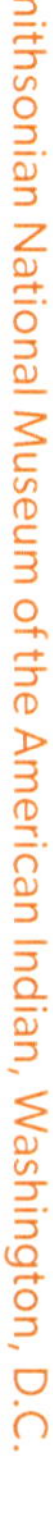

2009

Above: before painting with light. Right: Big Shot No. 24 which took place May 8, 2008 at 8:50pm. Exposure: 30 sec. at *f*/16.

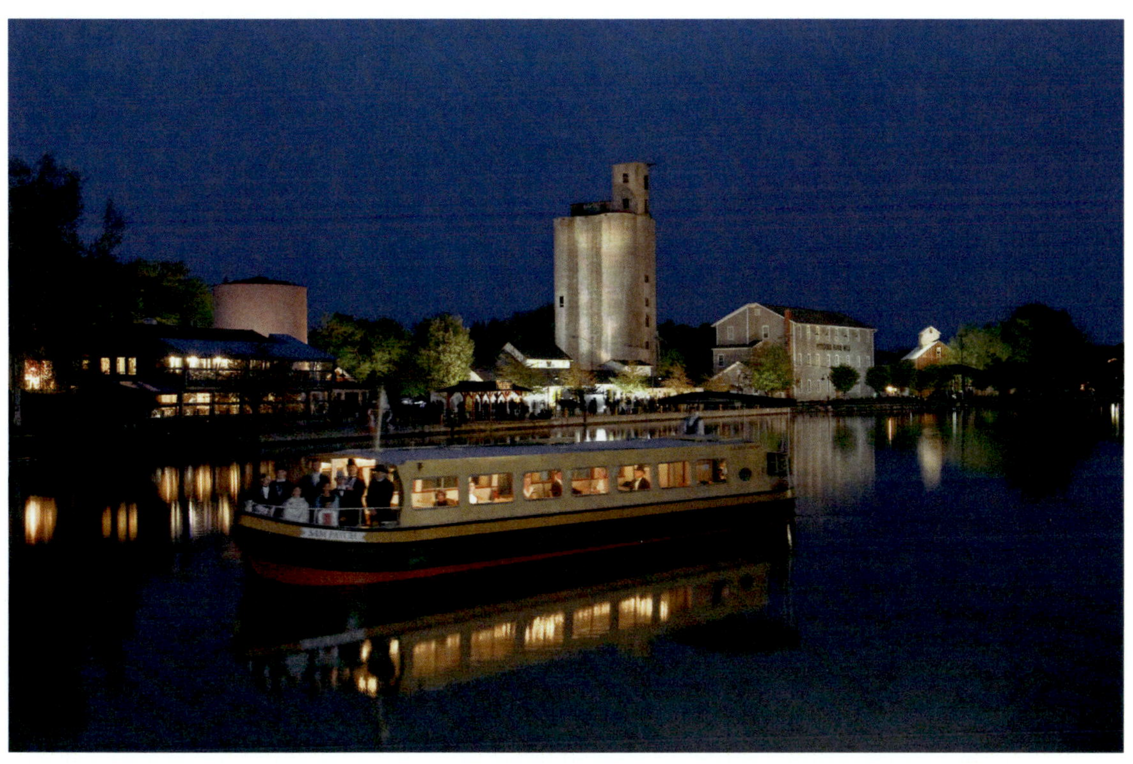

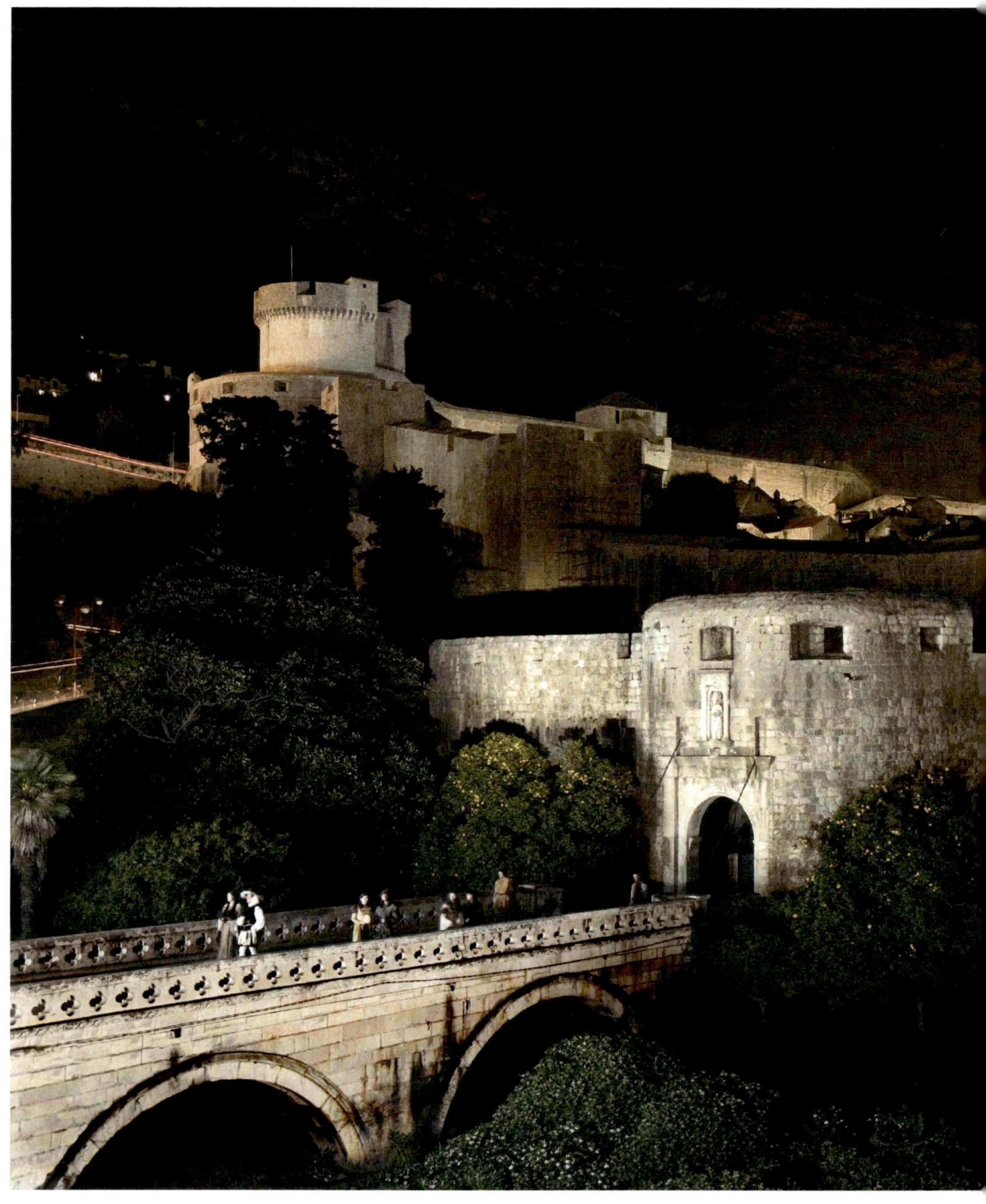

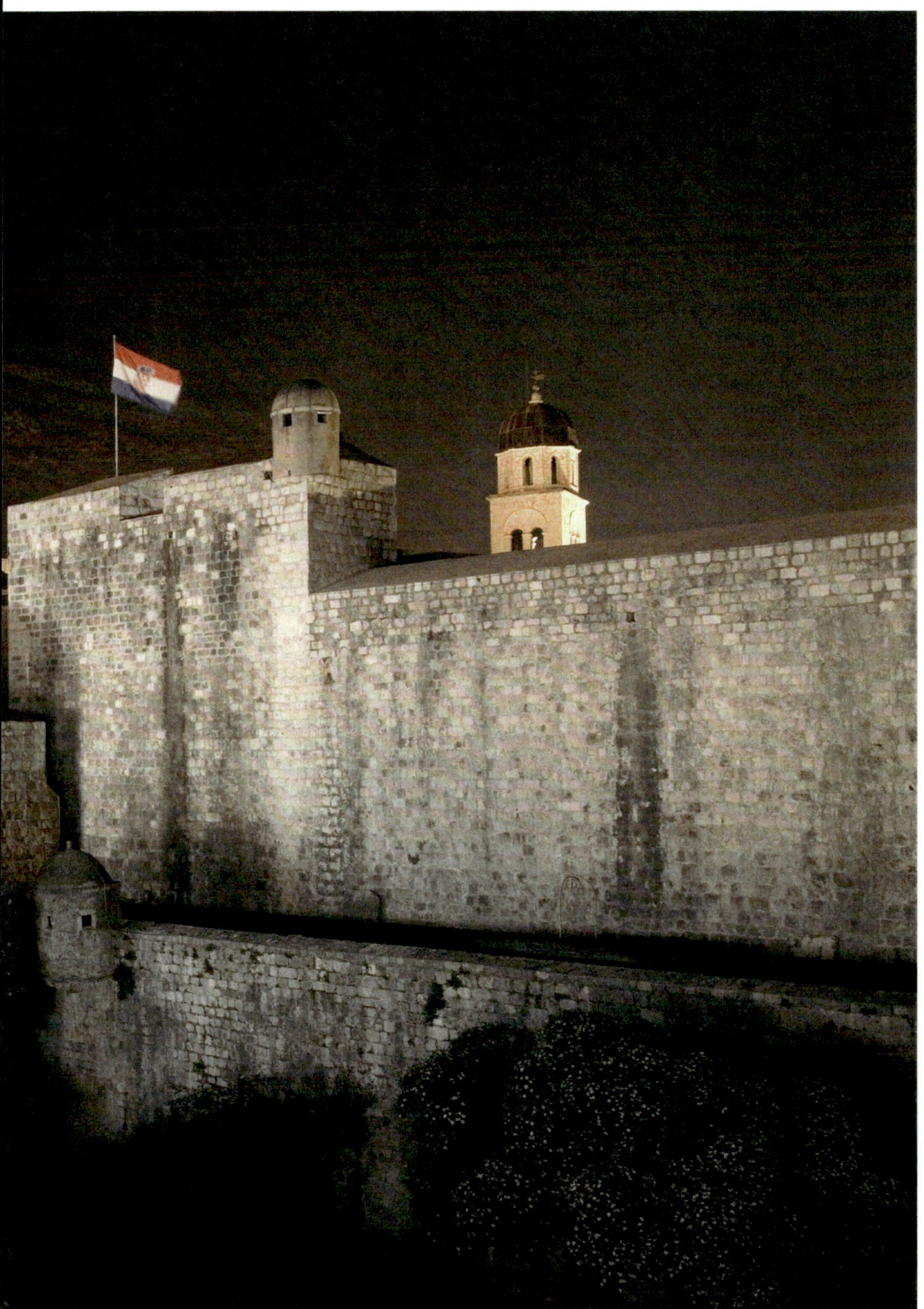

The Pile Gate in Dubrovnik's Old Town, Dubrovnik, Croatia

2007

Memorial Art Gallery of the University of Rochester, Rochester, NY

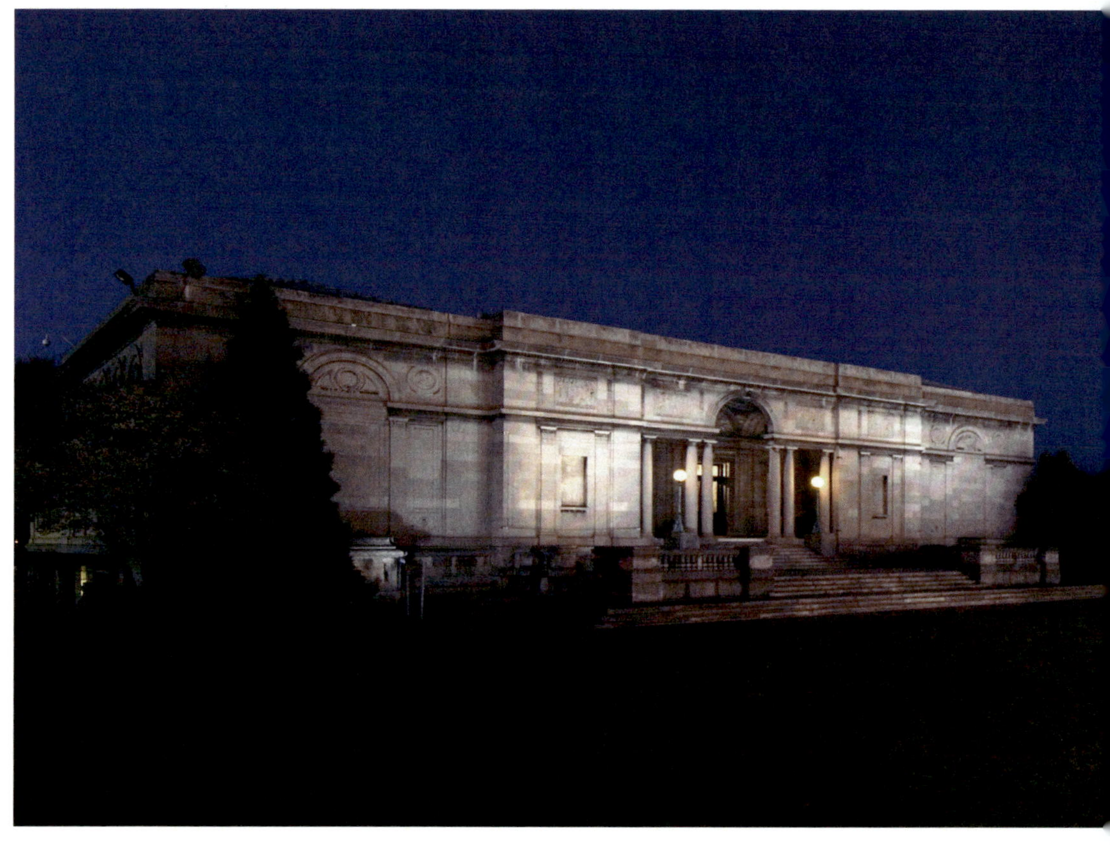

2006

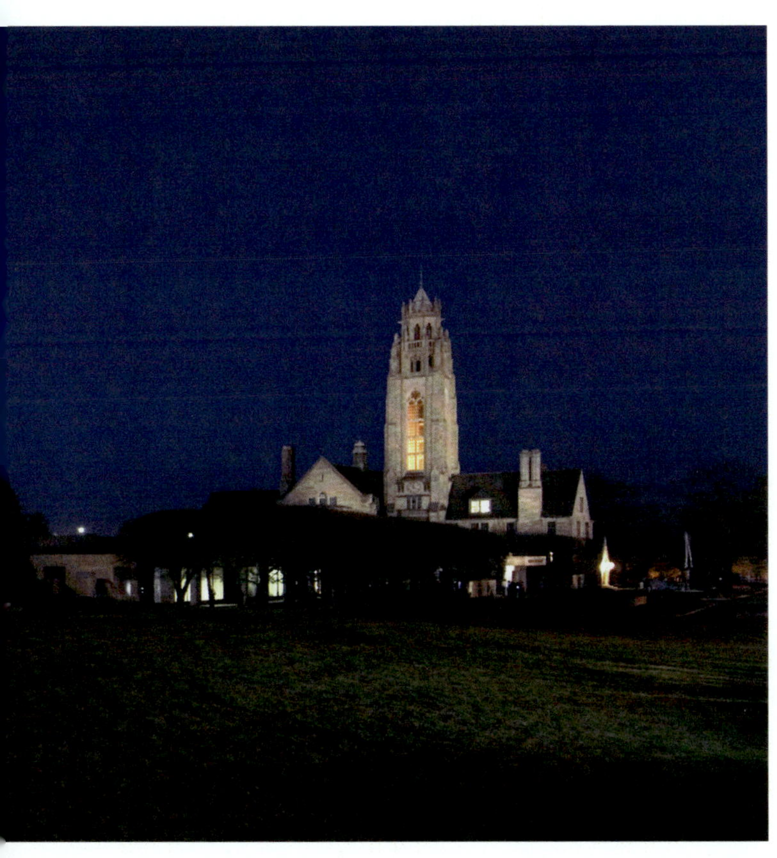

BIG SHOT NO. 22

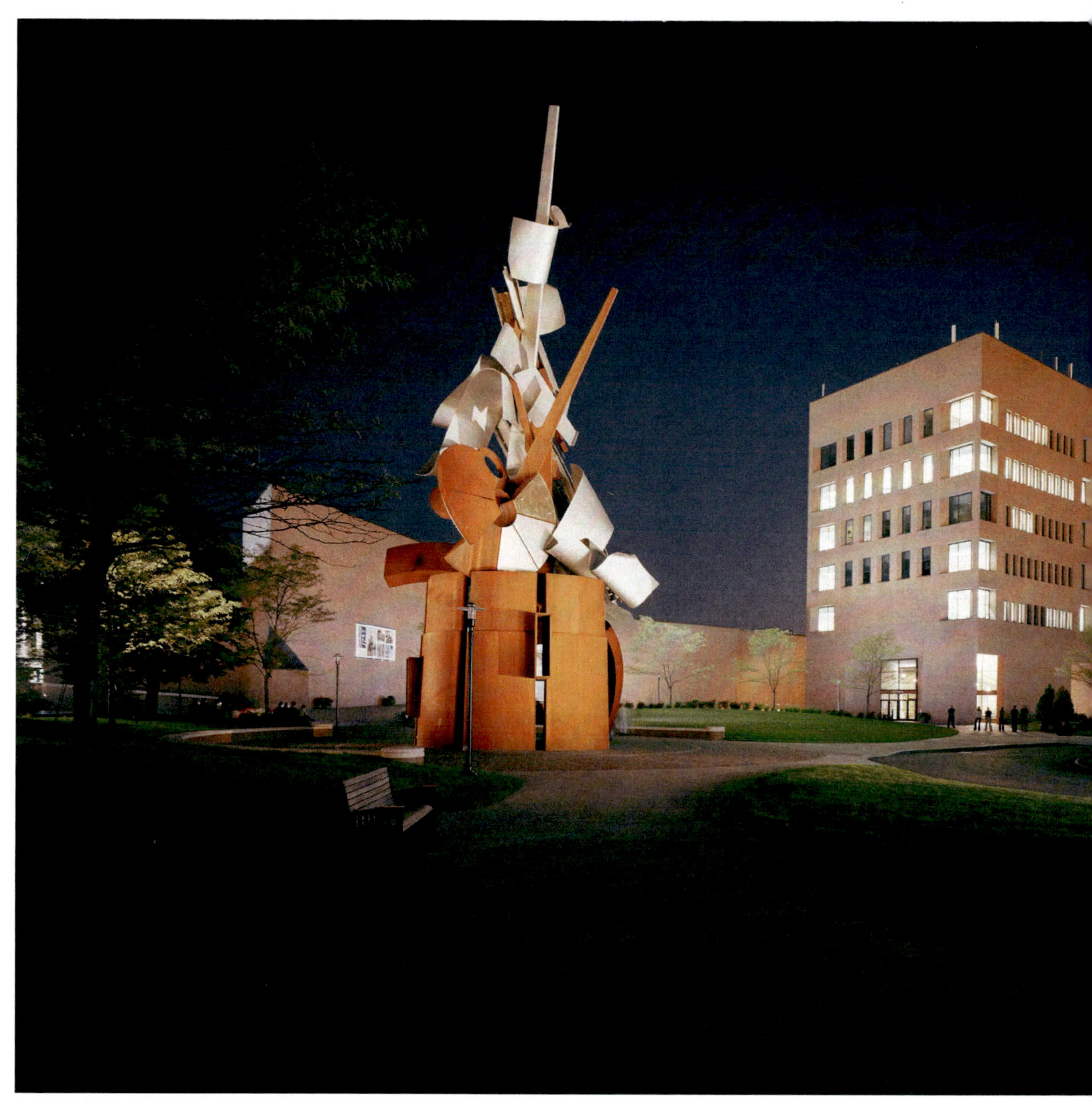

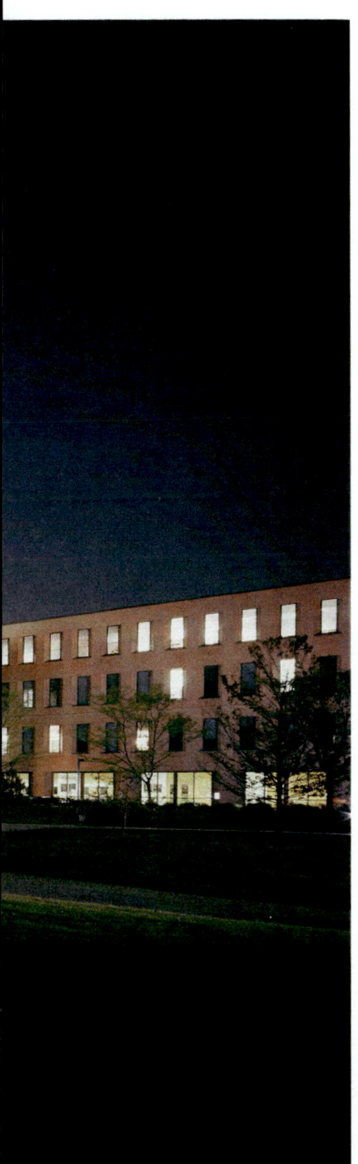

BIG SHOT NO. 21

Sentinel Sculpture and Administration Circle, RIT Campus, Rochester, NY

2004

The Royal Palace, Stockholm, Sweden

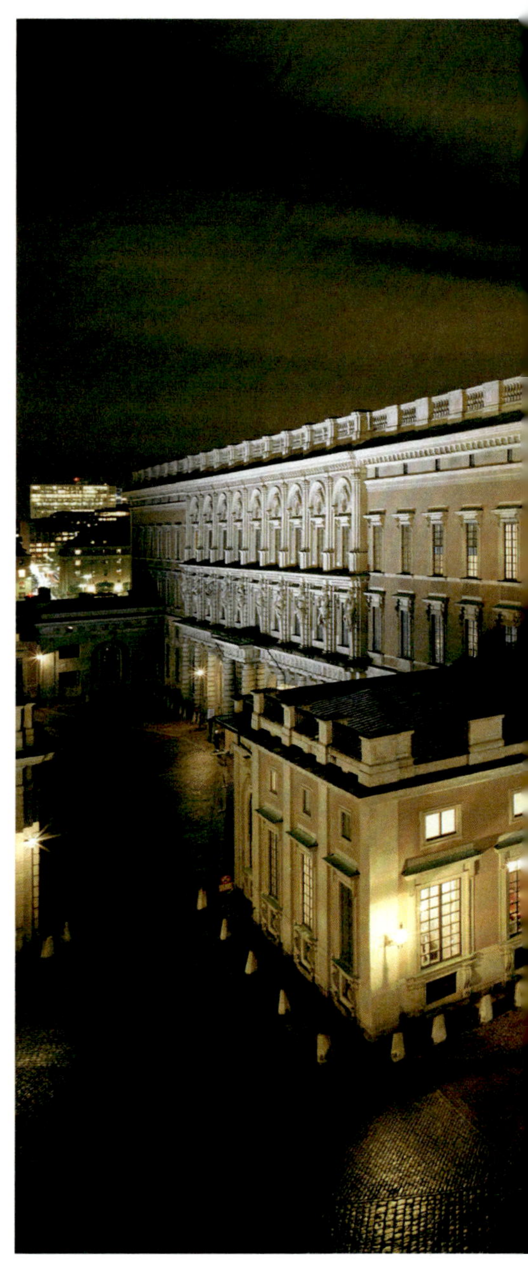

2003

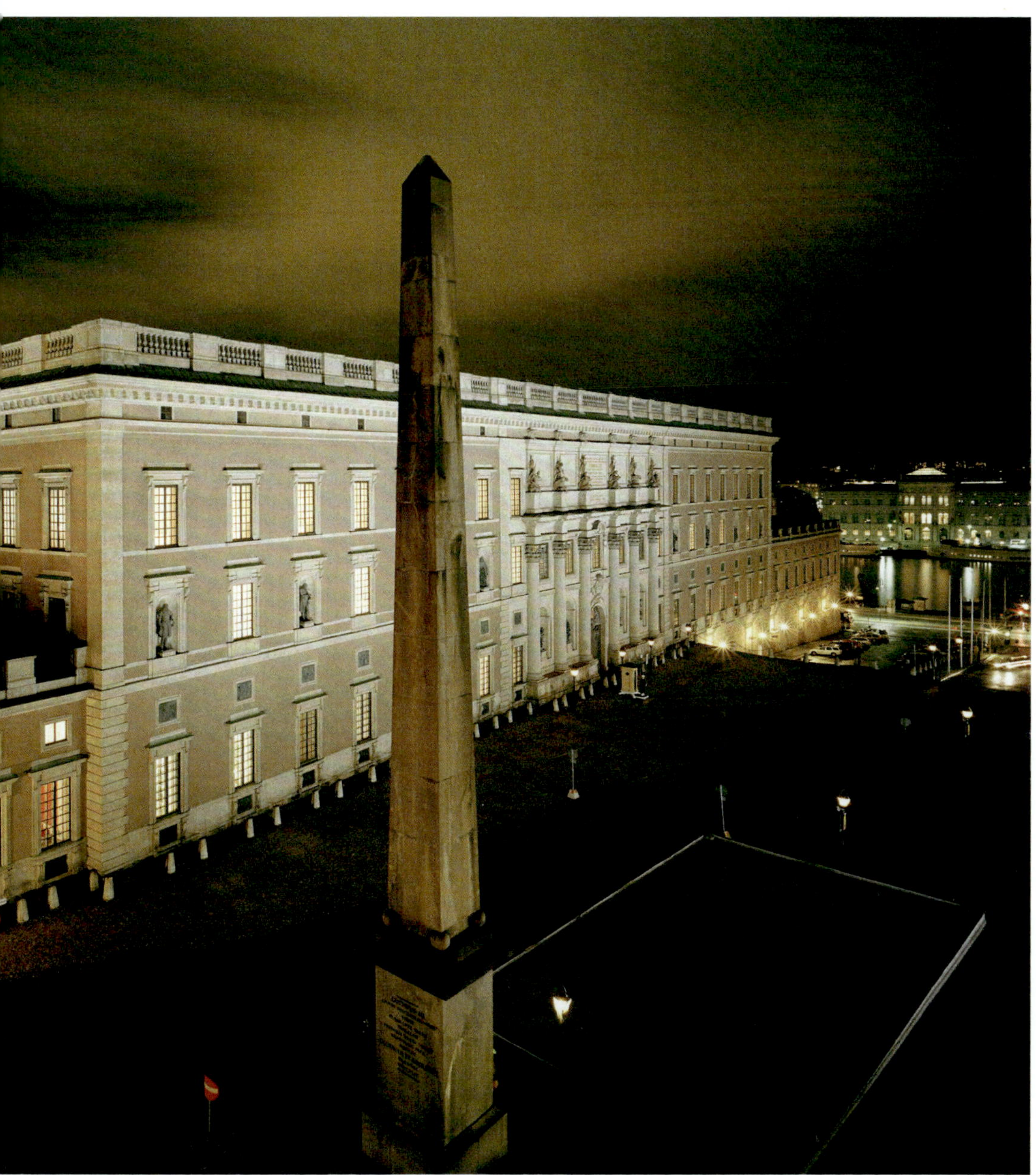

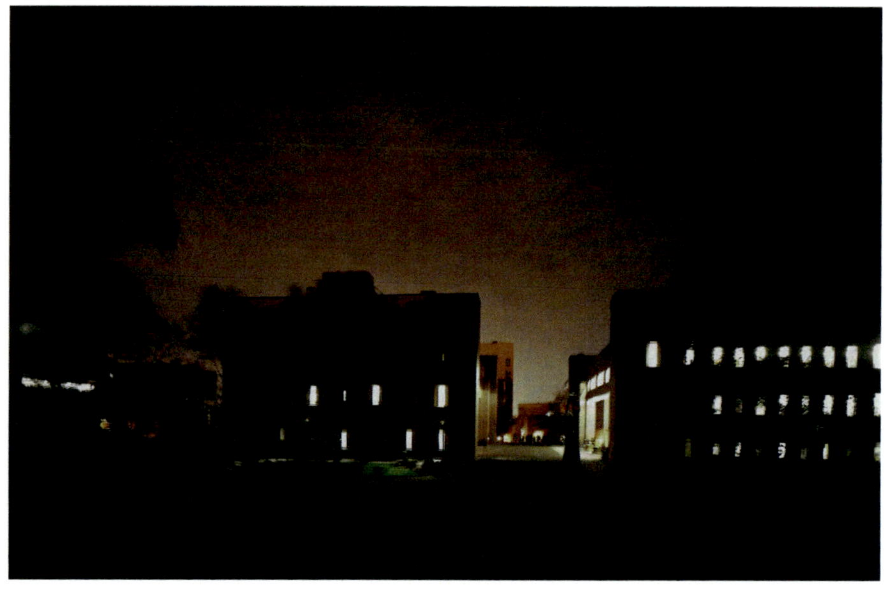

Above: before painting with light. Right: Big Shot No. 19 which took place November 7, 2002 at 11:00pm. Exposure: 1.5 min. at *f*/11.

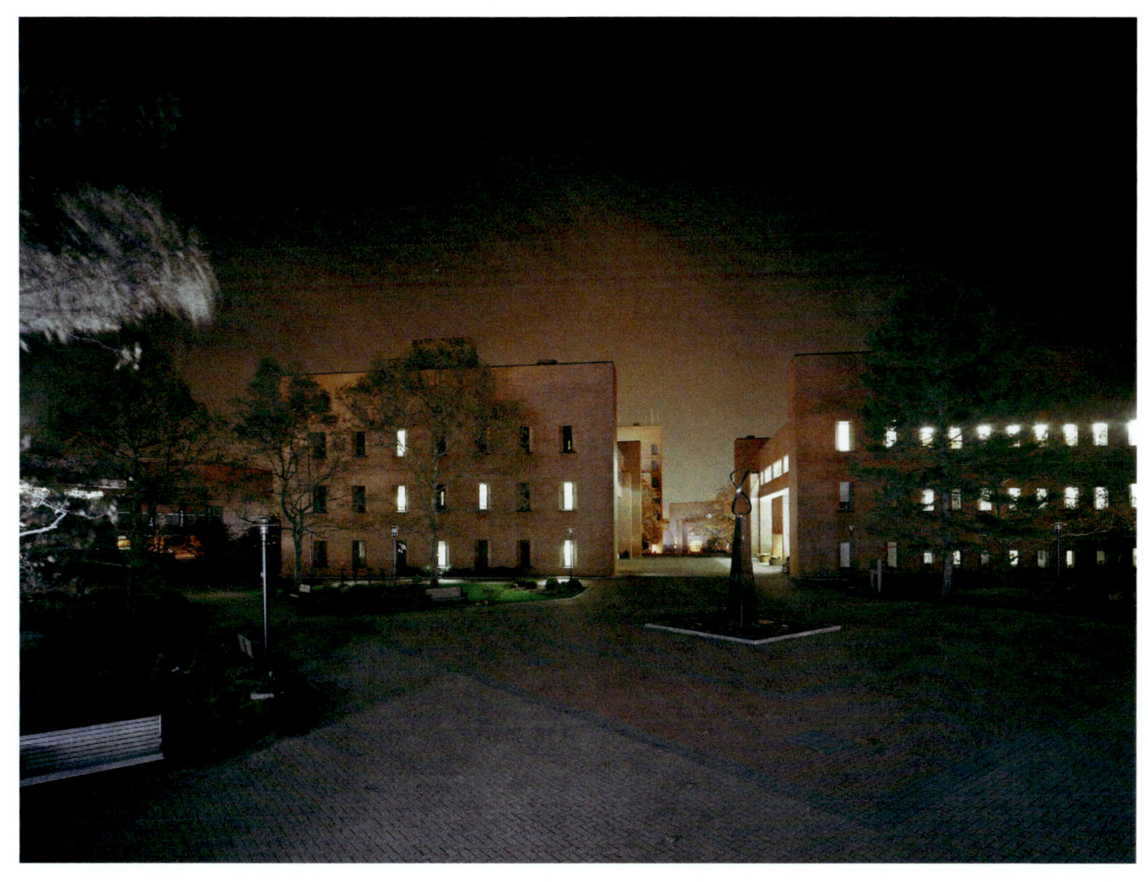

BIG SHOT NO. 19

BIG SHOT NO. 18

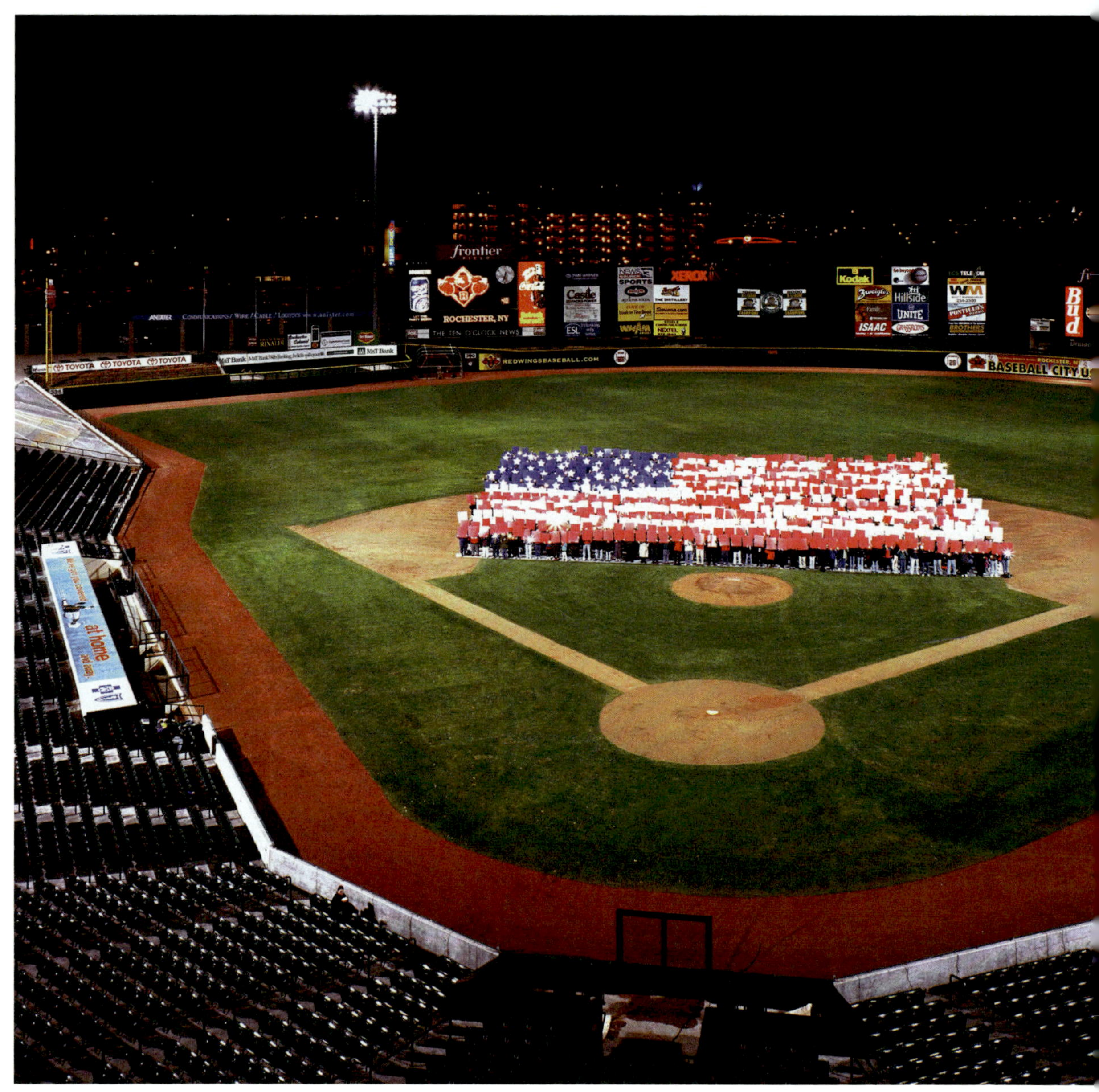

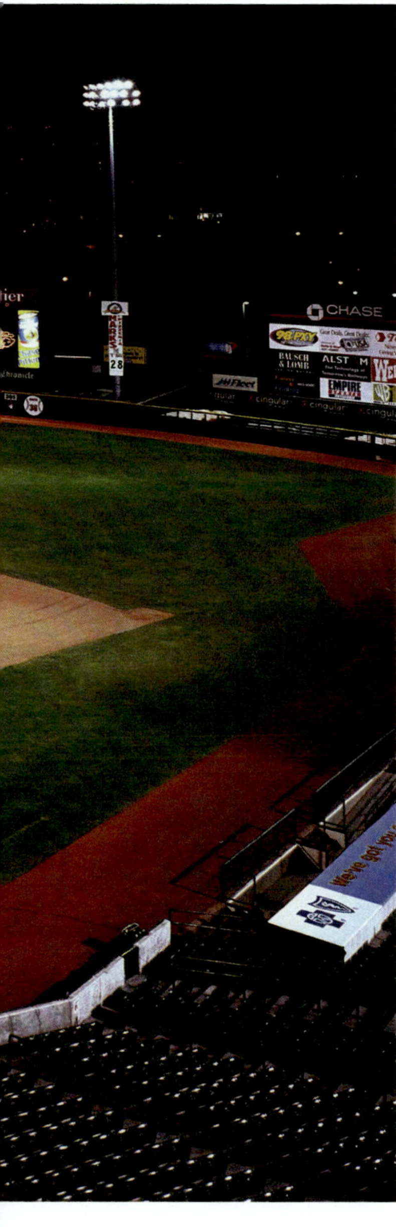

'Rochester Human Flag' at Frontier Field, Rochester, NY

2001

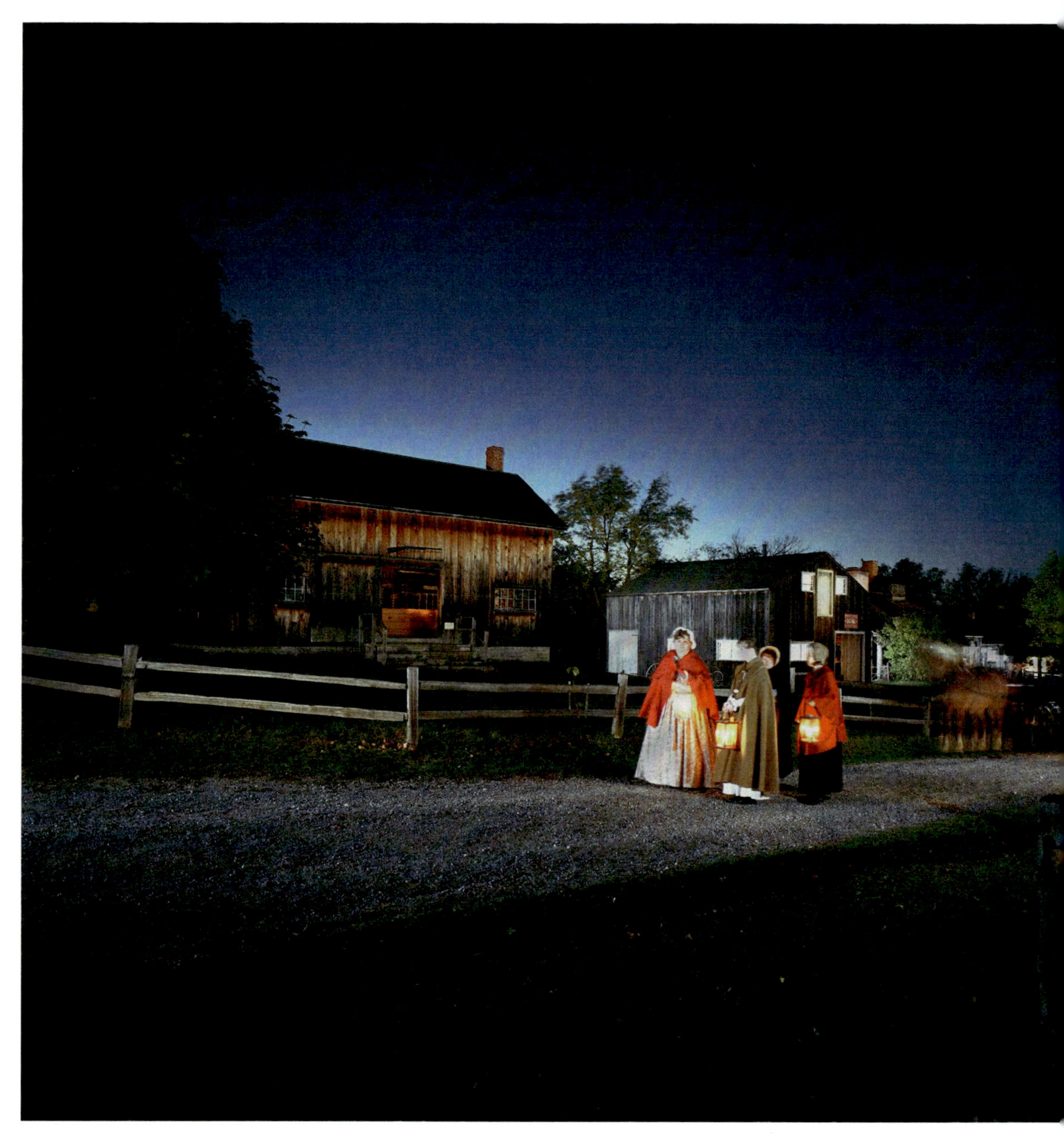

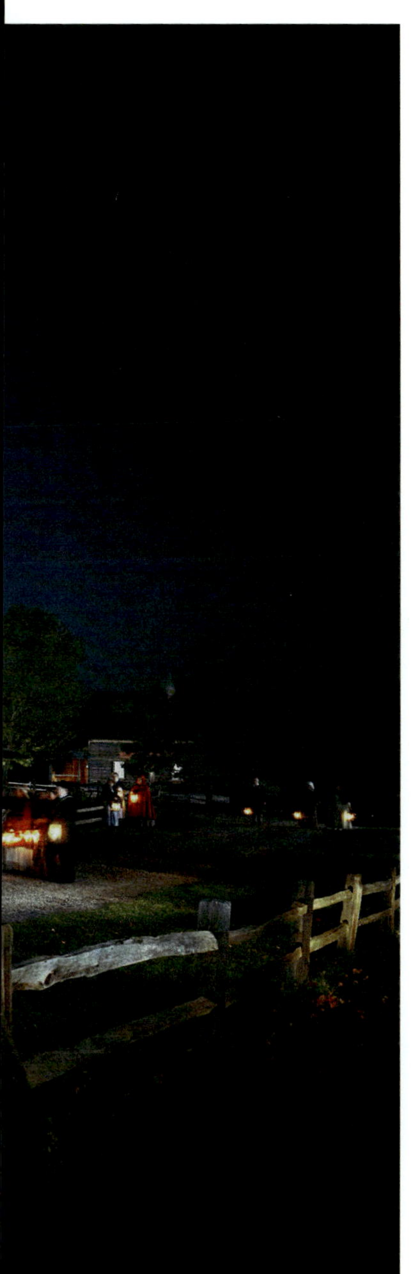

BIG SHOT NO. 17

Genesee Country Village & Museum, Mumford, NY

2001

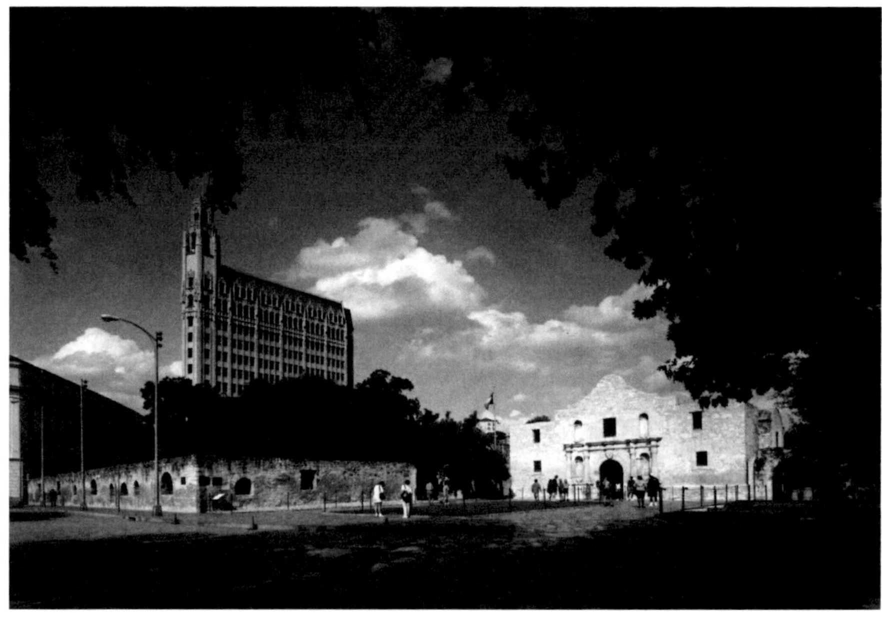

Above: Daytime view. Right: Big Shot No. 16 which took place at 7:15pm CST March 10, 2001. Exposure: 30 seconds at *f*/16

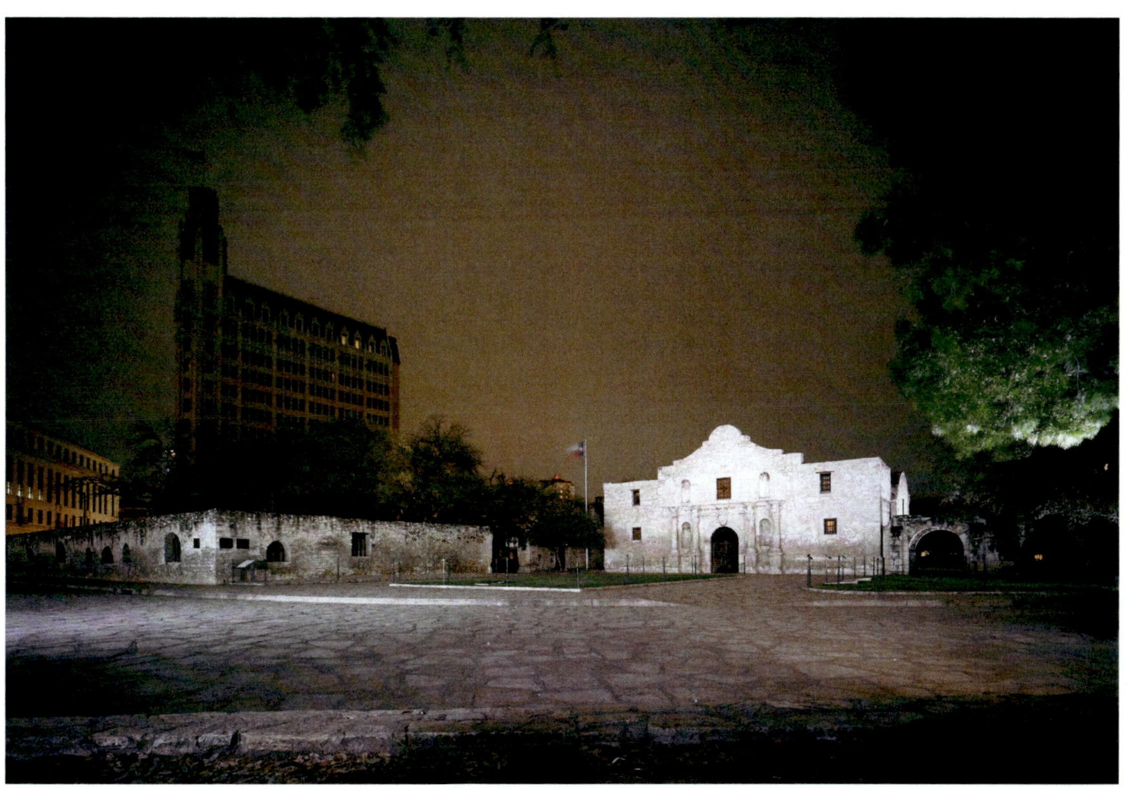

Liberty Pole, Main Street, Rochester, NY

2000

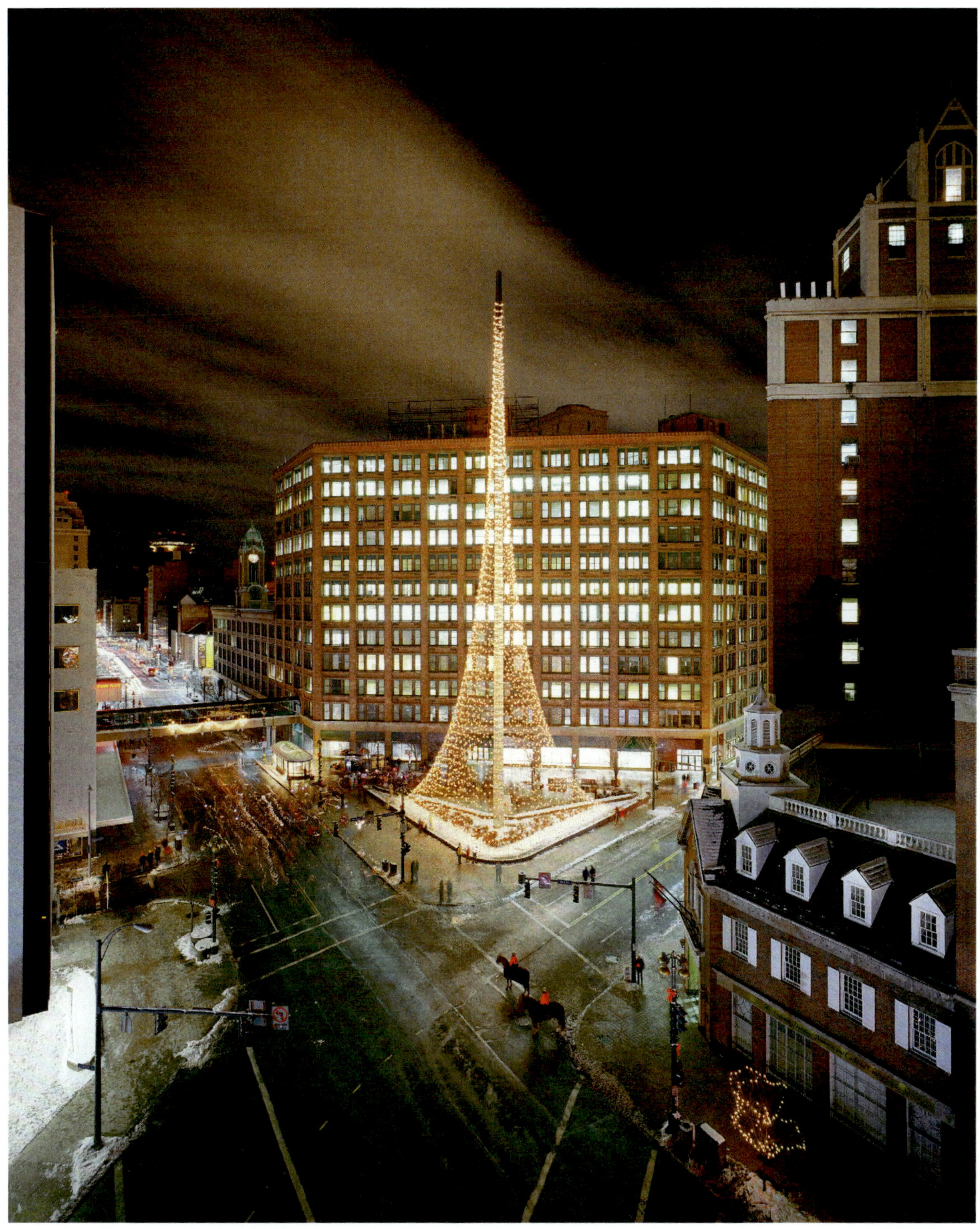

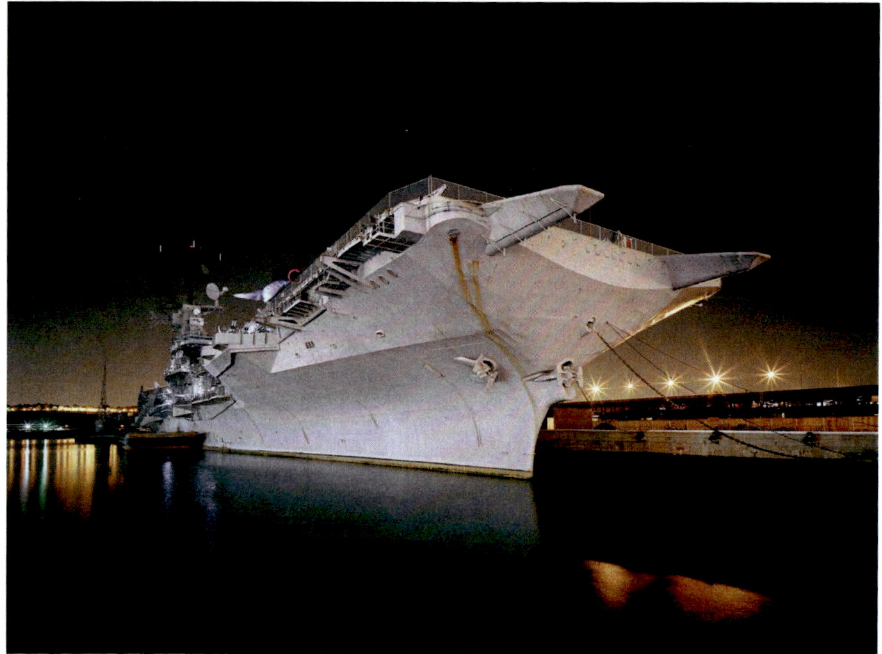

Above: Second Big Shot photograph, not previously published. Right: Big Shot No. 14 which took place October 28, 1999 at 9:05pm. Exposure: 2 min. at *f*/11

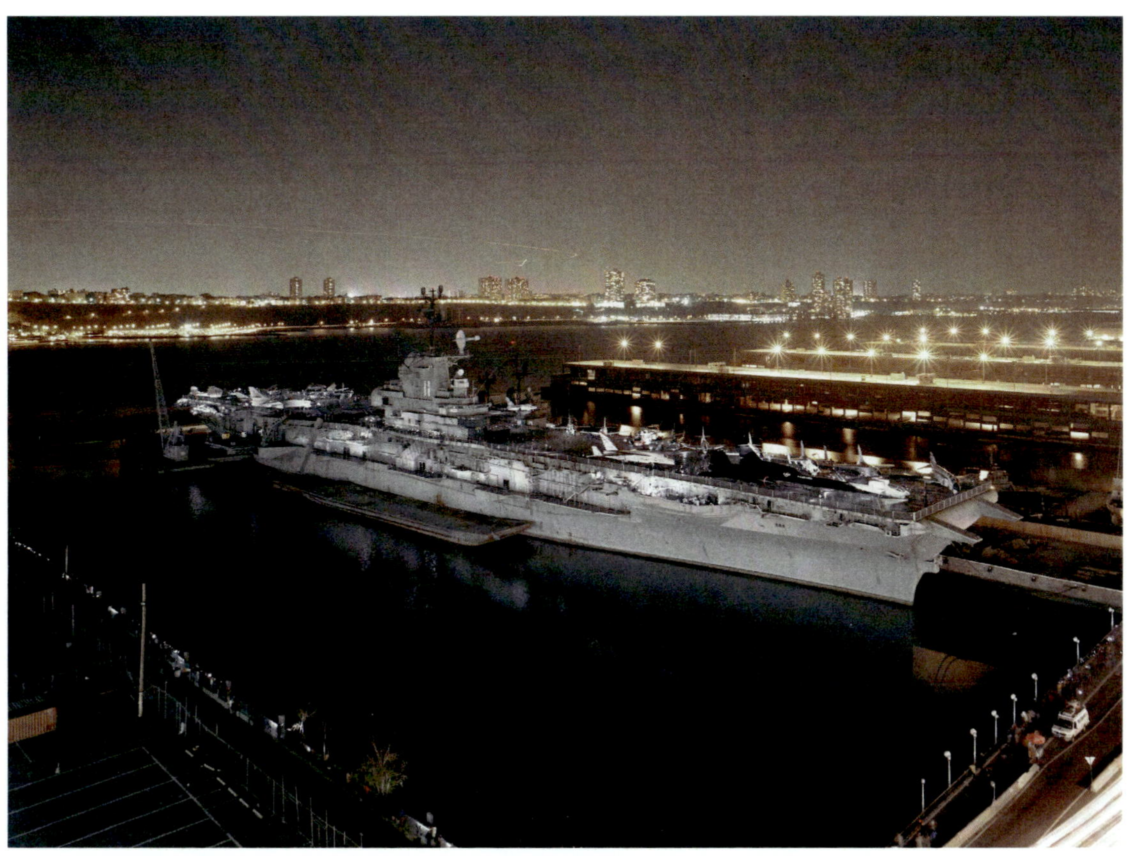

Ontario County Courthouse, Canandaigua, NY

1998

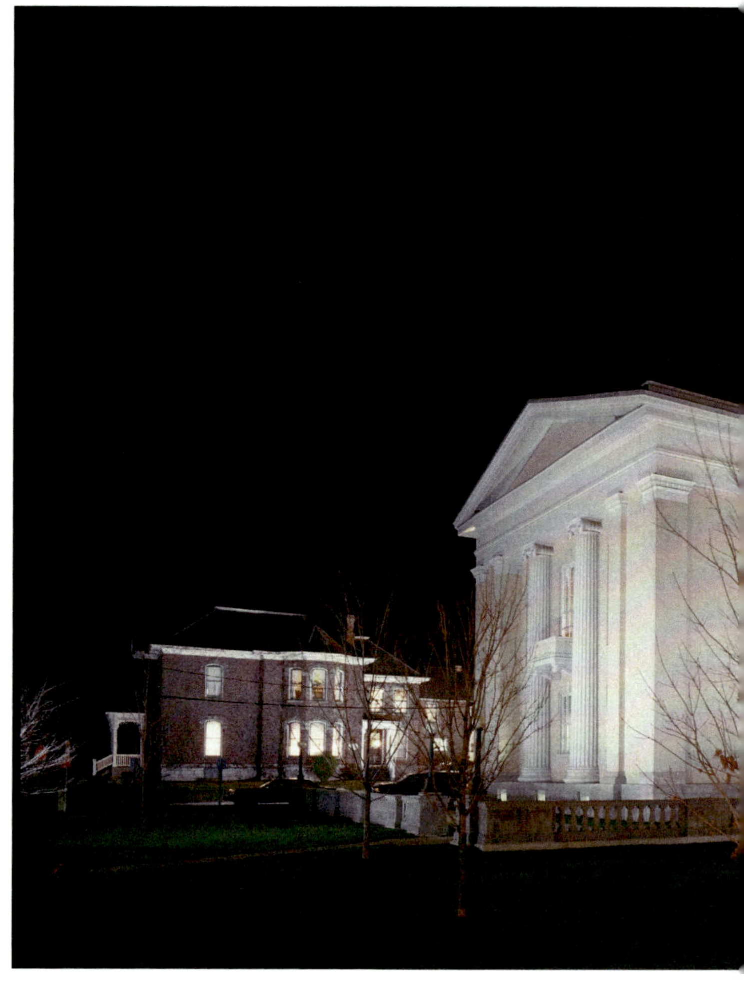

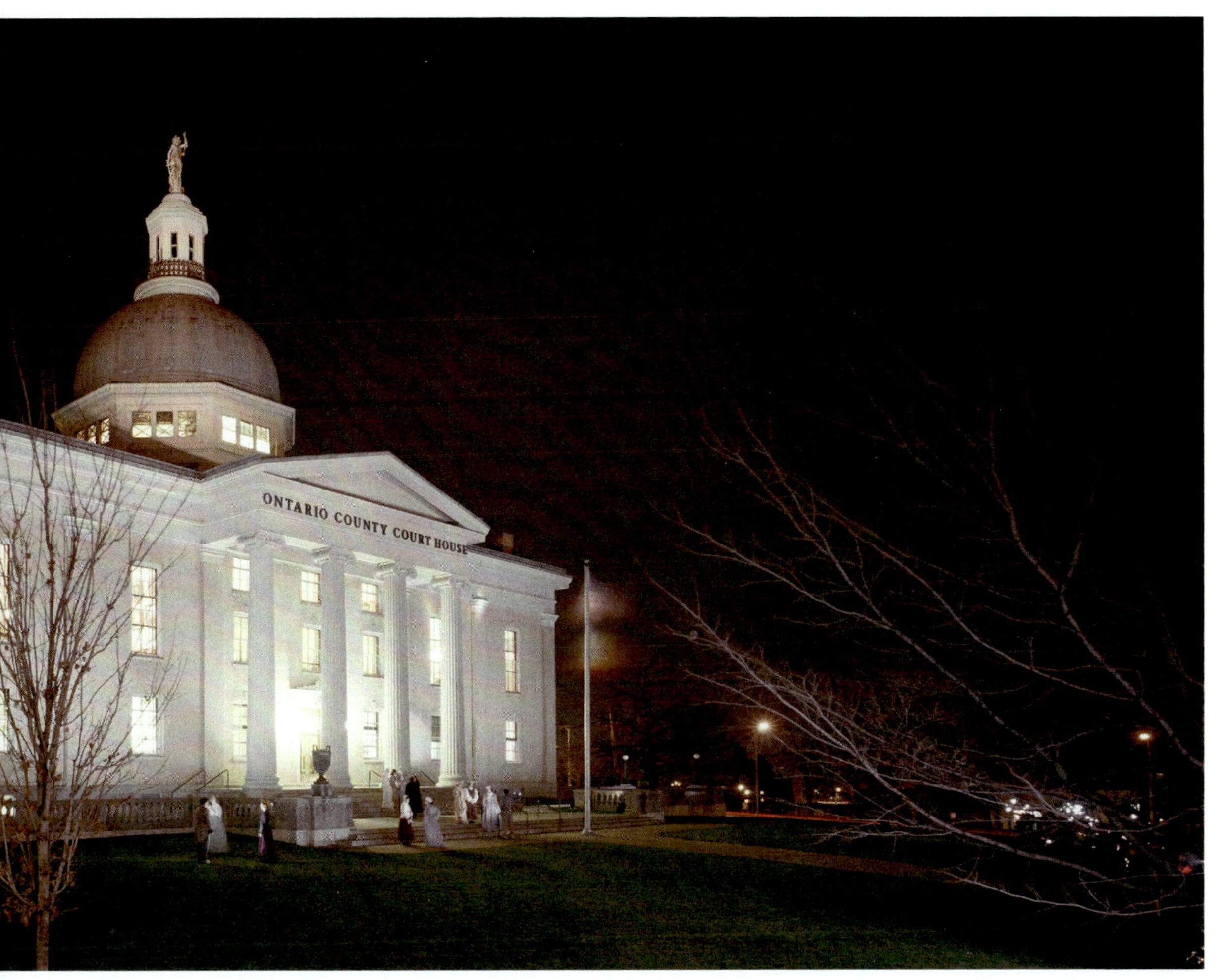
ONTARIO COUNTY COURT HOUSE

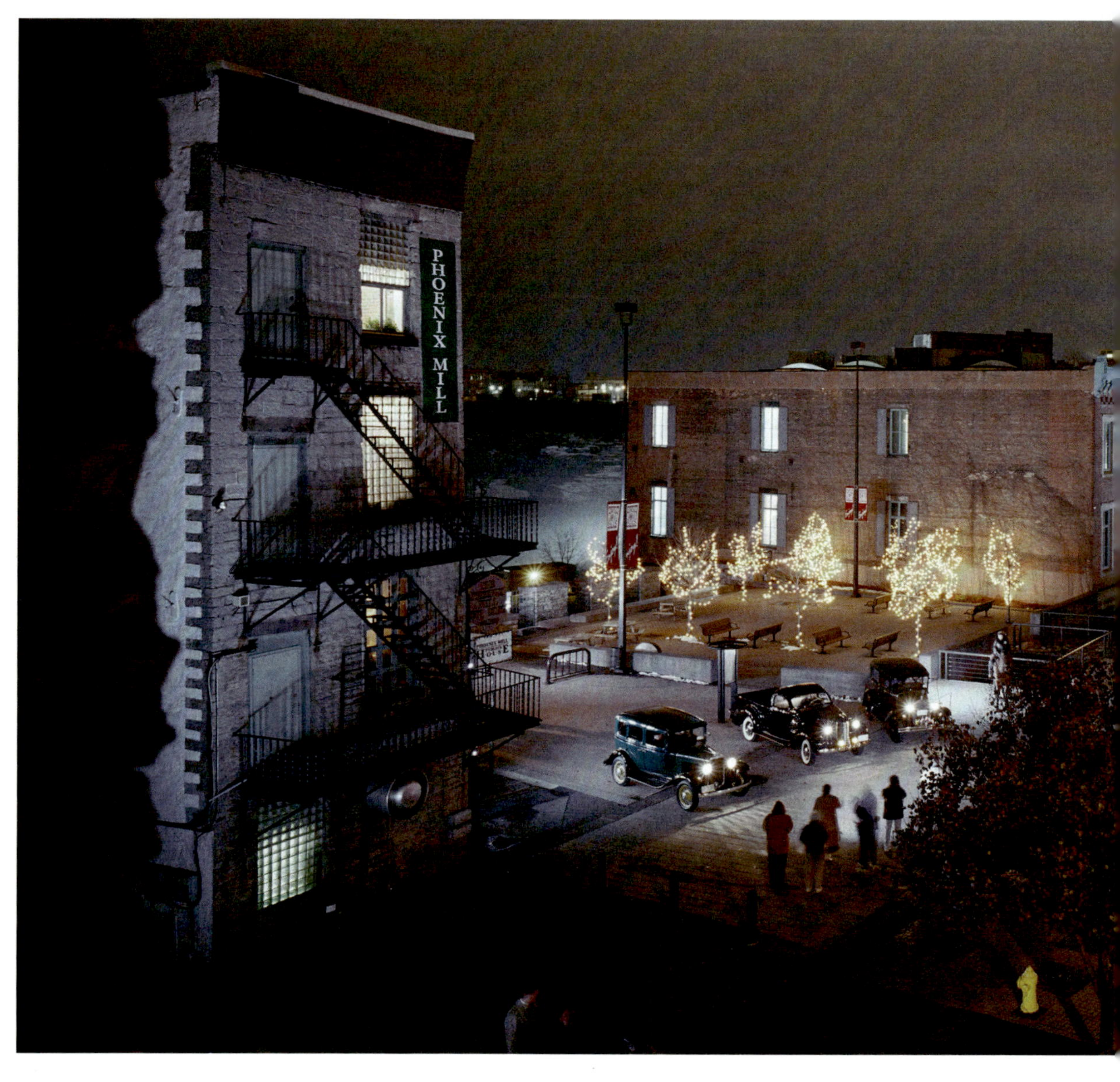

BIG SHOT NO. 12

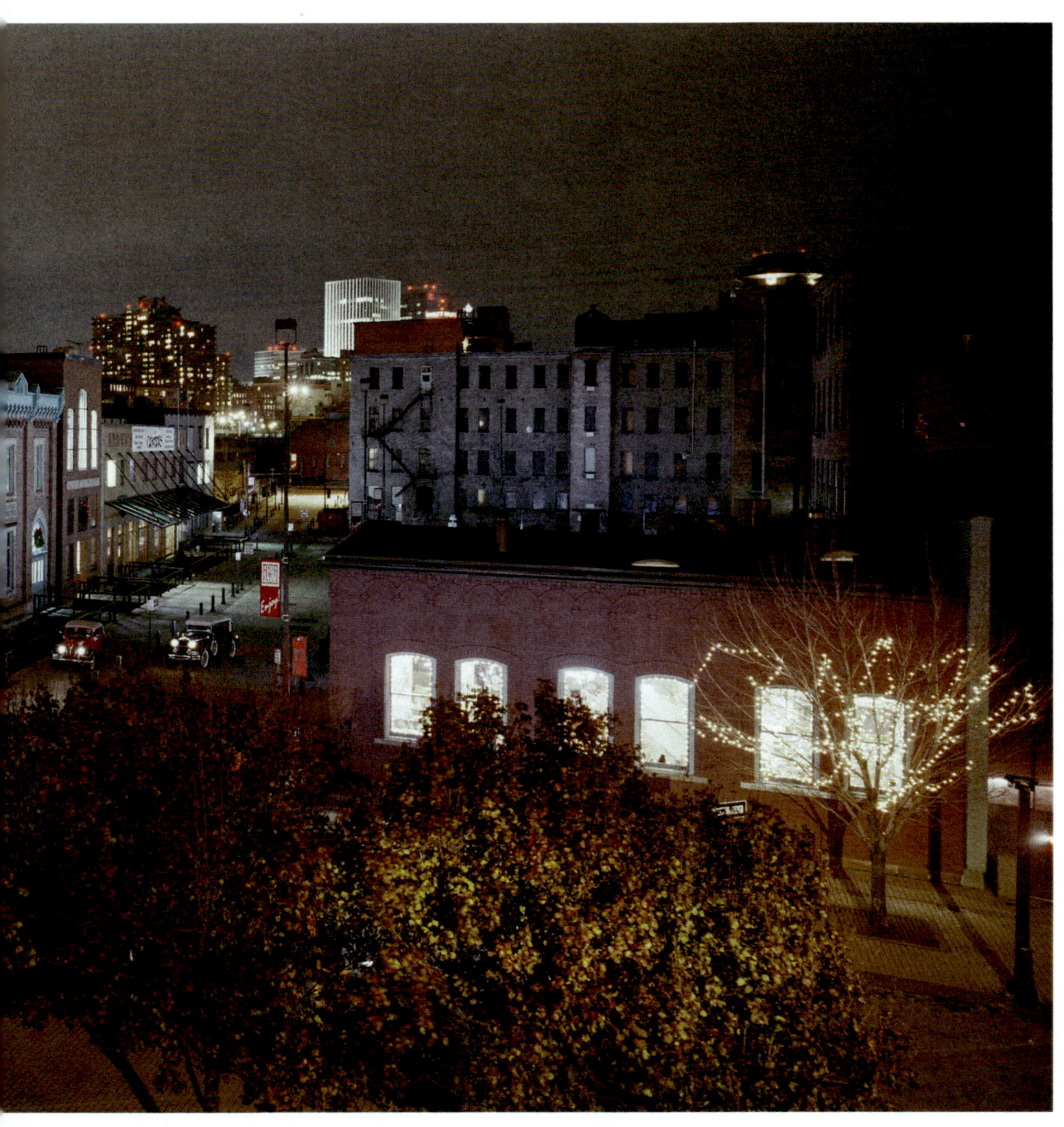

Brown's Race at High Falls, Rochester, NY

1997

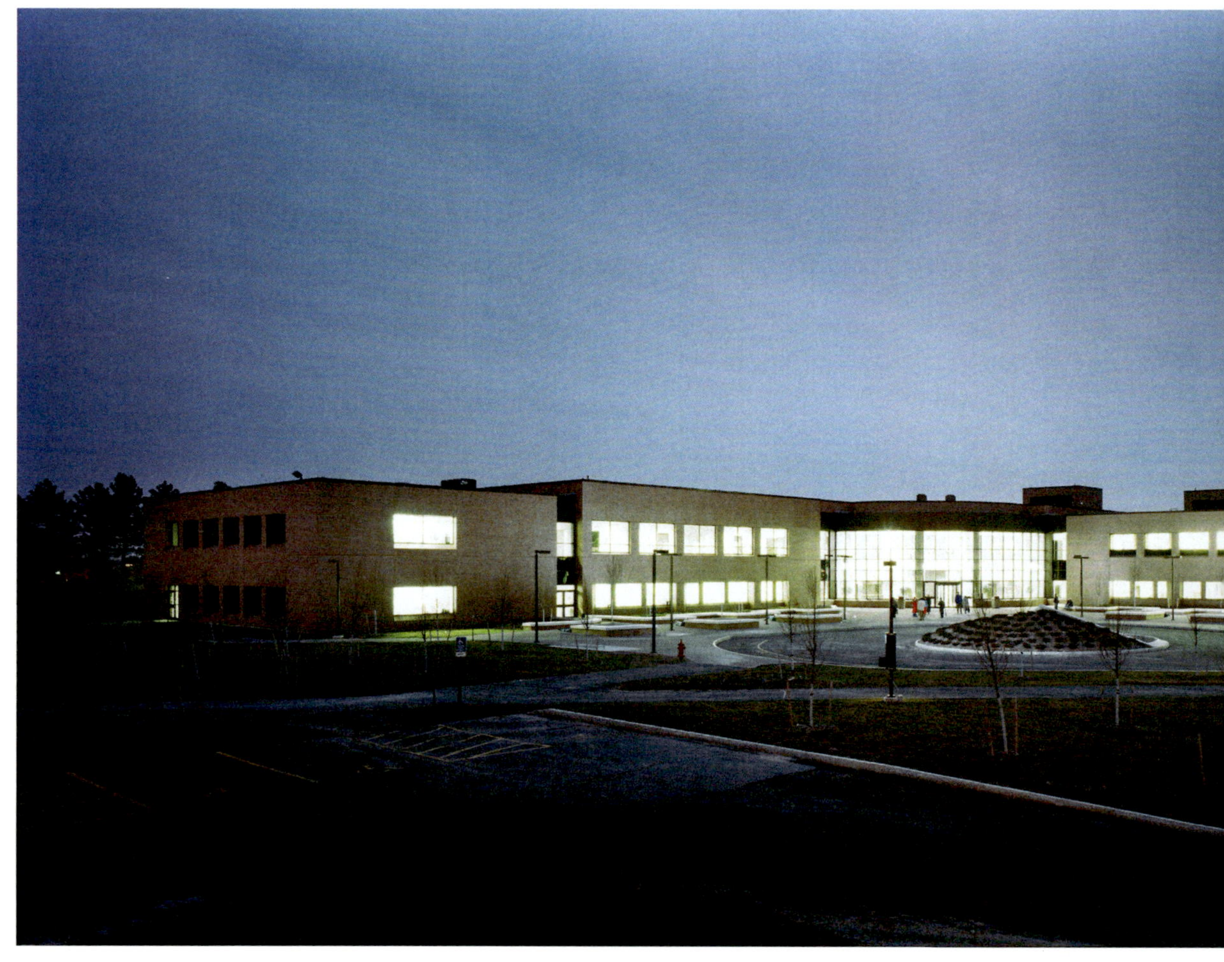

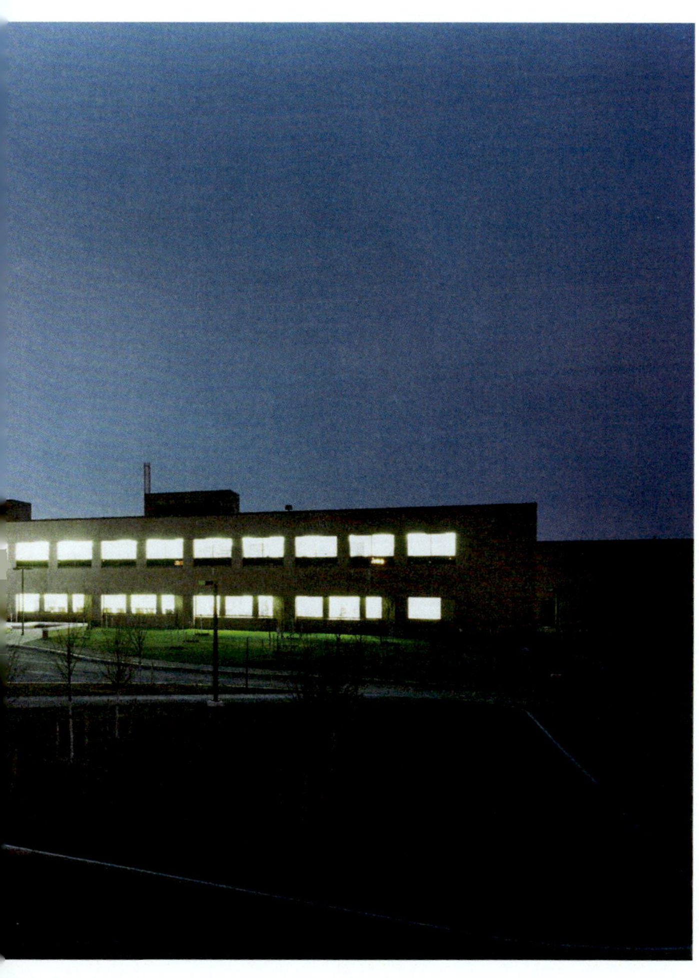

Center for Integrated Manufacturing Studies, RIT Campus, Rochester, NY

1997

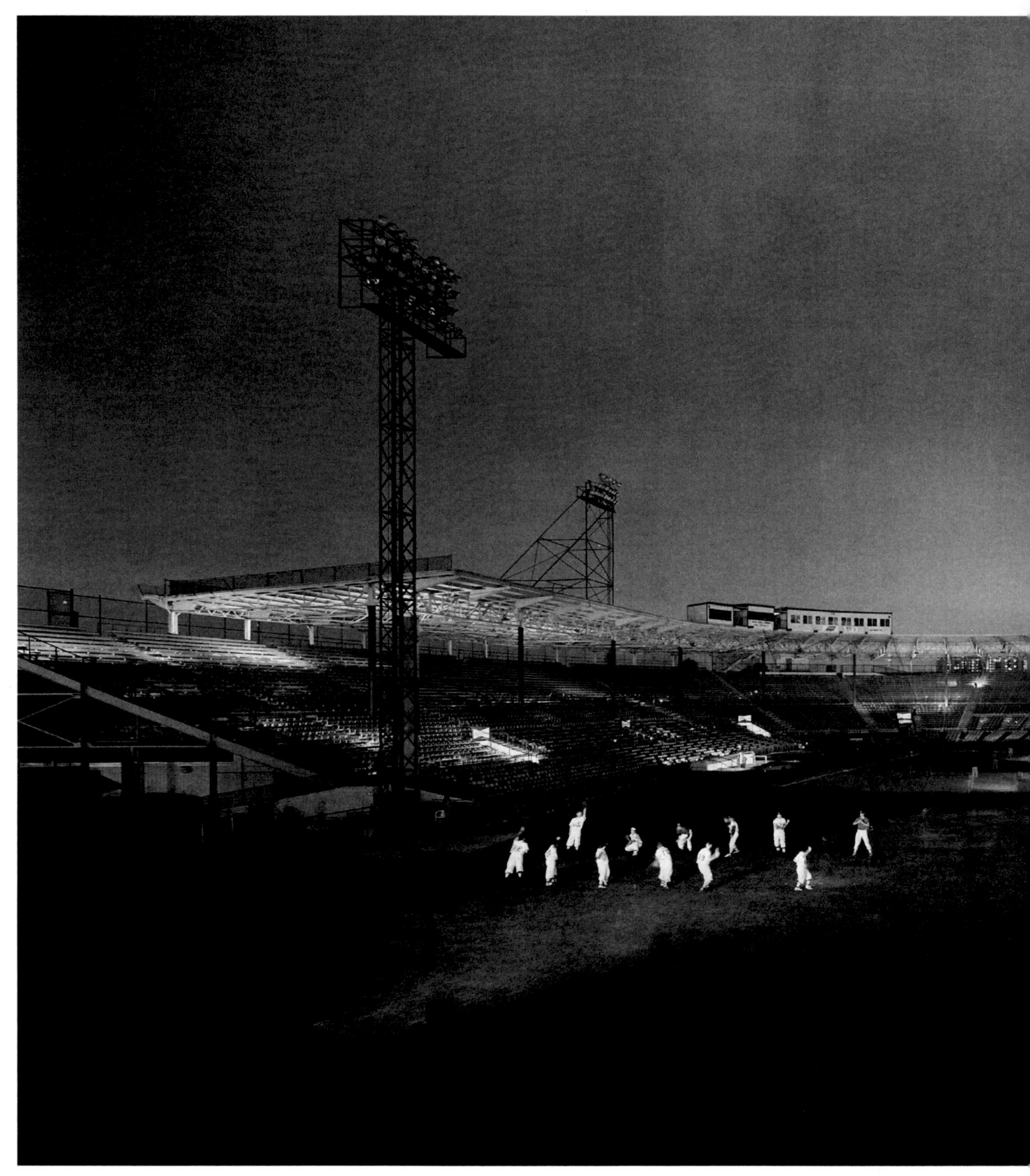

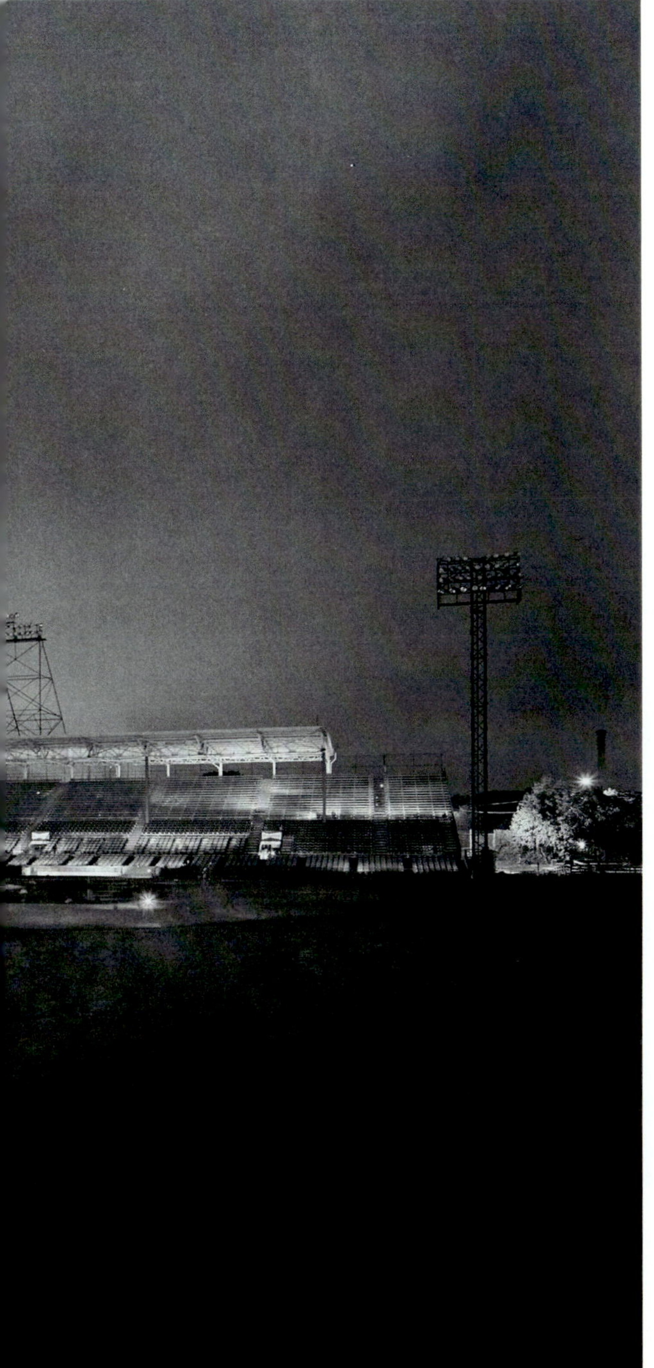

BIG SHOT NO. 10

Silver Stadium, Rochester, NY

1996

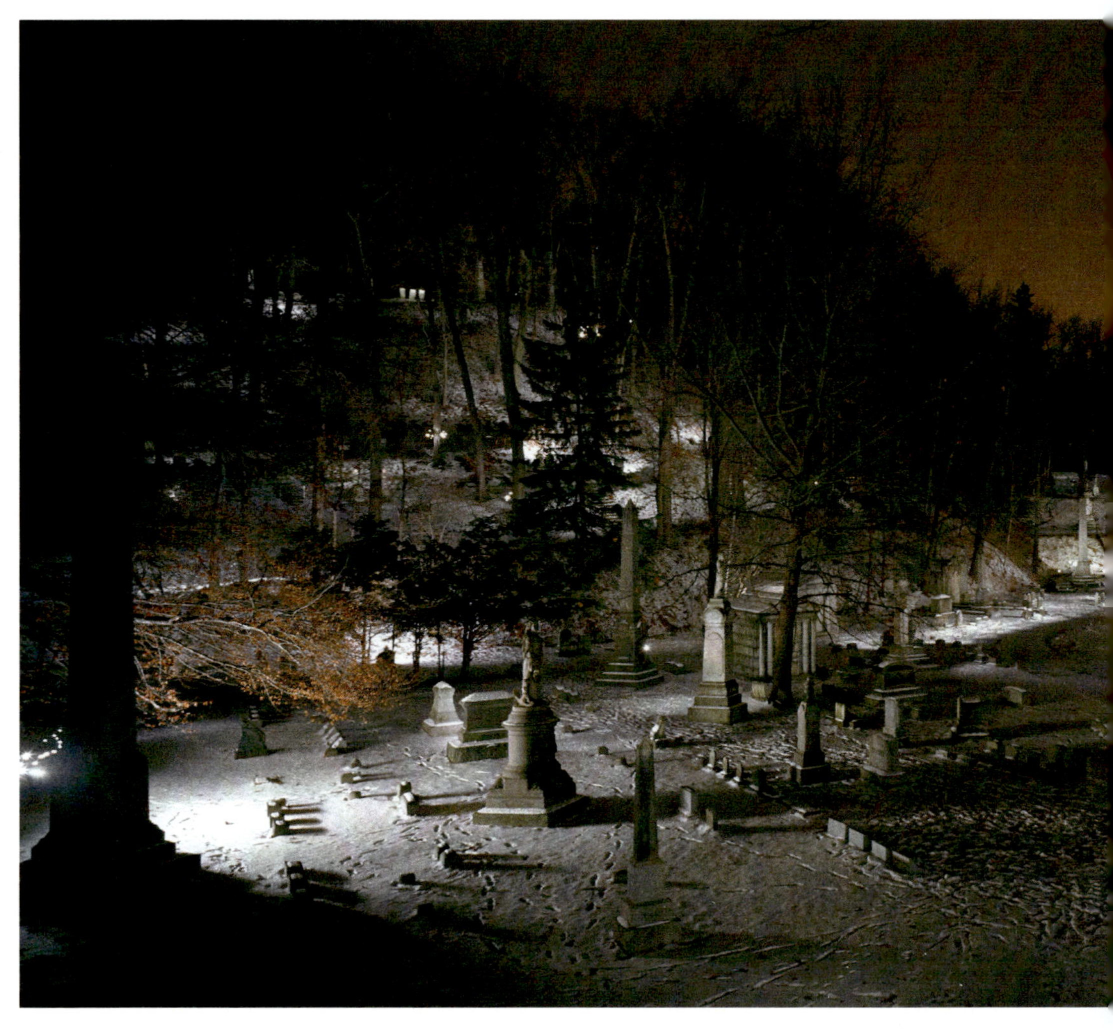

BIG SHOT NO. 9

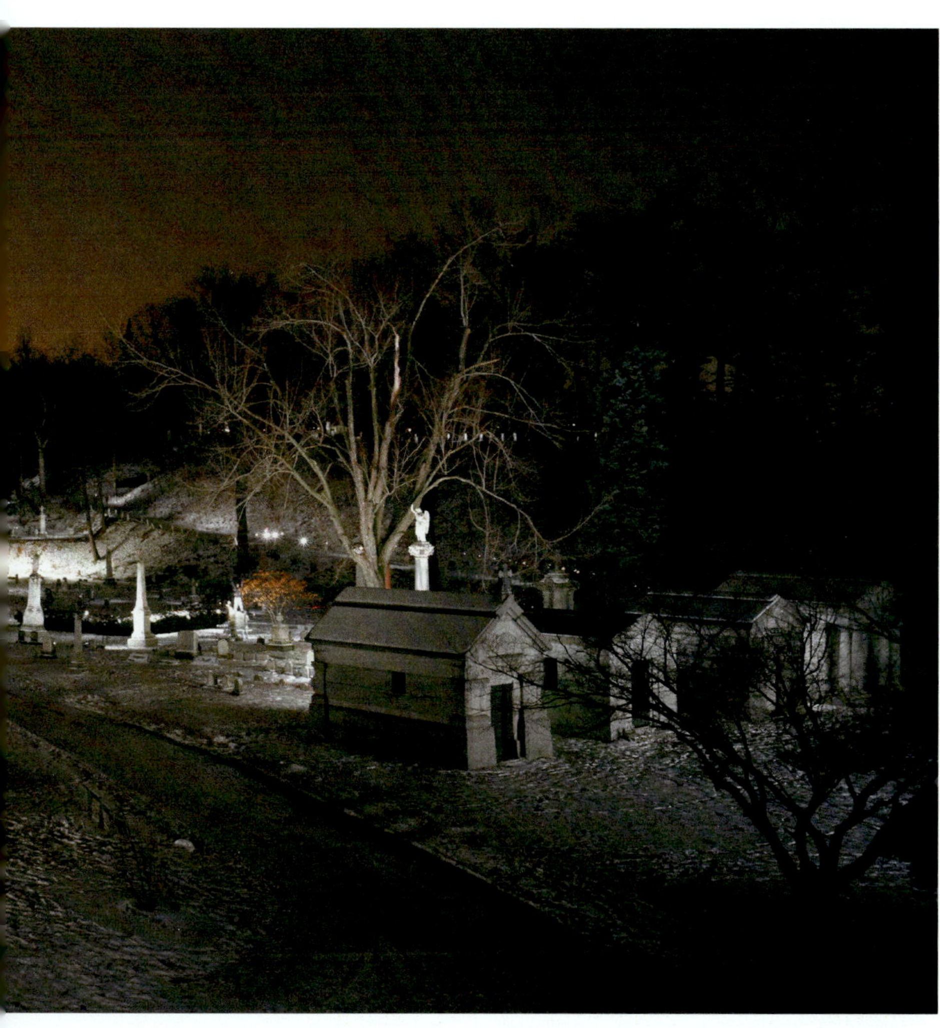

Mount Hope Cemetery, Rochester, NY

1995

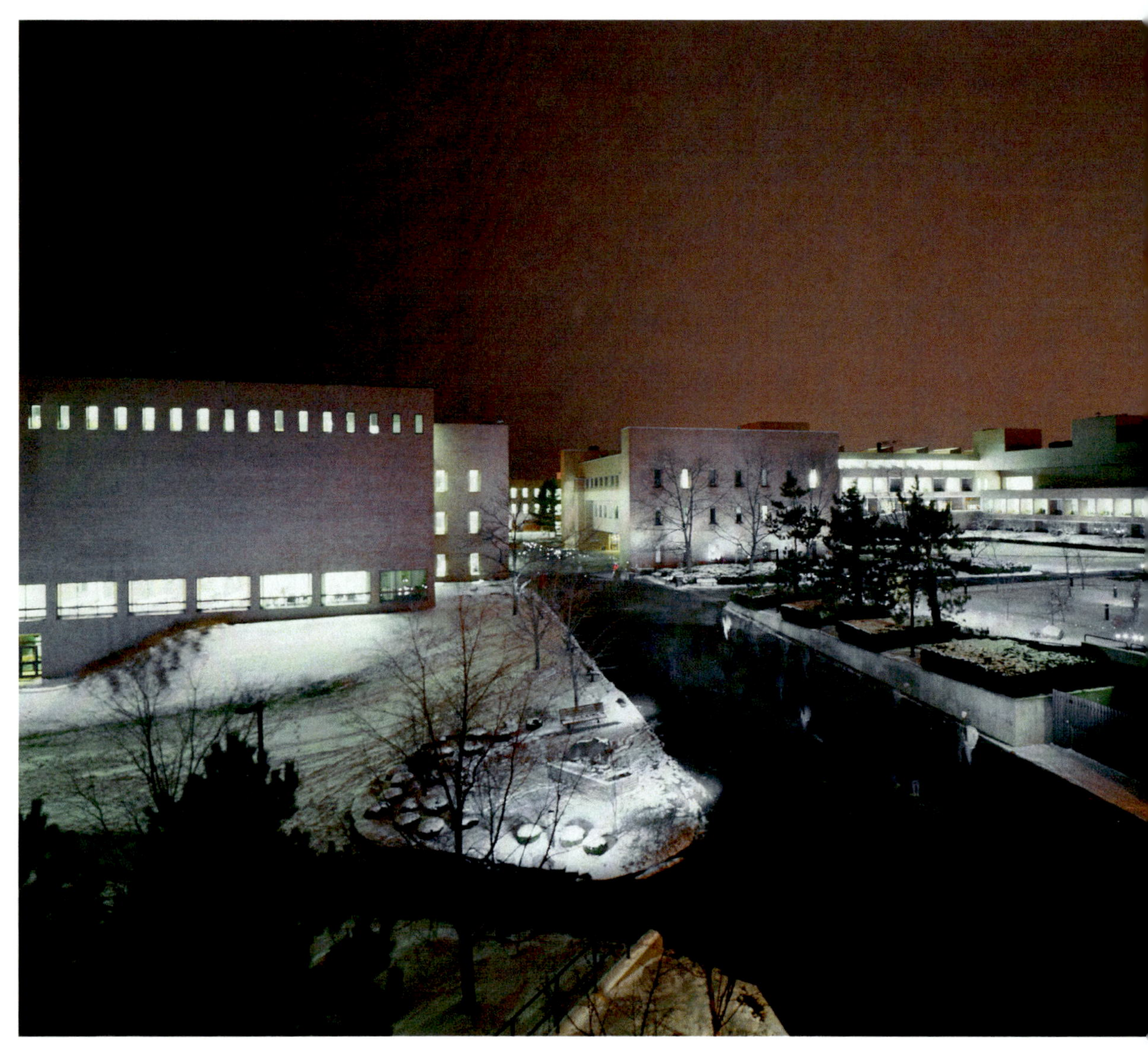

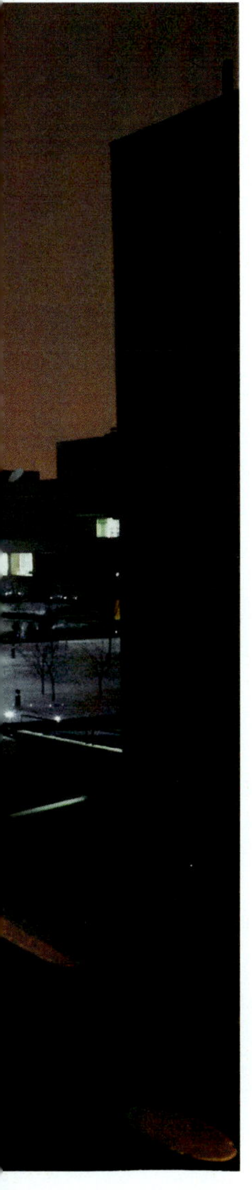

BIG SHOT NO. 8

RIT Campus looking west, Rochester, NY

1995

Rochester Museum & Science Center, Rochester, NY

1993

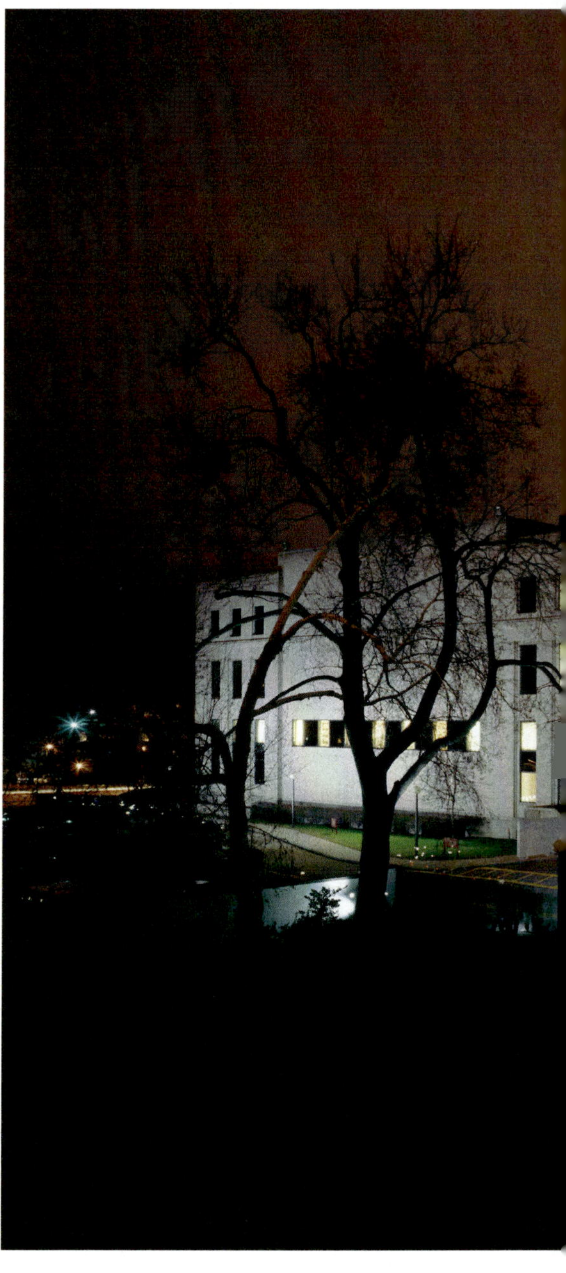

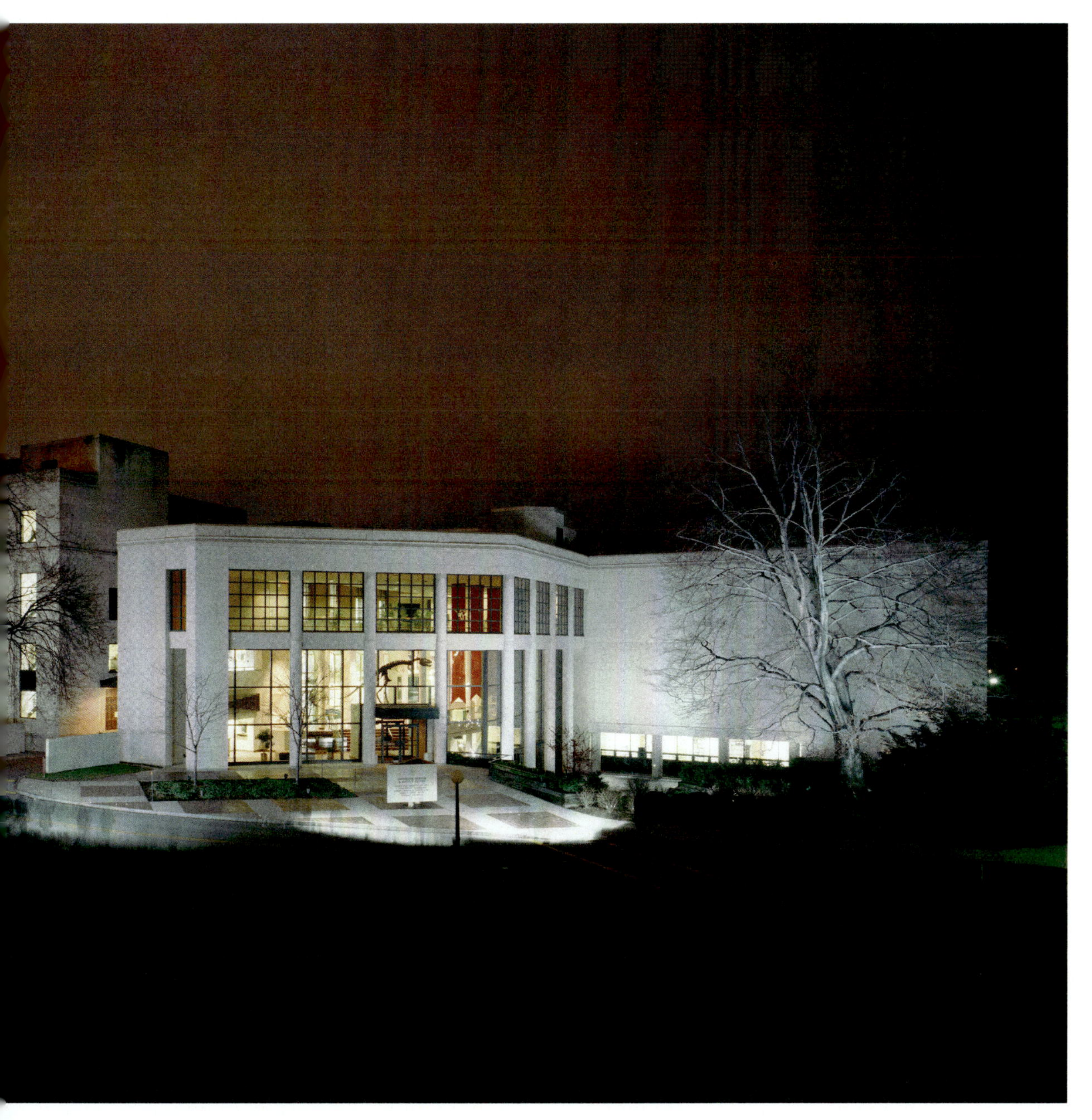

BIG SHOT NO. 7

Rundel Memorial Library, Rochester, NY

1992

BIG SHOT NO. 6

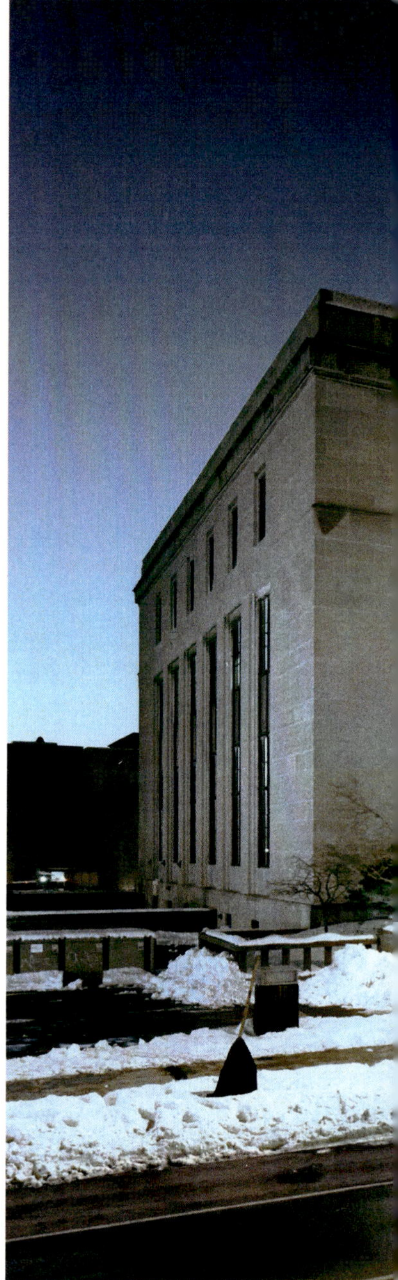

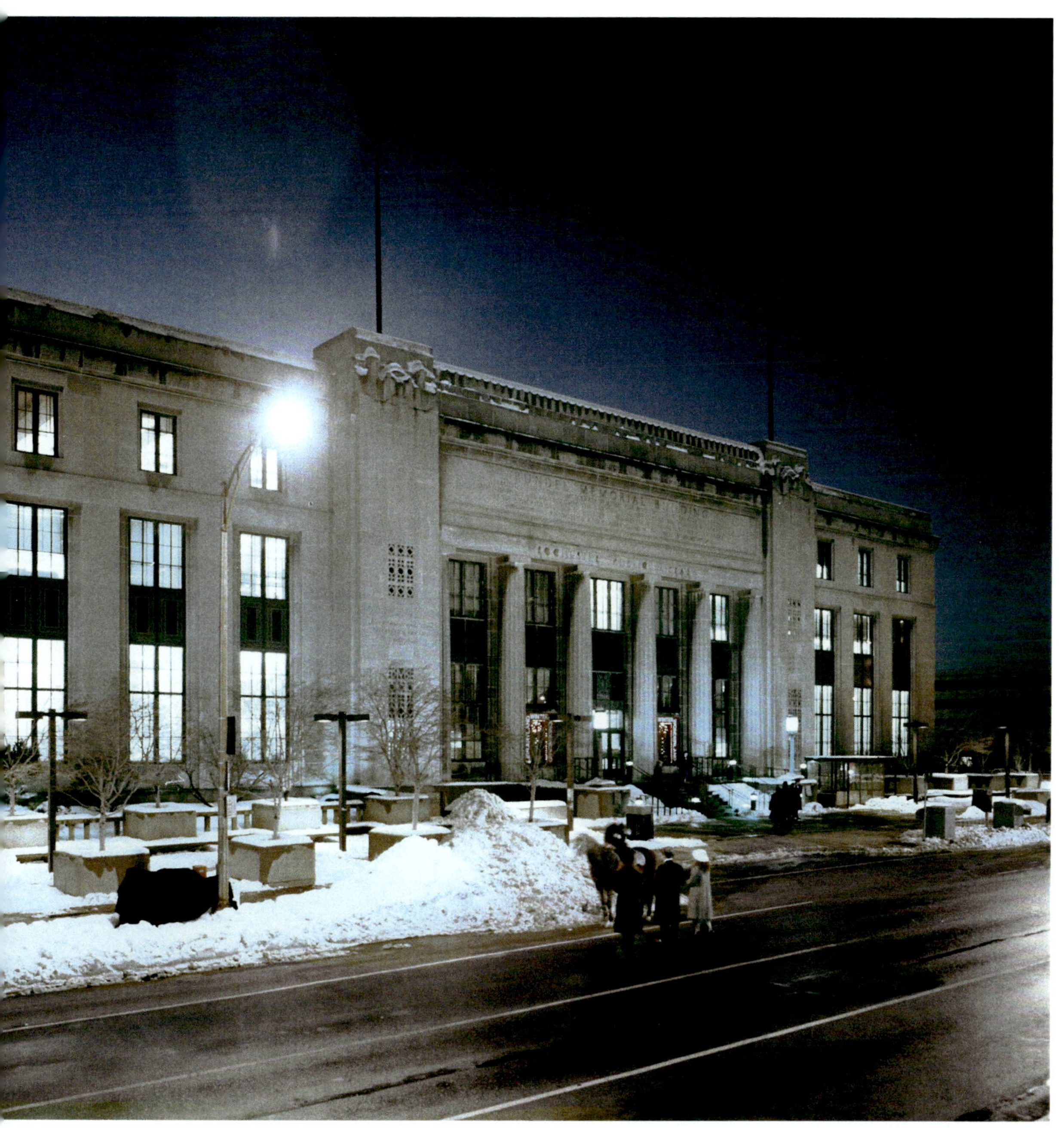

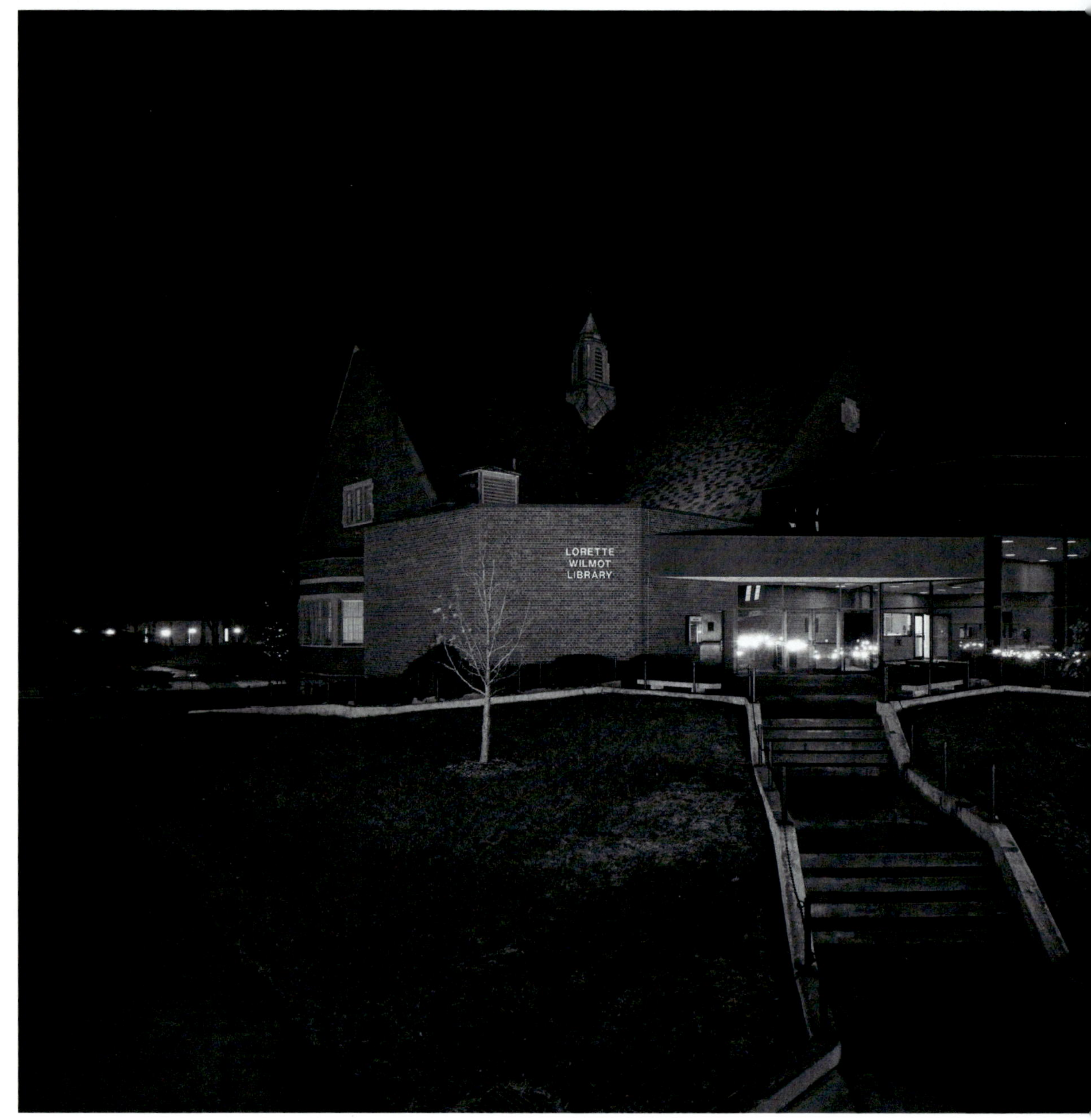
LORETTE
WILMOT
LIBRARY

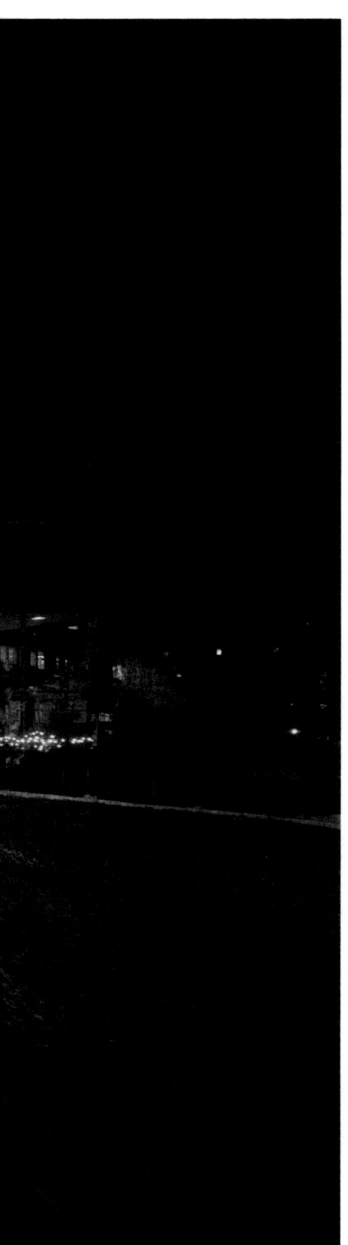

Lorette Wilmot Library, Nazareth College, Rochester, NY

1991

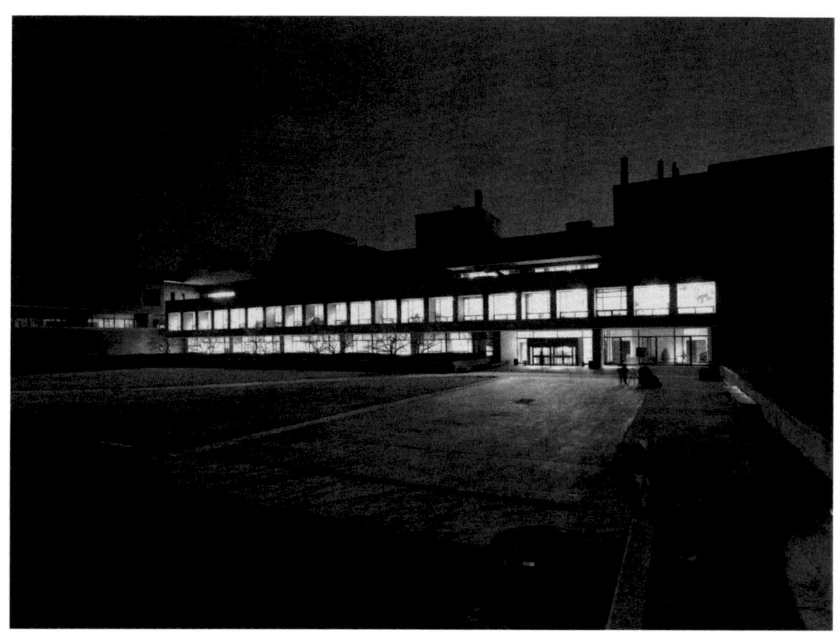

Above: before painting with light. Right: Big Shot No. 4 which took place December 8, 1990. Exposure: 12 sec. at *f*/11

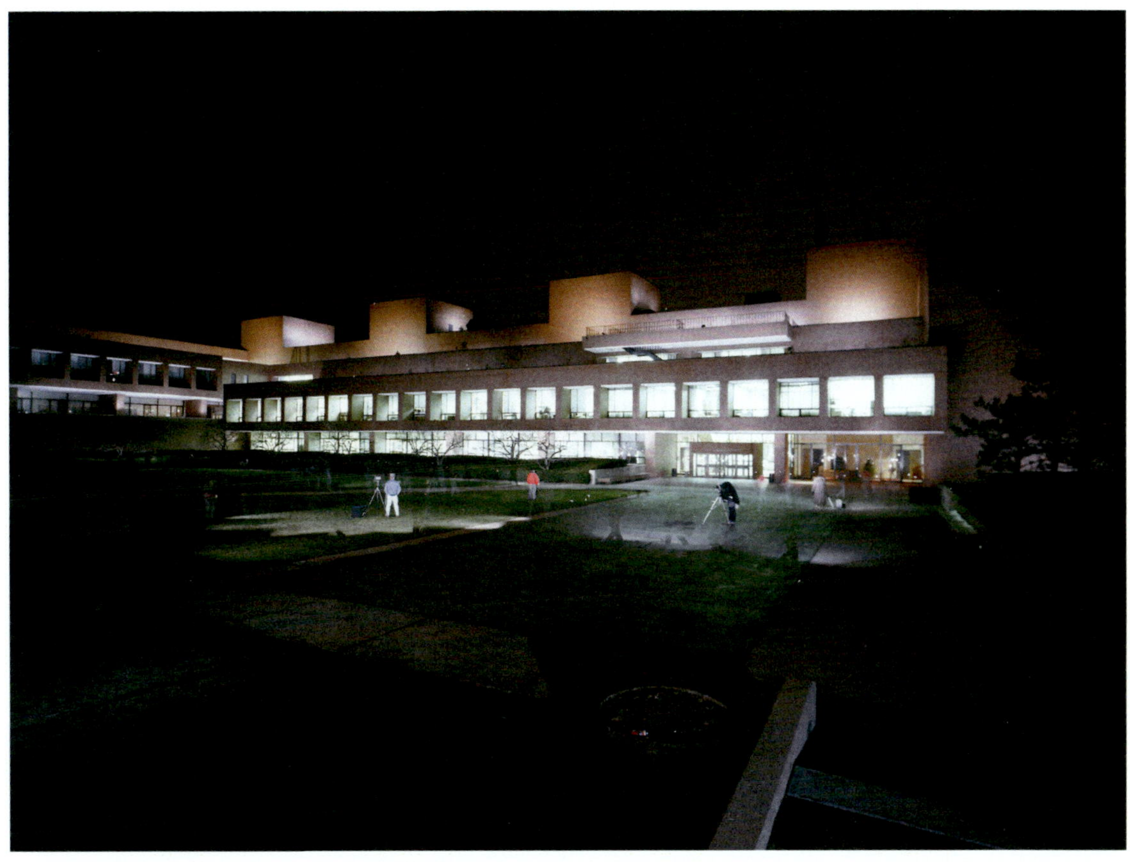

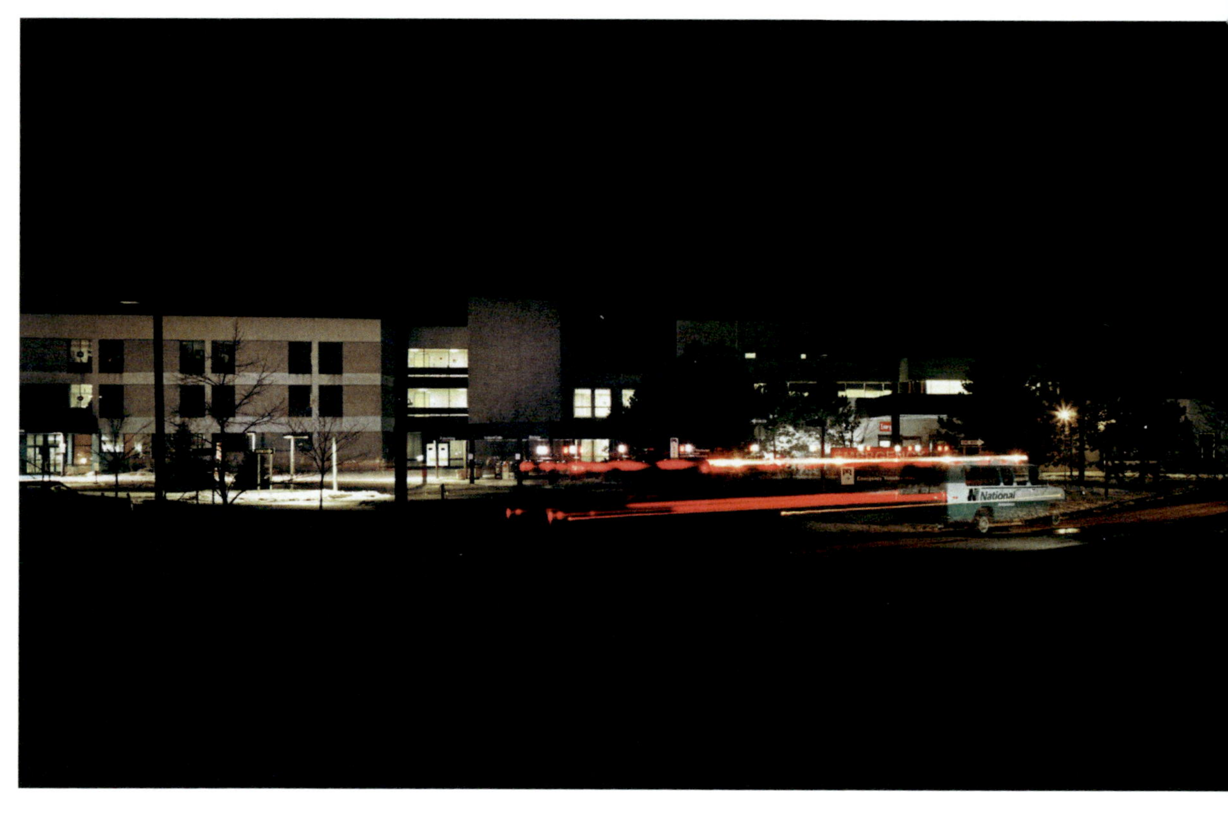
National

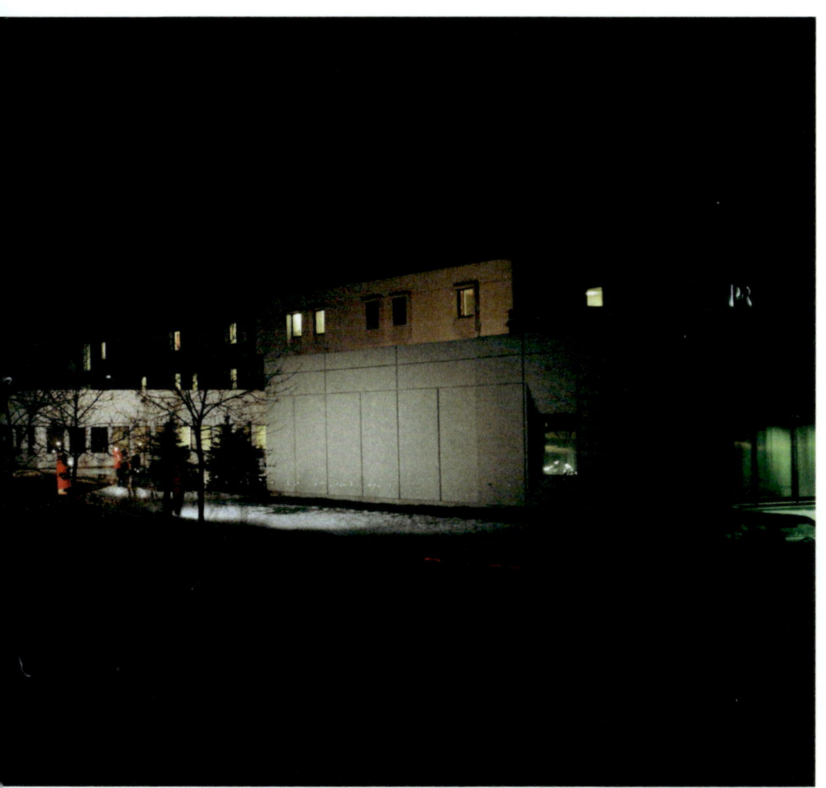

Park Ridge Hospital, Rochester, NY

1989

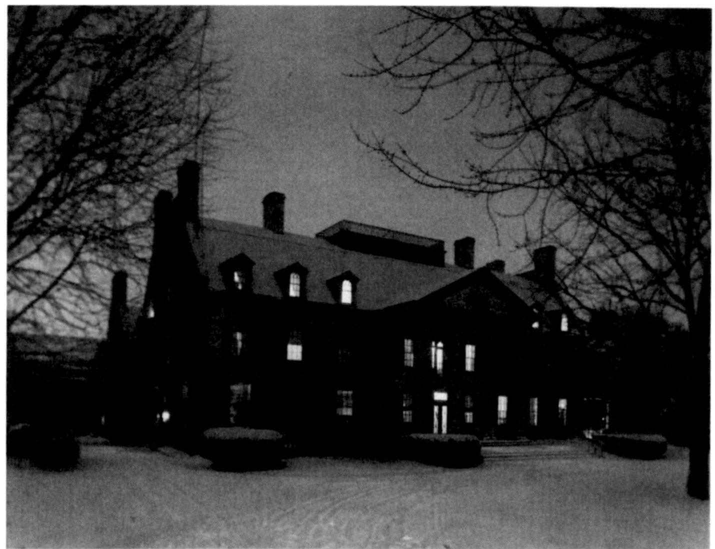

Above: before painting with light. Right: Big Shot No. 2 which took place December 10, 1988. Exposure: 12 sec. at $f/11$.

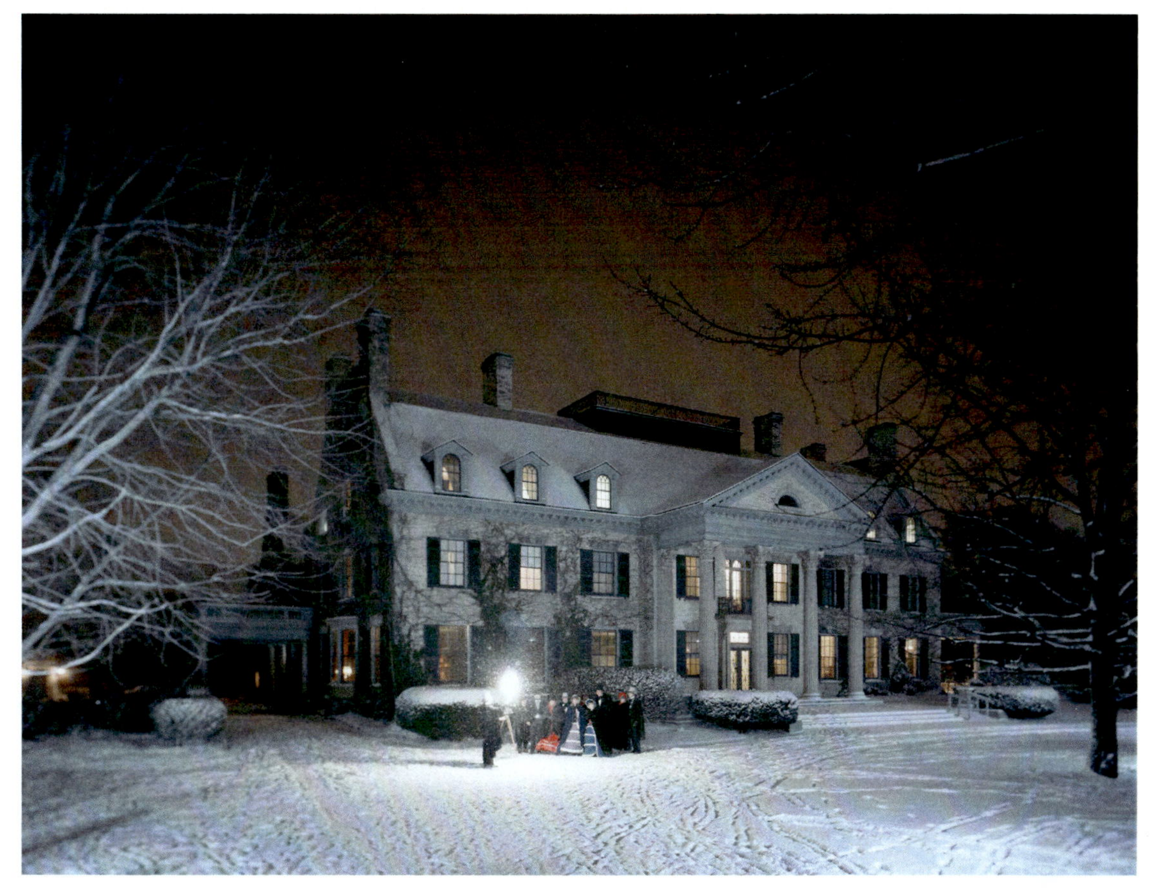

BIG SHOT NO. 2

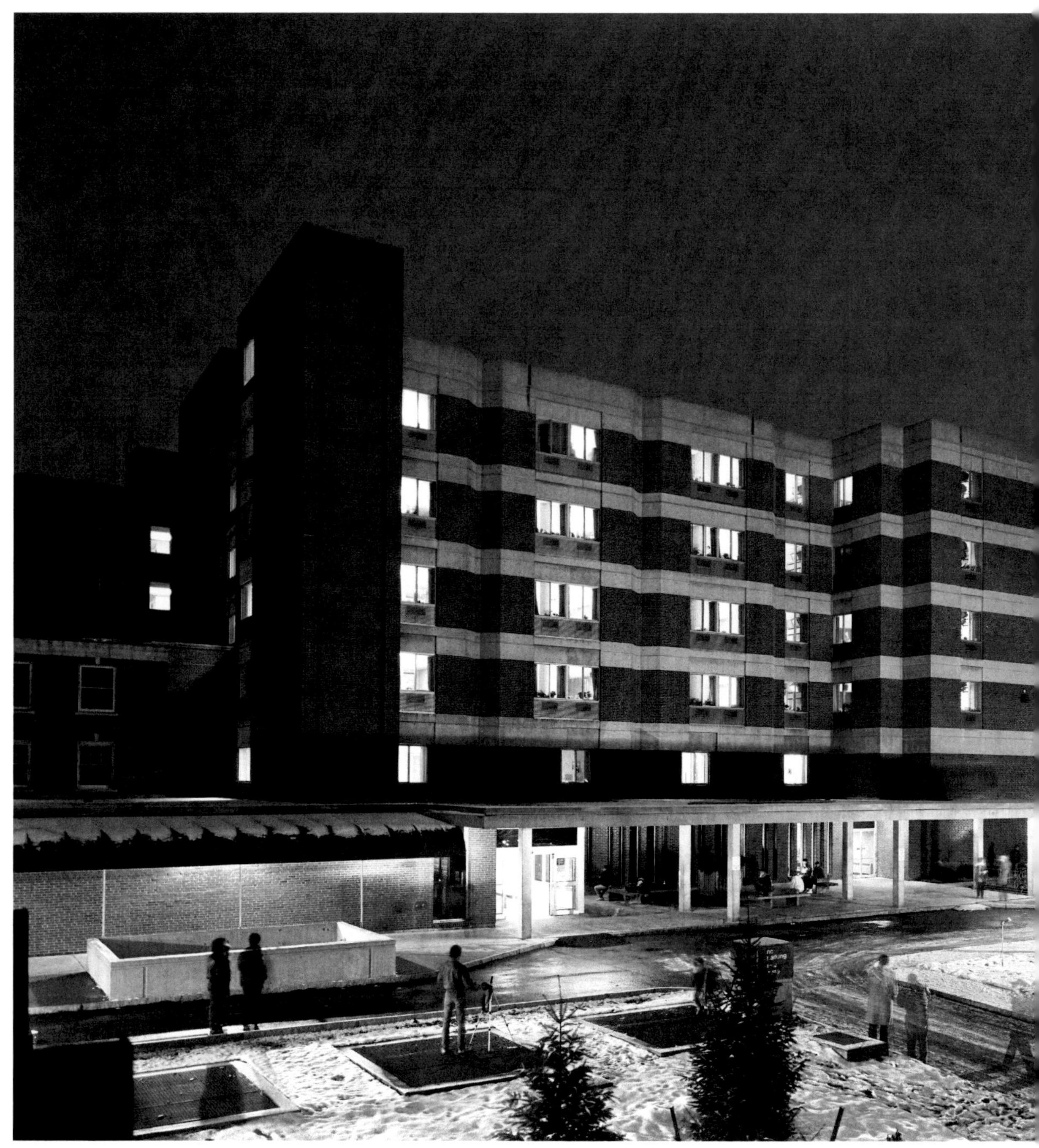

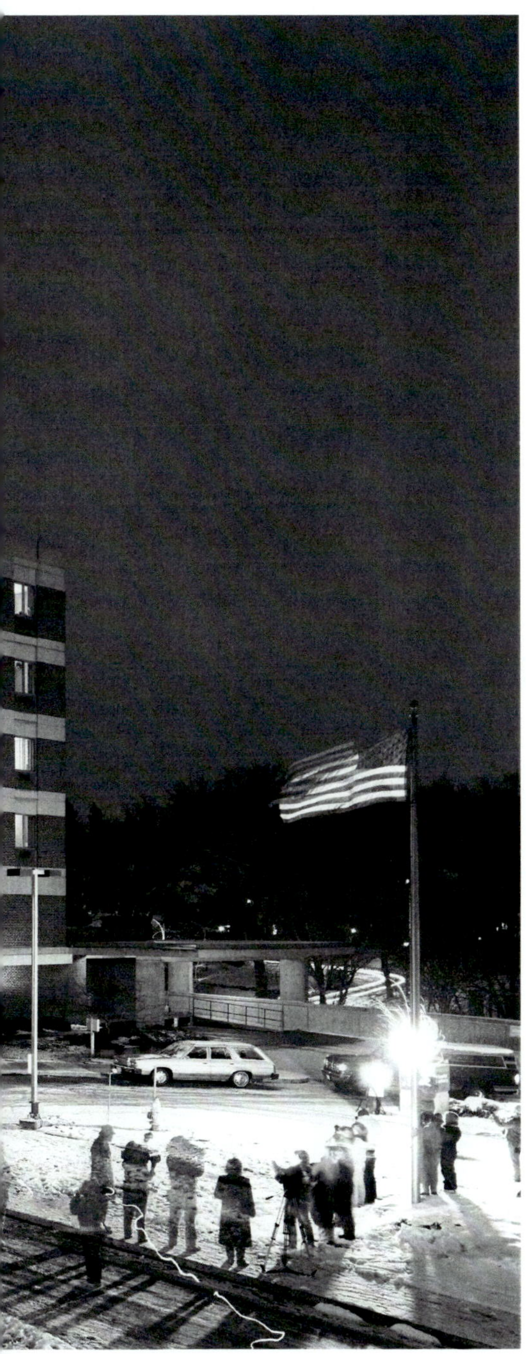

BIG SHOT NO. 1

Highland Hospital, Rochester, NY

1987

Big Shot Beginnings

On December 4, 1987, RIT's Biomedical Photographic Communications department, housed in the Photography School, produced the first Big Shot photograph of Rochester's Highland Hospital by employing a 4 × 5 film camera and with help from 37 students and members of the university community. The initial conception for Big Shot photographs derived from a collaboration of Professors Bill DuBois and Michael Peres, who wished to create a challenging extracurricular event for their students to study the display of light in a nighttime setting. Professor Dawn Tower DuBois operated the camera at the first Big Shot. She continued this contribution in succeeding images of the longtime project. Given the technology of the day, a magnesium flash powder tray, along with handheld flash units, were used to provide illumination needed to produce the extended nighttime exposure of the Hospital.

The Big Shot project was loosely based on a 1950s large-scale public lighting endeavor undertaken by Sylvania, a consumer electronics company known for its flash bulb products. As lighting sources changed over the lifetime of the RIT project, so too did the technologies used to capture and disseminate the Big Shot photographs. Film-based and darkroom processes were replaced by digital technologies and traditional print practices were succeeded by computer imaging software and website display and dissemination. The Big Shot project's mission was to encourage students to work in teams, learning how to solve complicated lighting problems on location. They provided lighting with portable electronic flashes and flashlights.

Since the project's inception, the Big Shot has traveled to many national landmarks and twice crossed the Atlantic Ocean. Through their viewfinders, Big Shot photographers have captured such landmarks as the Alamo; the Intrepid Air Sea and Space Museum (formerly USS Intrepid); the Royal Palace in Stockholm, Sweden; the Pile Gate in Dubrovnik, Croatia; AT&T (formerly Cowboys) Football Stadium; Churchill Downs; and, closer to home, the George Eastman Museum.

1987–1995

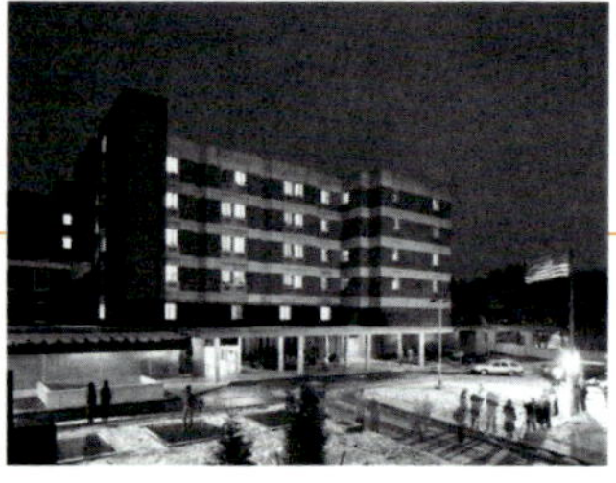
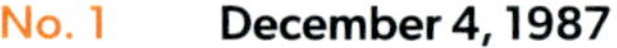

No. 1 **December 4, 1987**
Highland Hospital
Rochester, New York

TEMP.	34° F
CAMERA	Sinar F with 65 mm lens
EXPOSURE	30 seconds at *ƒ*/11
FILM	Kodak 4 × 5 T-Max 400
LIGHTING	Multiple flashes of electronic flash units and 1 old-fashioned flash-powder tray
TEAM	34 volunteers

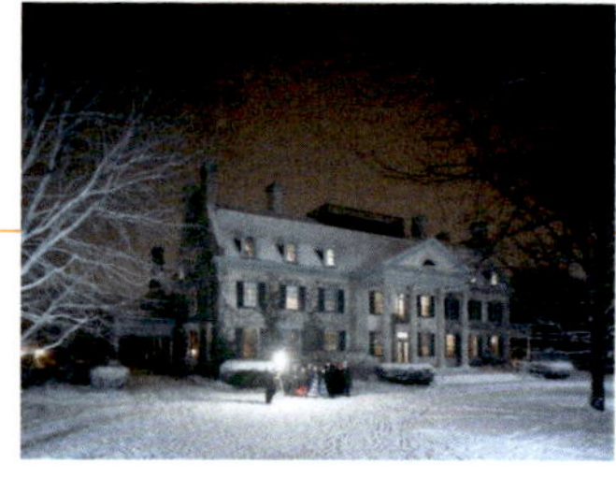

No. 2 **December 10, 1988**
George Eastman Museum
Rochester, New York

TEMP.	17° F
CAMERA	Sinar F with 65 mm lens
EXPOSURE	12 seconds at *ƒ*/11
FILM	Kodak 4 × 5 Vericolor 400
LIGHTING	Multiple flashes of electronic flash units and 1 old-fashioned flash-powder tray
TEAM	70 volunteers

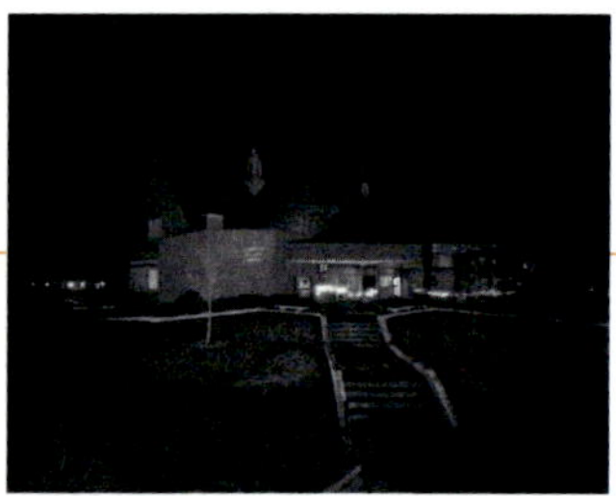

No. 5 **December 7, 1991**
Lorette Wilmot Library, Nazareth College
Rochester, New York

TEMP.	48° F
CAMERA	Sinar F with 65 mm lens
EXPOSURE	45 seconds at *ƒ*/16
FILM	Kodak 4 × 5 T-Max 400
LIGHTING	Multiple flashes of electronic flash units
TEAM	50 volunteers

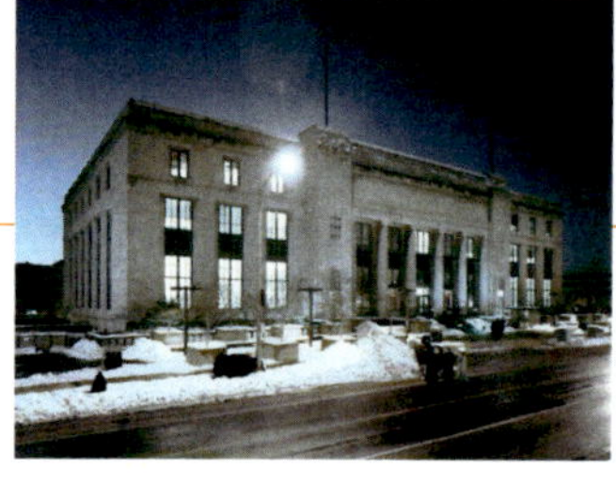

No. 6 **December 13, 1992**
Rundel Memorial Library
Rochester, New York

TEMP.	29° F
CAMERA	Sinar F with 65 mm lens
EXPOSURE	1 minute at *ƒ*/11
FILM	Kodak 4 × 5 Vericolor 400
LIGHTING	Multiple flashes of electronic flash units
TEAM	50 volunteers

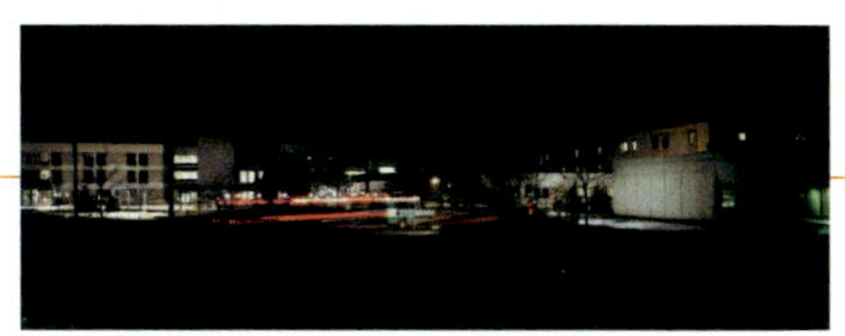

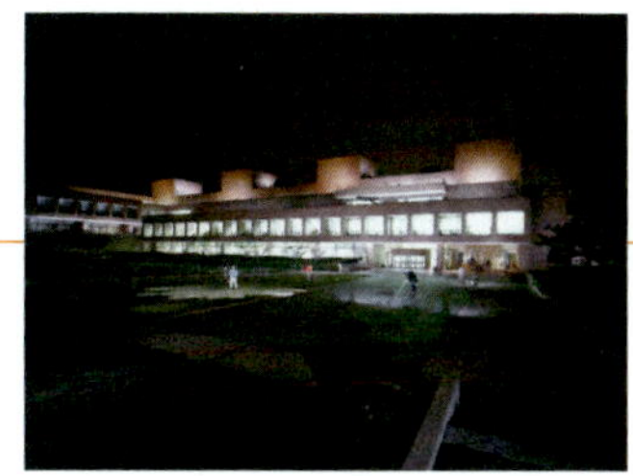

No. 3 December 9, 1989
Park Ridge Hospital
Rochester, New York

TEMP.	22° F
CAMERA	Sinar F with 65 mm lens
EXPOSURE	45 seonds. at *f*/16
FILM	Kodak 4 × 5 Vericolor 400
LIGHTING	Multiple flashes of electronic flash units and 1 old-fashioned flash-powder tray
TEAM	100 volunteers

No. 4 December 8, 1990
Frank E. Gannett Building, RIT Campus
Rochester, New York

TEMP.	38° F
CAMERA	Sinar F with 65 mm lens
EXPOSURE	45 seconds at *f*/11
FILM	Kodak 4 × 5 Vericolor 400
LIGHTING	Multiple flashes of electronic flash units and a few old-fashioned flash bulbs
TEAM	100 volunteers

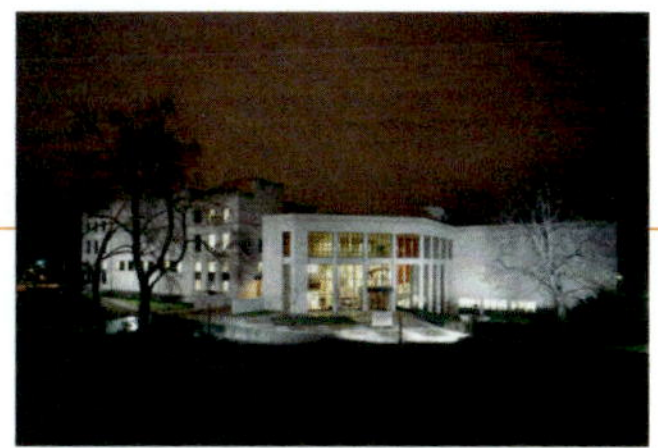

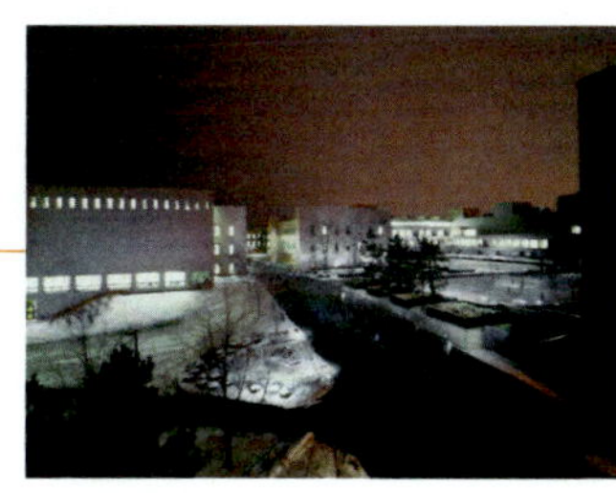

No. 7 December 5, 1993
Rochester Museum & Science Center
Rochester, New York

TEMP.	39° F
CAMERA	Sinar F with 65 mm lens
EXPOSURE	45 seconds at *f*/11
FILM	Kodak 4 × 5 Vericolor 400
LIGHTING	Multiple flashes of electronic flash units
TEAM	100 volunteers

No. 8 January 26, 1995
RIT Campus looking west
Rochester, New York

TEMP.	20° F
CAMERA	Sinar F with 65 mm lens
EXPOSURE	1 minute at *f*/11
FILM	Kodak 4 × 5 Vericolor 400
LIGHTING	Multiple flashes of electronic flash units
TEAM	175 volunteers

1995–2001

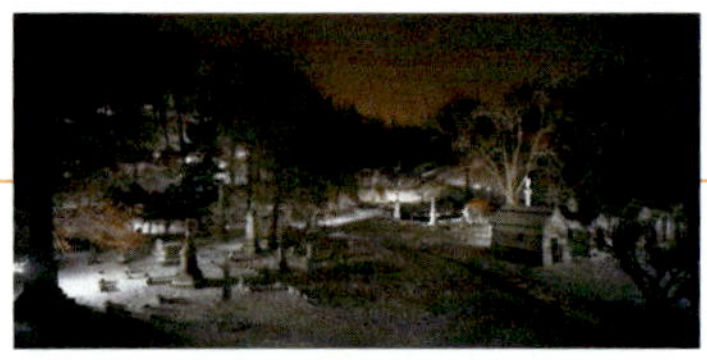

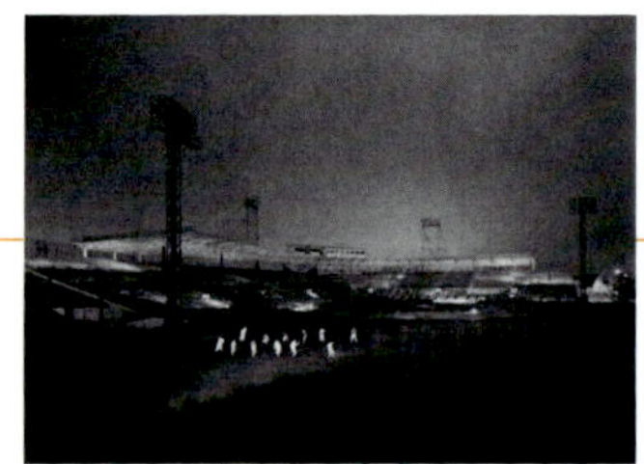

No. 9 **December 13, 1995**
Mount Hope Cemetery
Rochester, New York

TEMP.	22° F
CAMERA	Sinar F with 65 mm lens
EXPOSURE	2 minutes at *f*/11
FILM	Kodak Pro MC 400
LIGHTING	Multiple flashes of electronic flash units
TEAM	150 volunteers

No. 10 **October 9, 1996**
Silver Stadium
Rochester, New York

TEMP.	45° F
CAMERA	Sinar F with 65 mm lens
EXPOSURE	1.5 minutes at *f*/11
FILM	Kodak T-Max 400
LIGHTING	Multiple flashes of electronic flash units
TEAM	125 volunteers

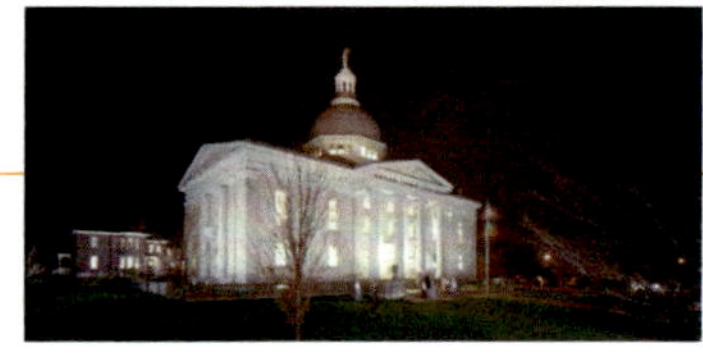

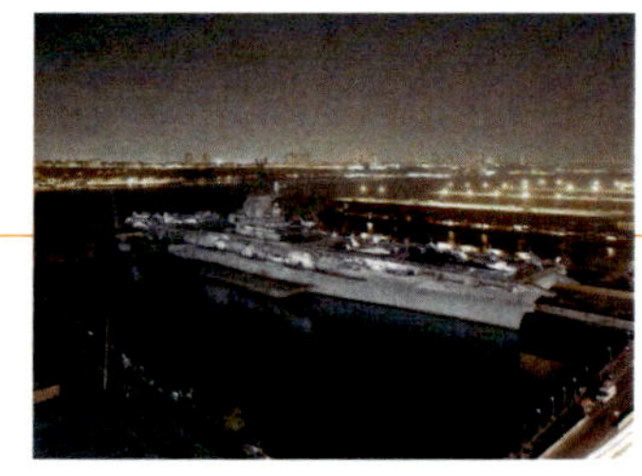

No. 13 **December 10, 1998**
Ontario County Courthouse
Canandaigua, New York

TEMP.	36° F
CAMERA	Sinar F with 65 mm lens
EXPOSURE	1.5 minutes at *f*/11
FILM	Kodak Portra 400 NC
LIGHTING	Multiple flashes of electronic flash units
TEAM	200 volunteers

No. 14 **October 28, 1999**
Intrepid Sea, Air & Space Museum
New York, New York

TEMP.	47° F
CAMERA	Sinar F with 65 mm lens
EXPOSURE	2 minutes at *f*/11
FILM	Kodak Portra 400 NC
LIGHTING	Multiple flashes of electronic flash units
TEAM	1200 volunteers

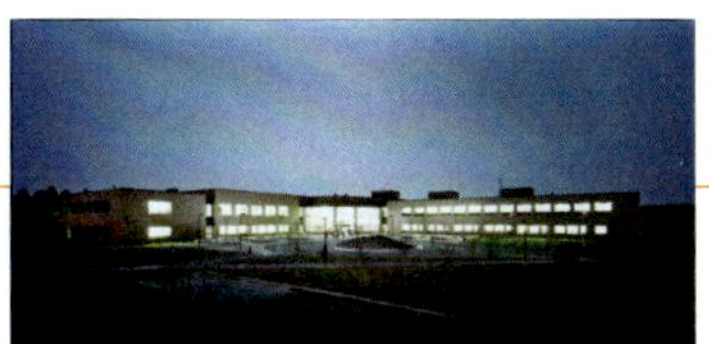

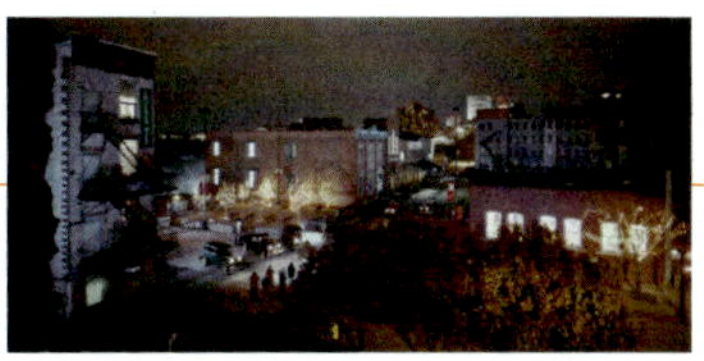

No. 11 **April 3, 1997**
Center for Integrated Manufacturing Studies
RIT Campus, Rochester, New York

TEMP.	48° F
CAMERA	Sinar F with 65 mm lens
EXPOSURE	1 minute at *f*/11
FILM	Kodak 400 NC
LIGHTING	Multiple flashes of electronic flash units
TEAM	50 volunteers

No. 12 **December 8, 1990**
Brown's Race at High Falls
Rochester, New York

TEMP.	34° F
CAMERA	Sinar F with 65 mm lens
EXPOSURE	1.5 minutes at *f*/11
FILM	Kodak 400 NC
LIGHTING	Multiple flashes of electronic flash units
TEAM	200 volunteers

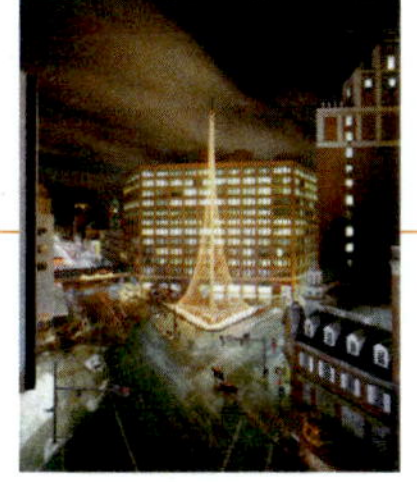

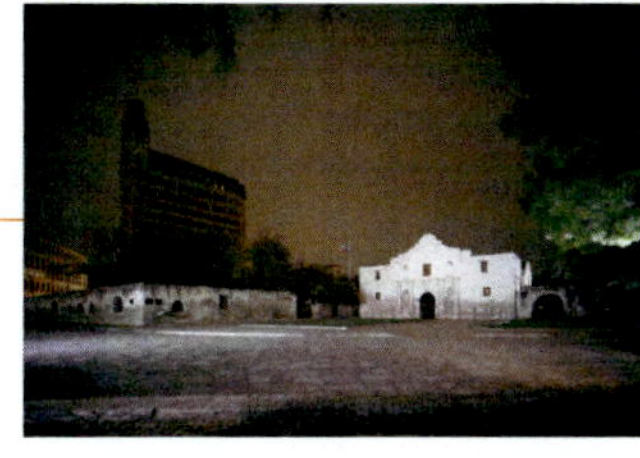

No. 15 **December 2, 2000**
Liberty Pole, Main Street
Rochester, New York

TEMP.	18° F
CAMERA	Sinar F with 65 mm lens
EXPOSURE	1.5 minutes at *f*/11
FILM	Kodak 4 × 5 Portra 400
LIGHTING	Multiple flashes of electronic flash units
TEAM	1100 volunteers

No. 16 **March 10, 2001**
The Alamo
San Antonio, Texas

TEMP.	61° F
CAMERA	Sinar F with 65 mm lens
EXPOSURE	30 seconds at *f*/16
FILM	Kodak 4 × 5 Portra 400
LIGHTING	Multiple flashes of electronic flash units
TEAM	1000 volunteers

2001–2008

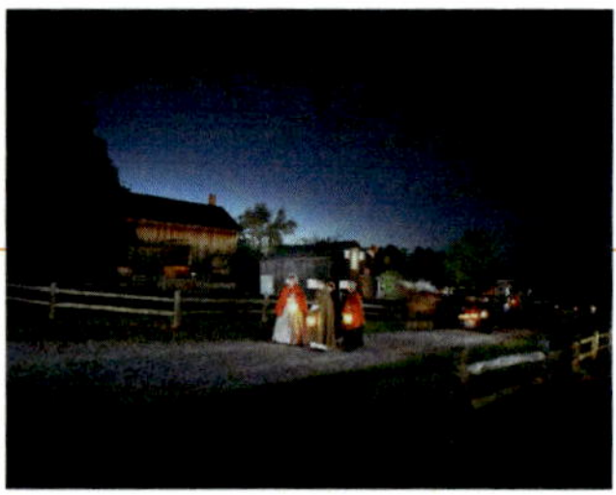

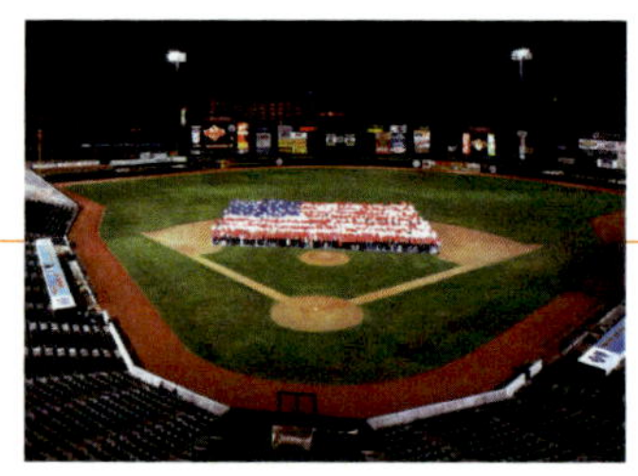

No. 17 **October 6, 2001**
Genesee Country Village & Museum
Mumford, New York

TEMP.	48° F
CAMERA	Sinar F with 65 mm lens
EXPOSURE	1.5 minutes at $f/11$
FILM	Kodak Portra 400 NC
LIGHTING	Multiple flashes of electronic flash units
TEAM	350 volunteers

No. 18 **November 11, 2001**
'Rochester Human Flag' at Frontier Field
Rochester, New York

TEMP.	40° F
CAMERA	Sinar 4 x 5 with 65 mm lens
FILM	Kodak Portra 400 NC
LIGHTING	Illumination provided by the stadium lighting, no painting with light was implemented
TEAM	1000 volunteers

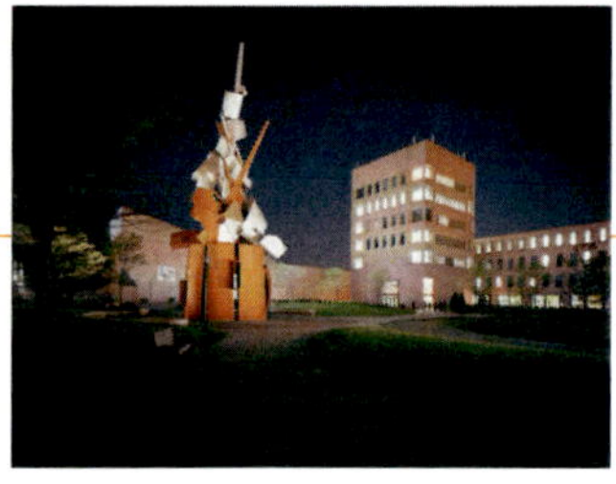

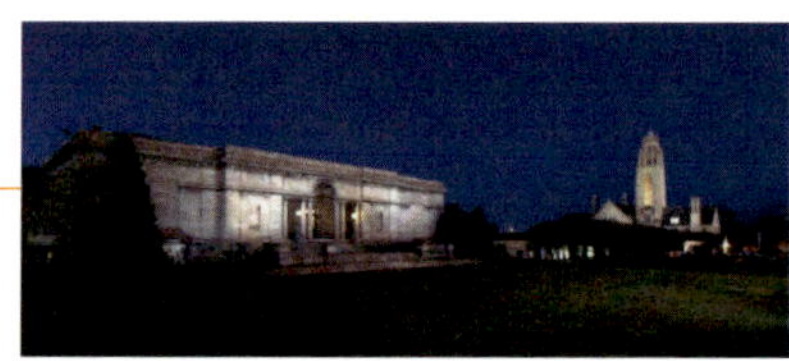

No. 21 **September 12, 2004**
Sentinel Sculpture and Administration Circle
RIT Campus, Rochester, New York

TEMP.	68° F
CAMERA	Sinar F with 65 mm lens
EXPOSURE	45 seconds at $f/16$
FILM	Kodak Portra 400 NC
LIGHTING	Multiple flashes of electronic flash units and flashlights
TEAM	1000 volunteers

No. 22 **May 1, 2006**
Memorial Art Gallery of the University of Rochester
Rochester, New York

TEMP.	62° F
CAMERA	Nikon D200 with 65 mm lens
EXPOSURE	30 seconds at $f/8$
FILM	First Big Shot with Direct Digital Capture
LIGHTING	Multiple flashes of electronic flash units and flashlights
TEAM	750 volunteers

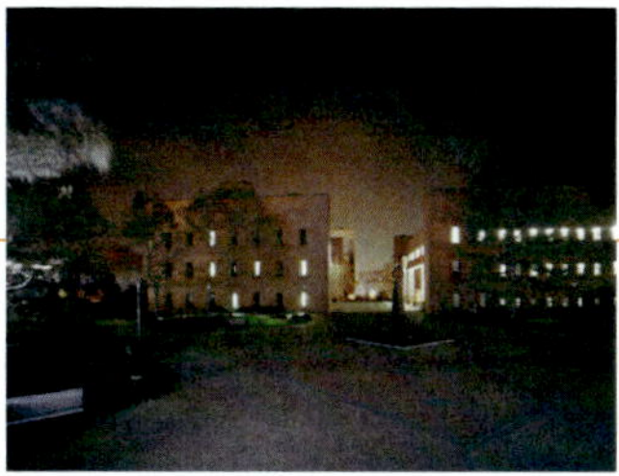

No. 19 **November 7, 2002**
RIT Campus Infinity Quad
Rochester, New York

TEMP.	37° F
CAMERA	Sinar F with 65 mm lens
EXPOSURE	1.5 minutes at *f*/11
FILM	Kodak Portra 400 NC
LIGHTING	Multiple flashes of electronic flash units
TEAM	500 volunteers

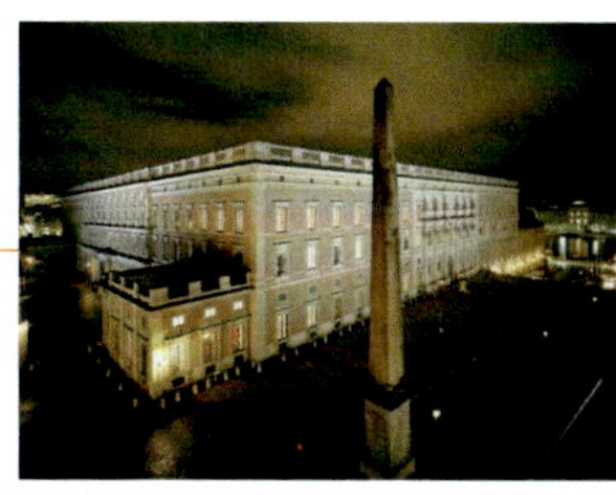

No. 20 **October 9, 2003**
The Royal Palace
Stockholm, Sweden

TEMP.	17° C
CAMERA	Sinar F with 65 mm lens
EXPOSURE	45 seconds at *f*/16
FILM	Kodak Portra 400 NC
LIGHTING	Multiple flashes of electronic flash units
TEAM	350 volunteers

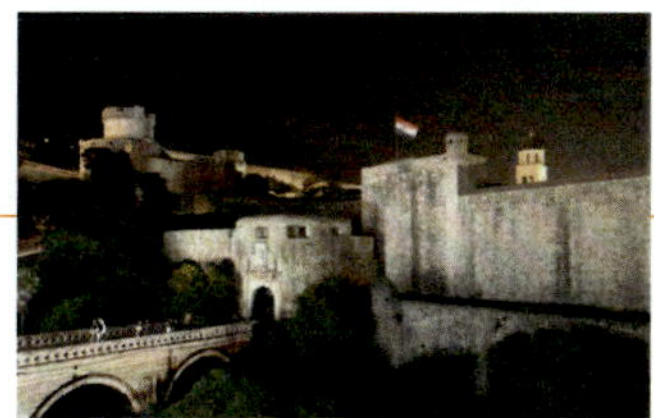

No. 23 **April 12, 2007**
The Pile Gate in Dubrovnik's Old Town
Dubrovnik, Croatia

TEMP.	17° C
CAMERA	Nikon D200 with 20 mm lens
EXPOSURE	90 seconds at *f*/11
LIGHTING	Multiple flashes of electronic flash units and flashlights
TEAM	478 volunteers

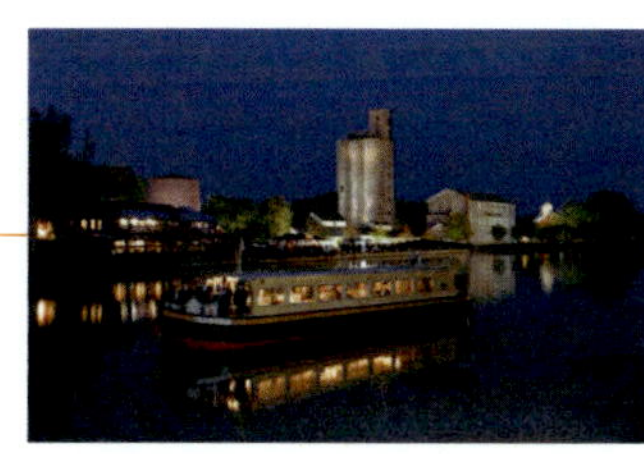

No. 24 **May 8, 2008**
Erie Canal & Schoen Place
Pittsford, New York

TEMP.	52° F
CAMERA	Nikon D3 with 40 mm lens
EXPOSURE	30 seconds at *f*/16 ISO 200
LIGHTING	Multiple flashes of electronic flash units
TEAM	615 volunteers

2009-2016

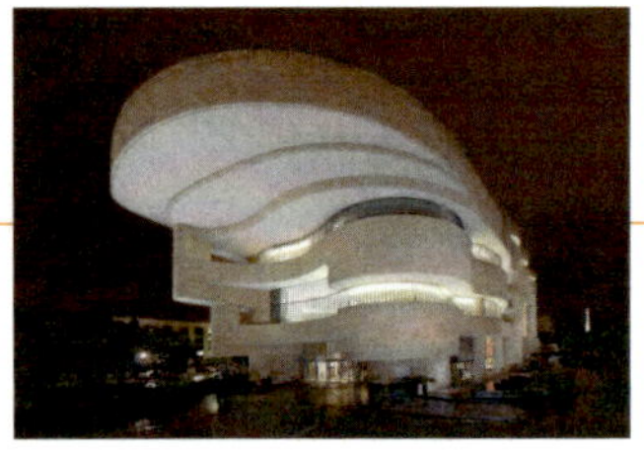

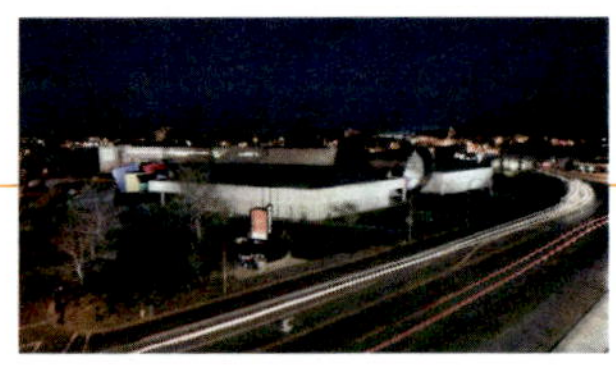

No. 25 **September 26, 2009**
Smithsonian National Museum of the American Indian, Washington, D.C.

TEMP.	60° F
CAMERA	Nikon D3X with 14mm lens
EXPOSURE	20 seconds at *f*/11 ISO 100
LIGHTING	Multiple flashes of electronic flash units and flashlights
TEAM	815 volunteers

No. 26 **May 5, 2011**
National Museum of Play at The Strong
Rochester, New York

TEMP.	56° F
CAMERA	Nikon D3X with 14mm lens
EXPOSURE	15 seconds at *f*/11 ISO 200
LIGHTING	Multiple flashes of electronic flash units and flashlights
TEAM	1003 volunteers

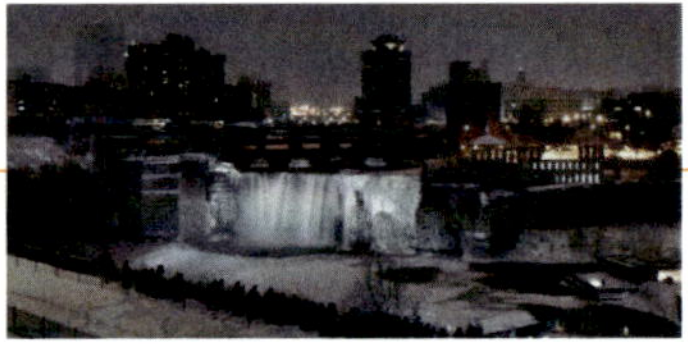

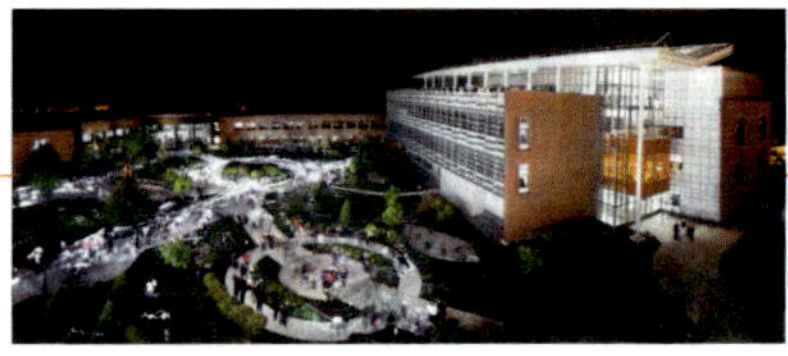

No. 29 **February 9, 2014**
High Falls
Rochester, New York

TEMP.	19° F
CAMERA	Nikon D800 with 24-70/*f* 2.8mm lens
EXPOSURE	30 seconds at *f*/22 ISO 200
LIGHTING	Multiple flashes of electronic flash units, flashlights and Profoto electronic flash equipment
TEAM	750 volunteers

No. 30 **September 6, 2014**
RIT Campus Golisano Institute for Sustainability Building, Louise M. Slaughter Building and Quad
Rochester, New York

TEMP.	67° F
CAMERA	2 x Nikon D810 cameras with 24/*f* 2.8mm lenses
EXPOSURE	30 seconds at *f*/11 ISO 200
GHTING	Multiple flashes of electronic flash units, flashlights and Profoto electronic flash equipment
TEAM	2900 volunteers

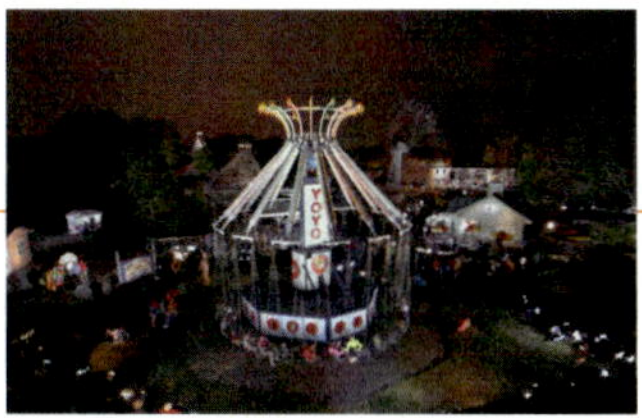

No. 27 **May 3, 2012**
Seabreeze Amusement Park
Rochester, New York

TEMP.	73° F
CAMERA	Nikon D800 with 14 mm lens
EXPOSURE	15 seconds at *f*/11 ISO 200
LIGHTING	Multiple flashes of electronic flash units and flashlights
TEAM	1500 volunteers

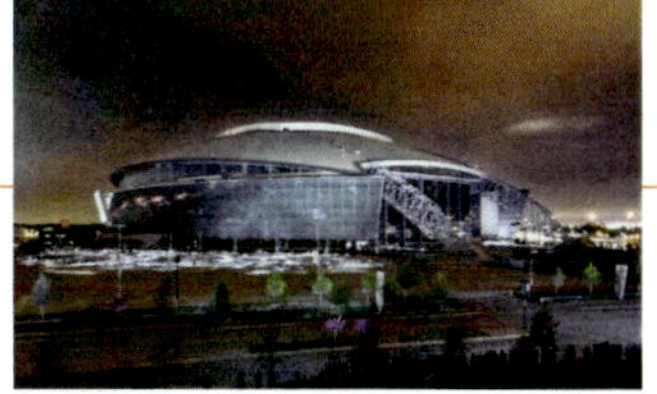

No. 28 **October 9, 2003**
Cowboys Stadium
Arlington, Texas

TEMP.	52° F
CAMERA	Nikon D800 with 14 mm lens
EXPOSURE	30 seconds at *f*/16
LIGHTING	Multiple flashes of electronic flash units and flashlights
TEAM	2430 volunteers

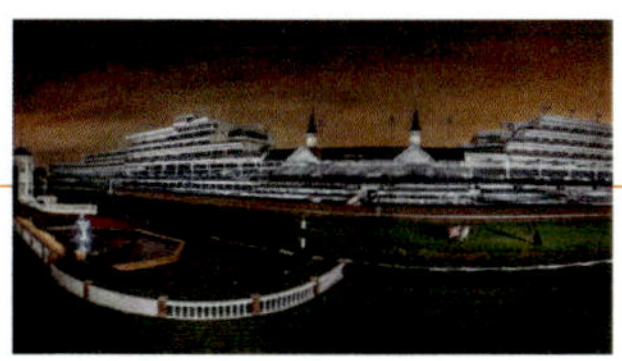

No. 31 **October 3, 2015**
Churchill Downs
Louisville, Kentucky

TEMP.	54° F
CAMERA	4 x Nikon D810 cameras with 8/*f* 1.8 mm lenses
EXPOSURE	30 seconds at *f*/11 ISO 100
TING	Multiple flashes of electronic flash units, flashlights and Profoto electronic flash equipment
TEAM	1800 volunteers

No. 32 **September 18, 2016**
Kodak World Headquarters Building
Rochester, New York

TEMP.	69° F
CAMERA	Nikon D810 camera with 28/*f* 1.8 mm lens
EXPOSURE	60 seconds at *f*/14 ISO 50
TING	Multiple flashes of electronic flash units, flashlights and Profoto electronic flash equipment
TEAM	2800 volunteers

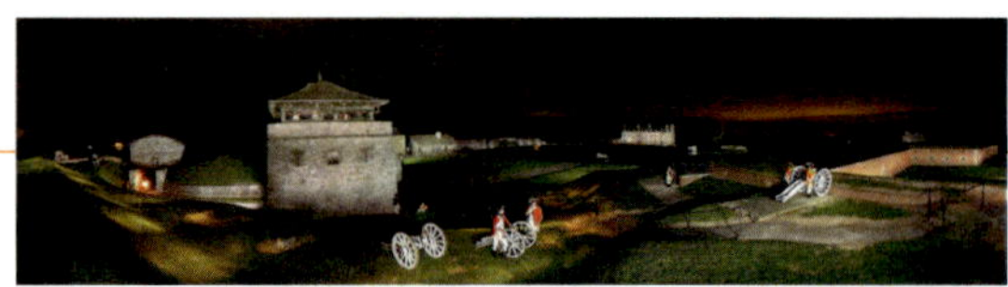

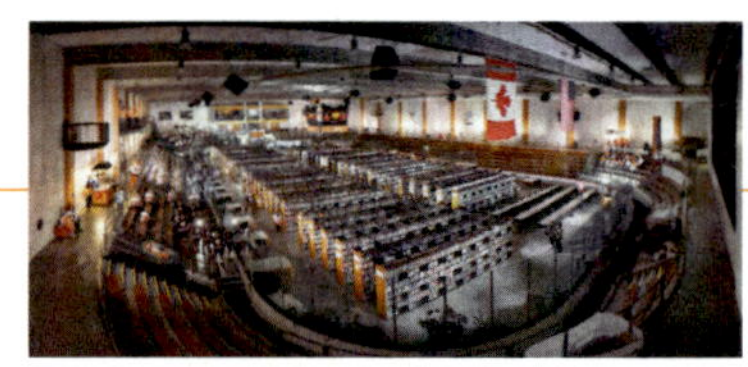

No. 33 September 29, 2018
Old Fort Niagara, Niagara State Park
Porter, New York

CAMERA	6 x Nikon D850 cameras with 20mm ƒ/1.8 lenses
EXPOSURE	90 seconds at ƒ/16 ISO 100
TING	Multiple flashes of electronic flash units, flashlights and Profoto electronic flash equipment
TEAM	825 volunteers

No. 34 April 2, 2022
Wallace On Ice, RIT Campus
Rochester, New York

CAMERA	4 x FujiFilm GFX 100 cameras with 20mm ƒ 2 lenses
EXPOSURE	60 seconds at ƒ/11 ISO 100
TING	Multiple flashes of electronic flash units, flashlights and Profoto electronic flash equipment
TEAM	200 volunteers

Big Shot Shutters Open! Shutters Closed!

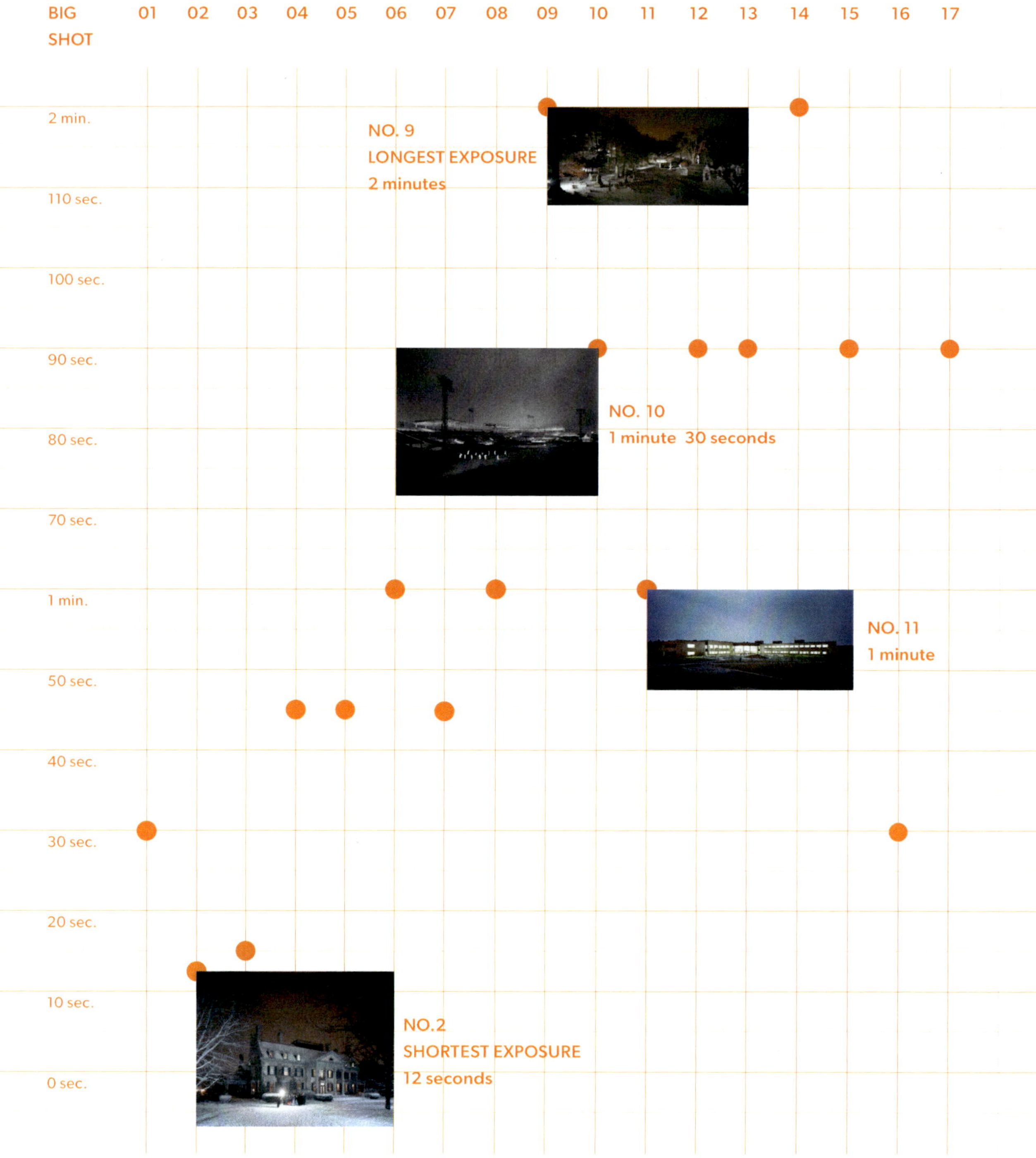

12 sec. to 2 min.

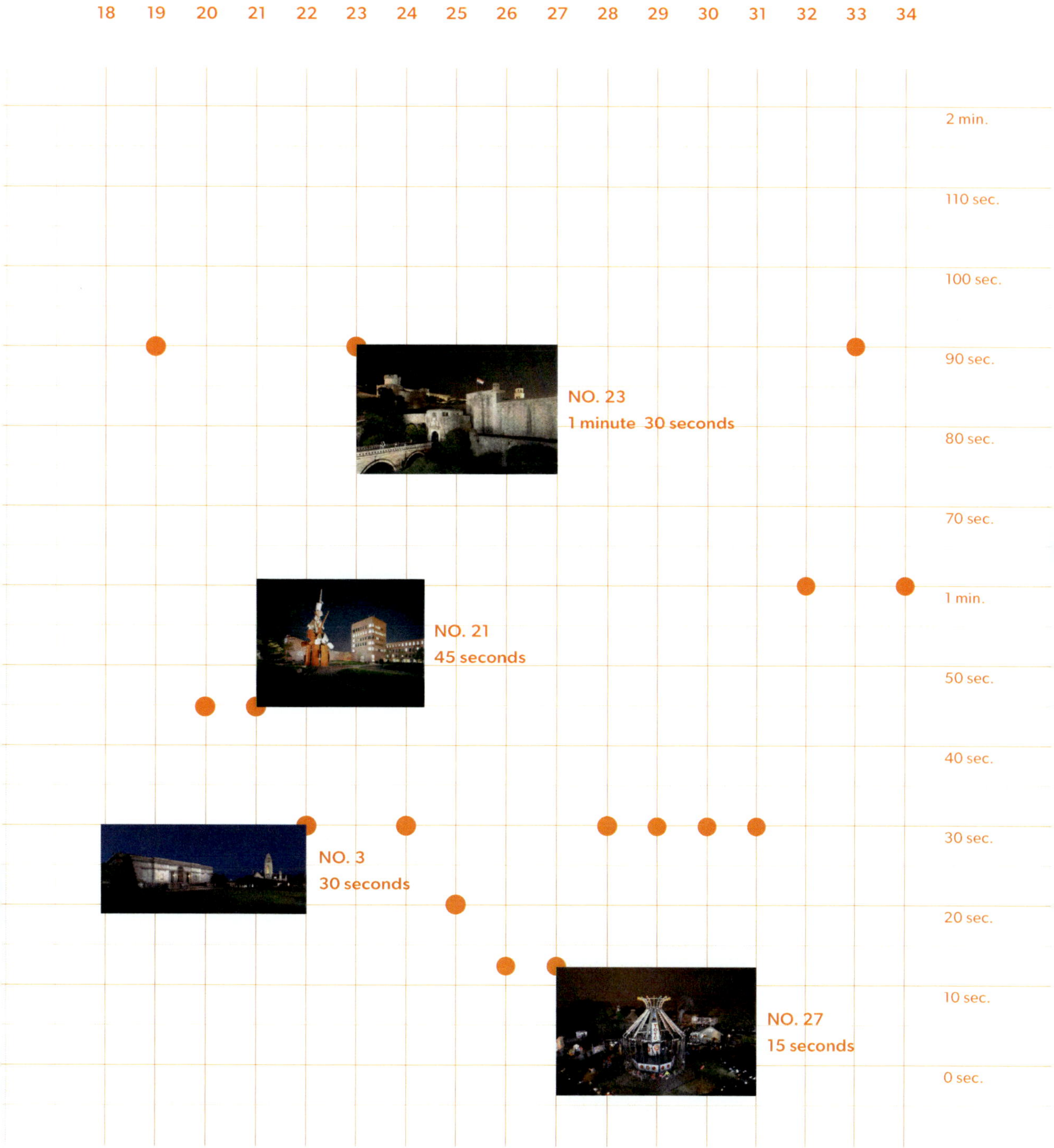

18 19 20 21 22 23 24 25 26 27 28 29 30 31 32 33 34

2 min.

110 sec.

100 sec.

90 sec.

NO. 23
1 minute 30 seconds

80 sec.

70 sec.

1 min.

NO. 21
45 seconds

50 sec.

40 sec.

30 sec.

NO. 3
30 seconds

20 sec.

10 sec.

NO. 27
15 seconds

0 sec.

Big Shot Exposure Time

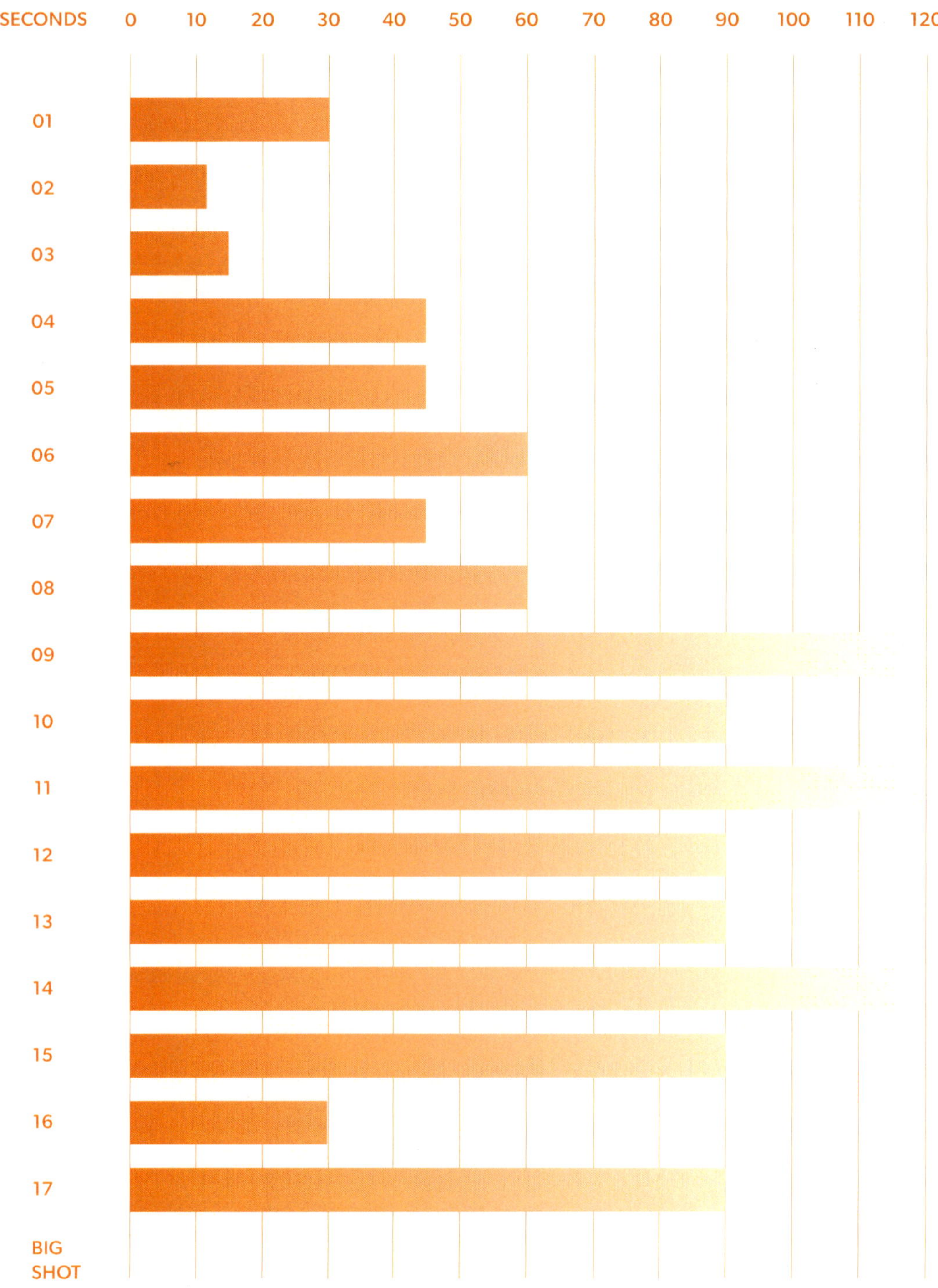

12 sec. to 2 min.

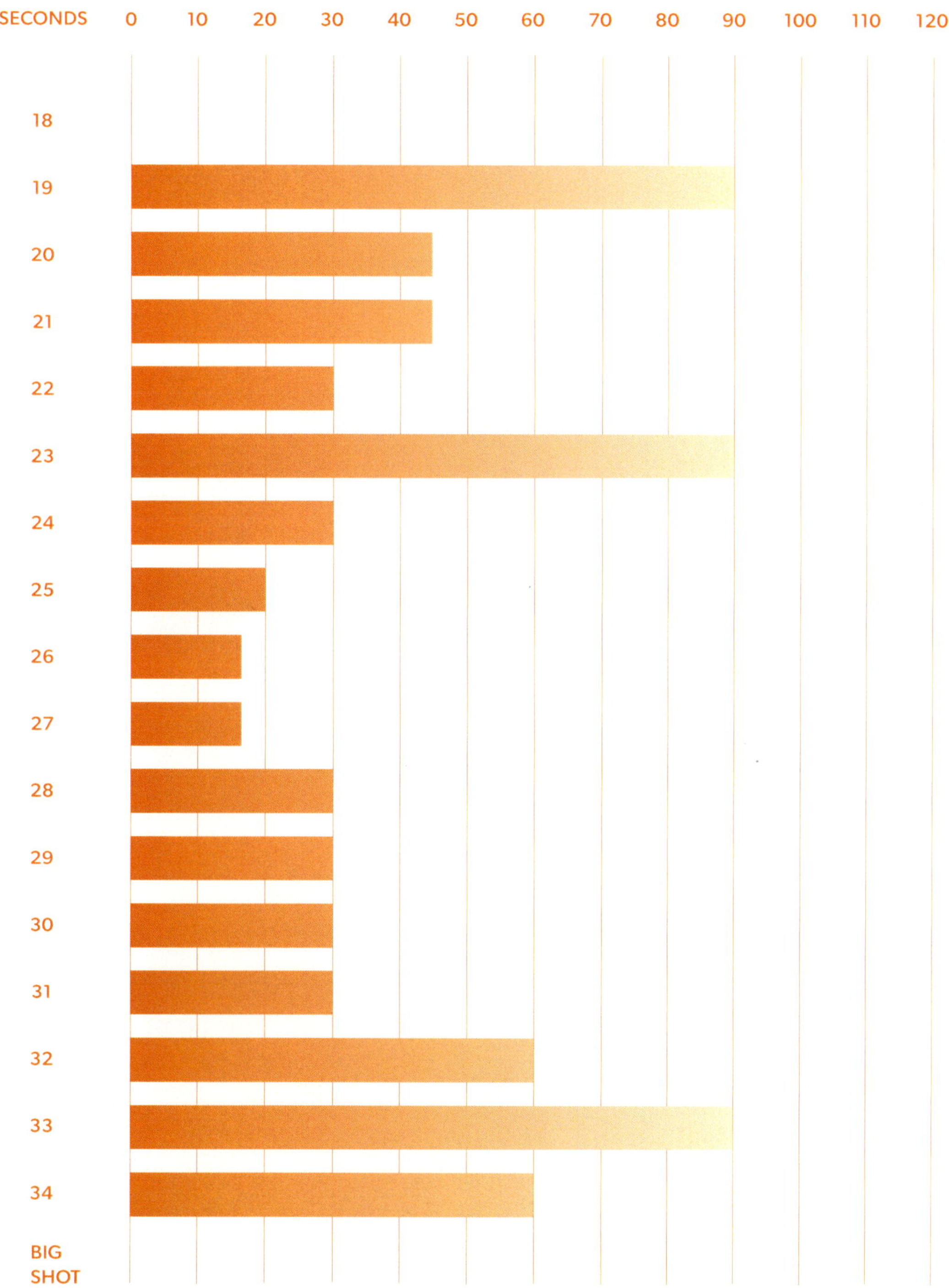

Big Shot Temperatures

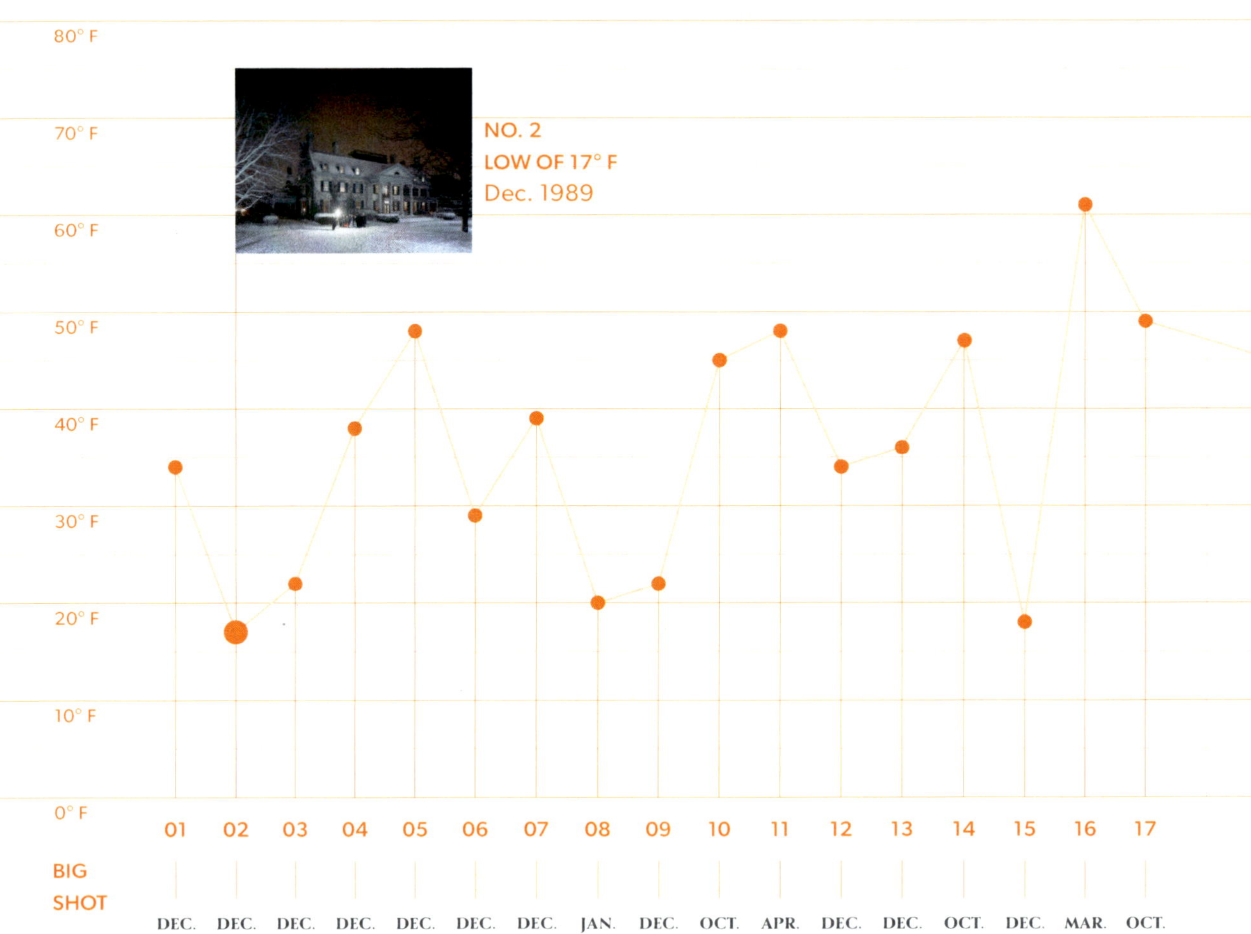

17°F to 68°F

NO. 27
HIGH OF 73° F
May 2012
80° F
70° F
60° F
50° F
40° F
30° F
20° F
10° F
0° F
18 NOV.
19 NOV.
20 OCT.
21 SEP.
22 MAY
23 APR.
24 MAY
25 SEP.
26 MAY
27 MAY
28 MAR.
29 FEB.
30 SEP.
31 OCT.
32 SEP.
33 SEP.
34 APR.

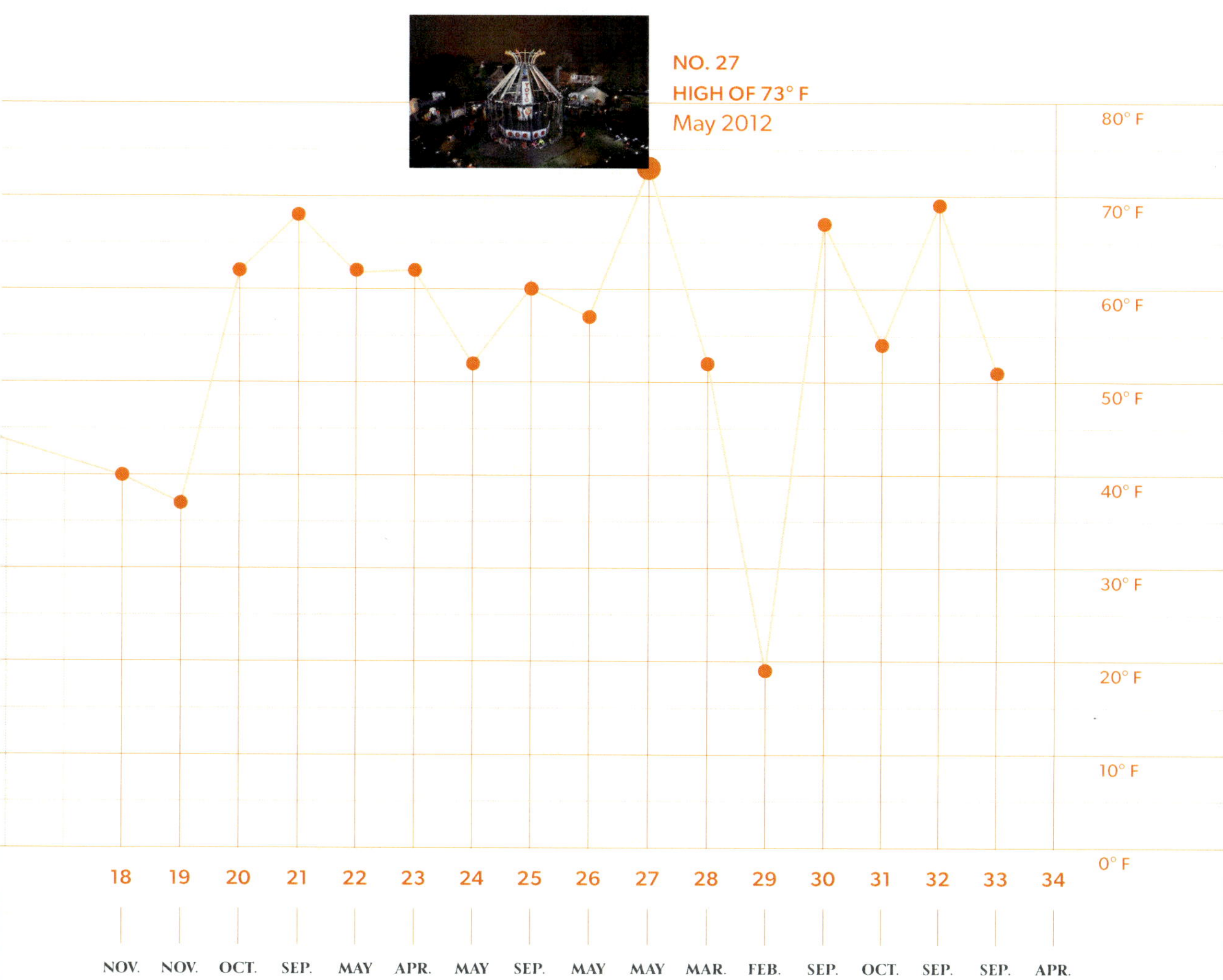

Big Shot Participant Milestones

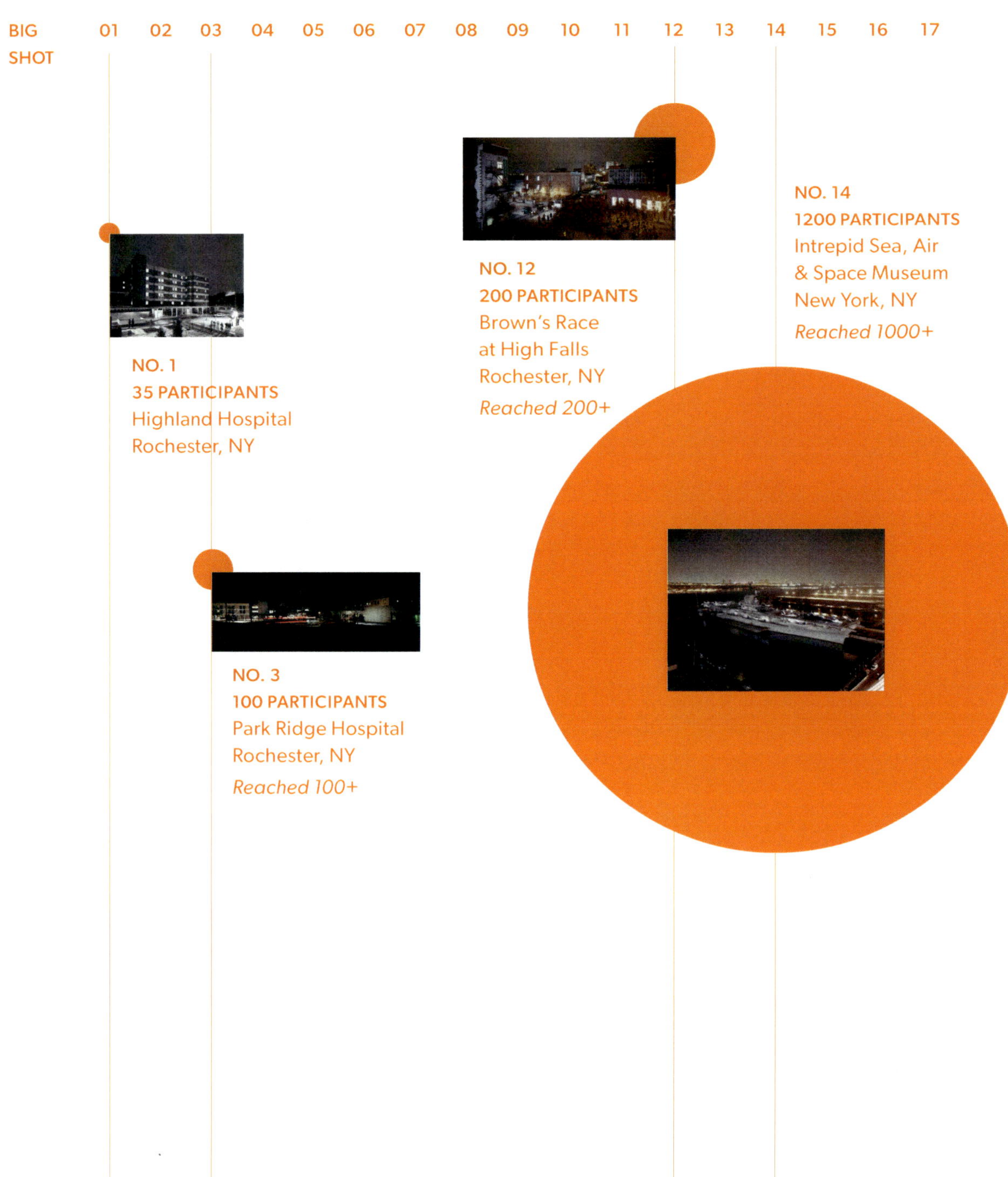

18 19 20 21 22 23 24 25 26 27 28 39 30 31 32 33 34

NO. 28
2430 PARTICIPANTS
Cowboys Stadium
Arlington, TX
Reached 2000+

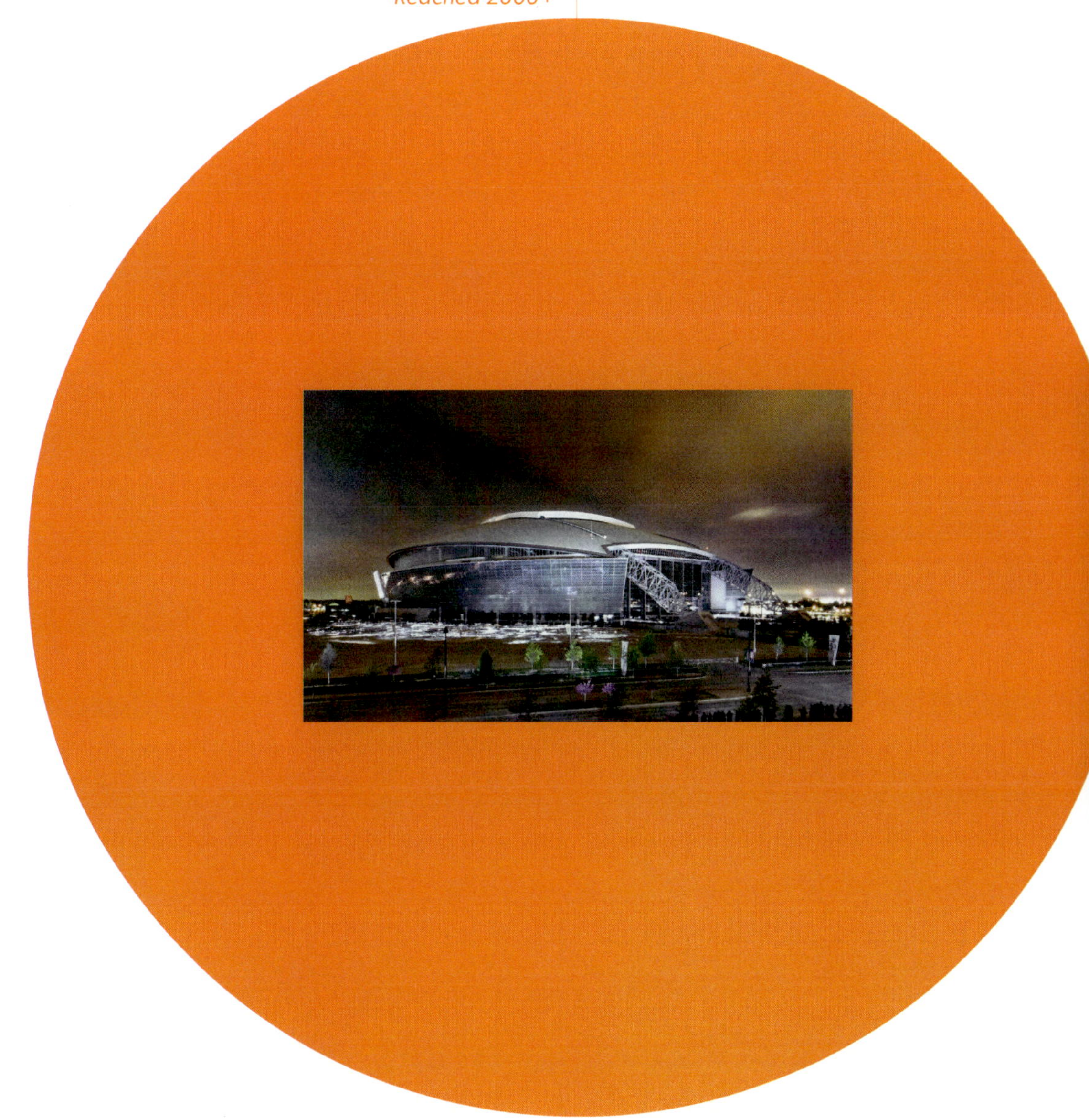

Big Shot Dates

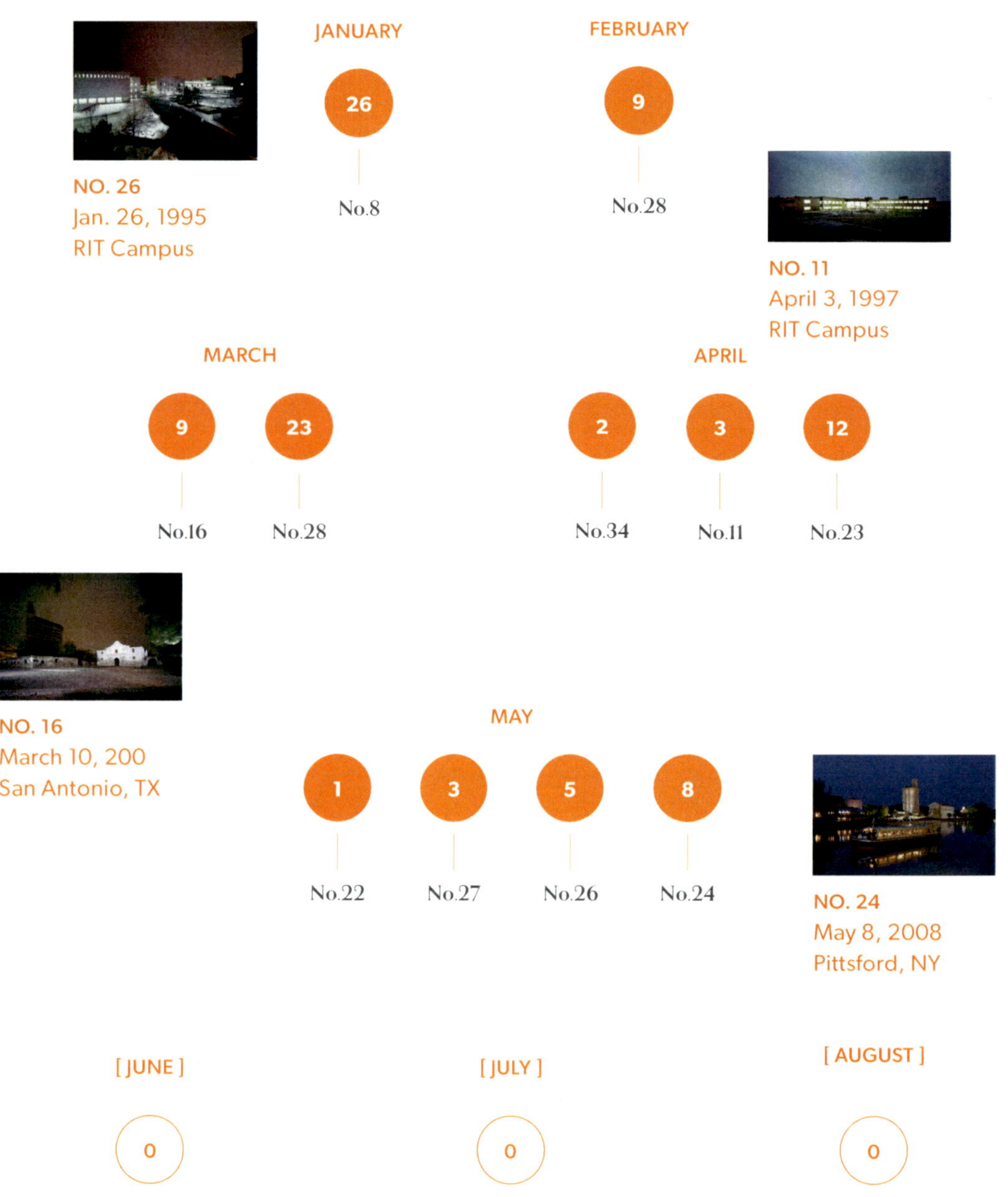

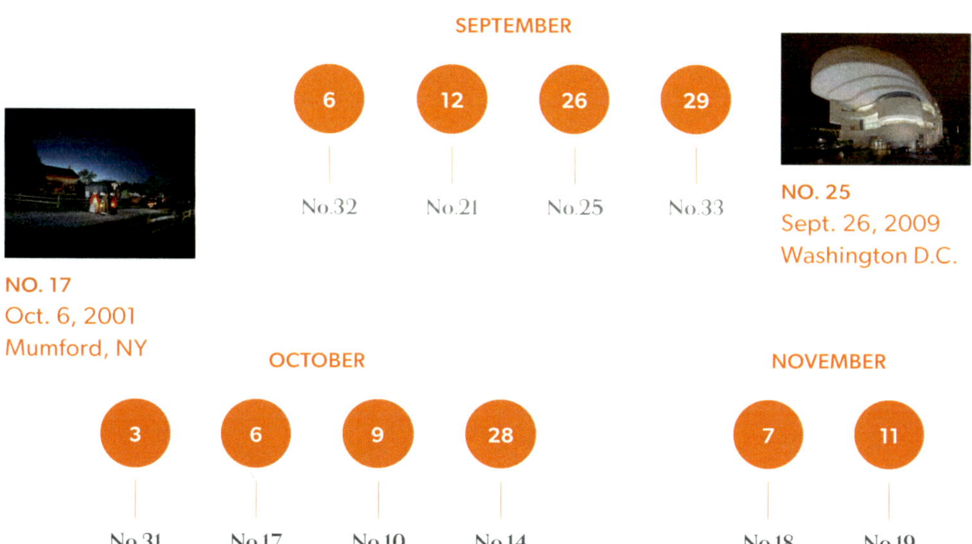

NO. 25
Sept. 26, 2009
Washington D.C.

NO. 17
Oct. 6, 2001
Mumford, NY

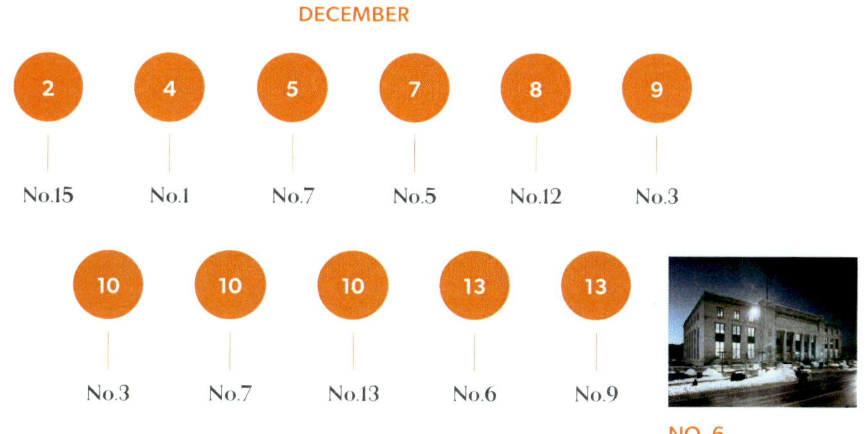

NO. 6
Dec. 13, 1992
Rochester, NY

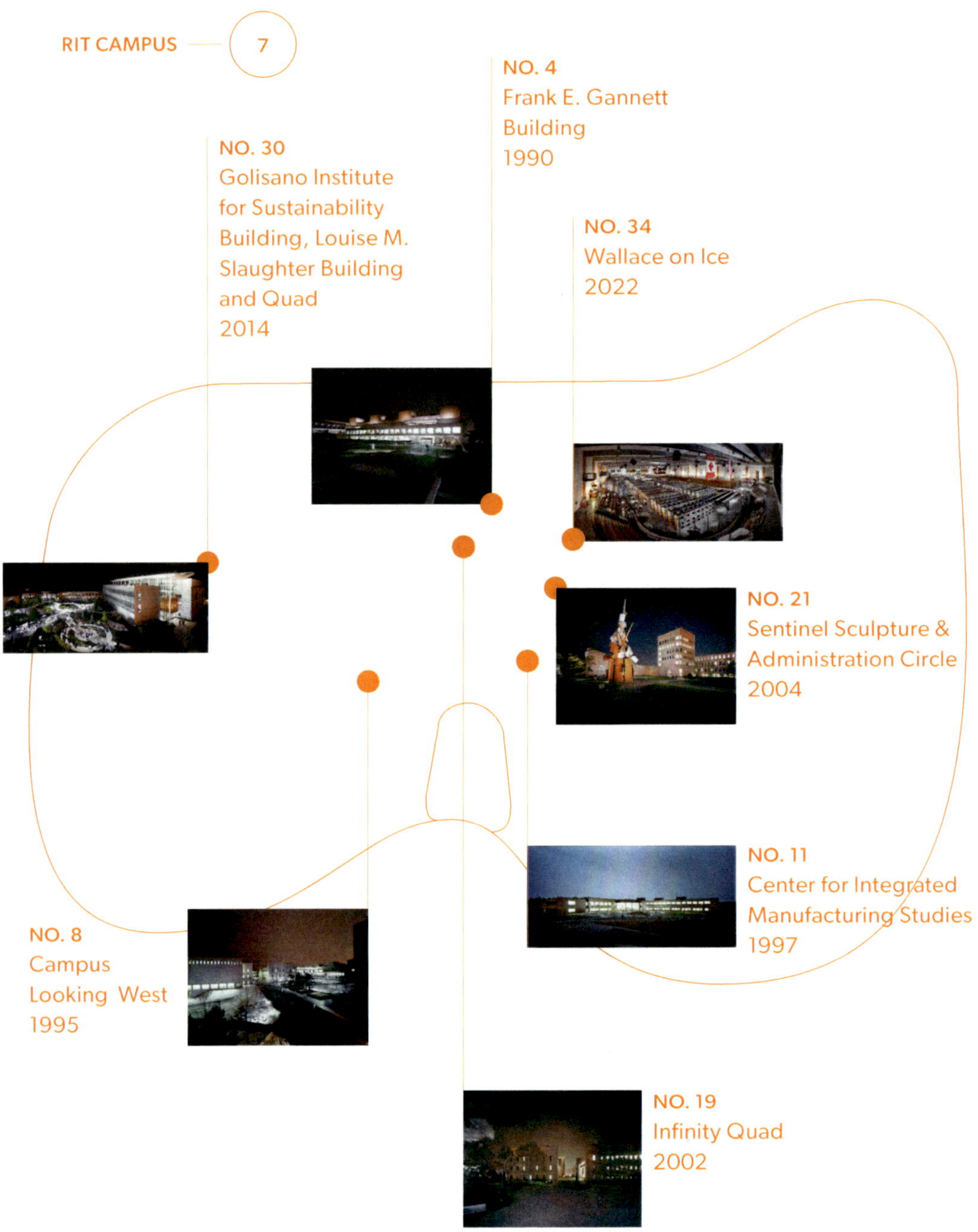
RIT CAMPUS
7
NO. 4
Frank E. Gannett
Building
1990
NO. 30
Golisano Institute
for Sustainability
Building, Louise M.
Slaughter Building
and Quad
2014
NO. 34
Wallace on Ice
2022
NO. 21
Sentinel Sculpture &
Administration Circle
2004
NO. 11
Center for Integrated
Manufacturing Studies
1997
NO. 8
Campus
Looking West
1995
NO. 19
Infinity Quad
2002

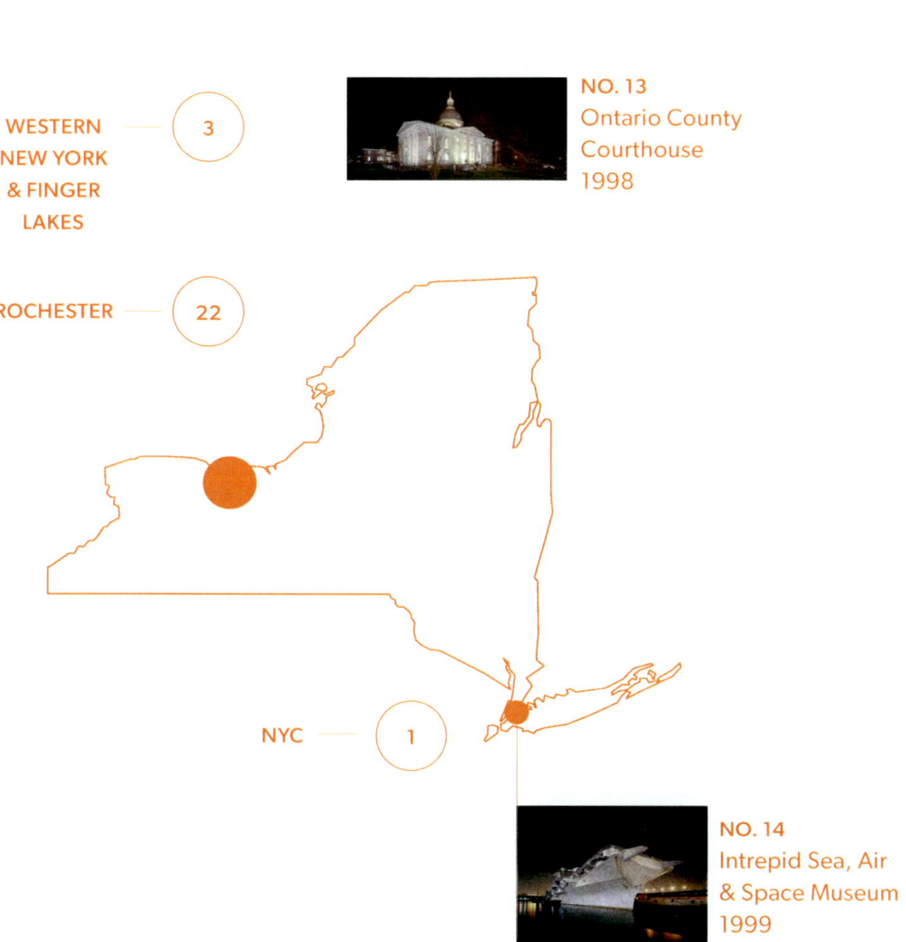
NEW YORK STATE
24
WESTERN NEW YORK & FINGER LAKES
3
NO. 13
Ontario County Courthouse
1998
ROCHESTER
22
NYC
1
NO. 14
Intrepid Sea, Air & Space Museum
1999

Downtown Rochester

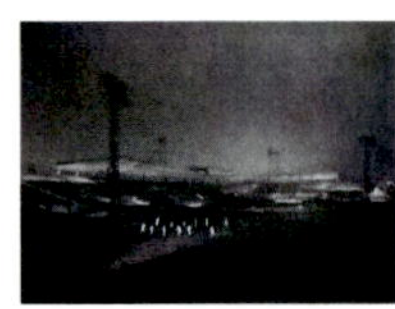
NO. 10
Silver Stadium
1996

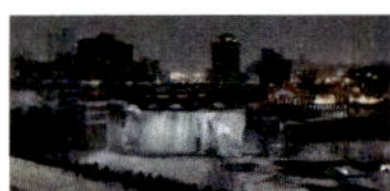
NO. 29
High Falls
2014

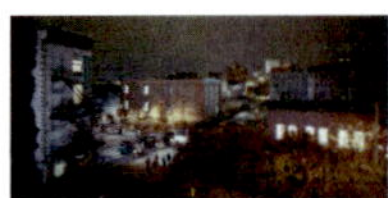
NO. 12
Brown's Race at High Falls
1997

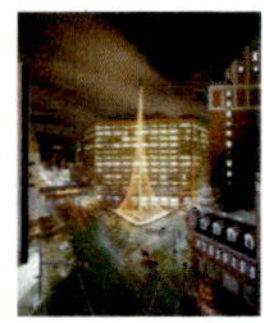
NO. 15
Liberty Pole, Main Street
2000

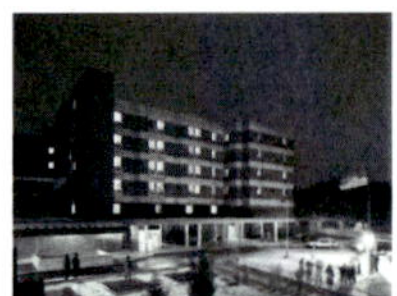
NO. 1
Highland Hospital
1987

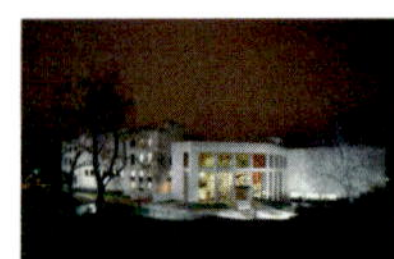
NO. 7
Rochester Museum & Science Center
1993

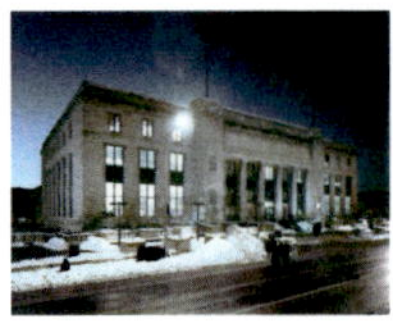
NO. 6
Rundel Memorial Library

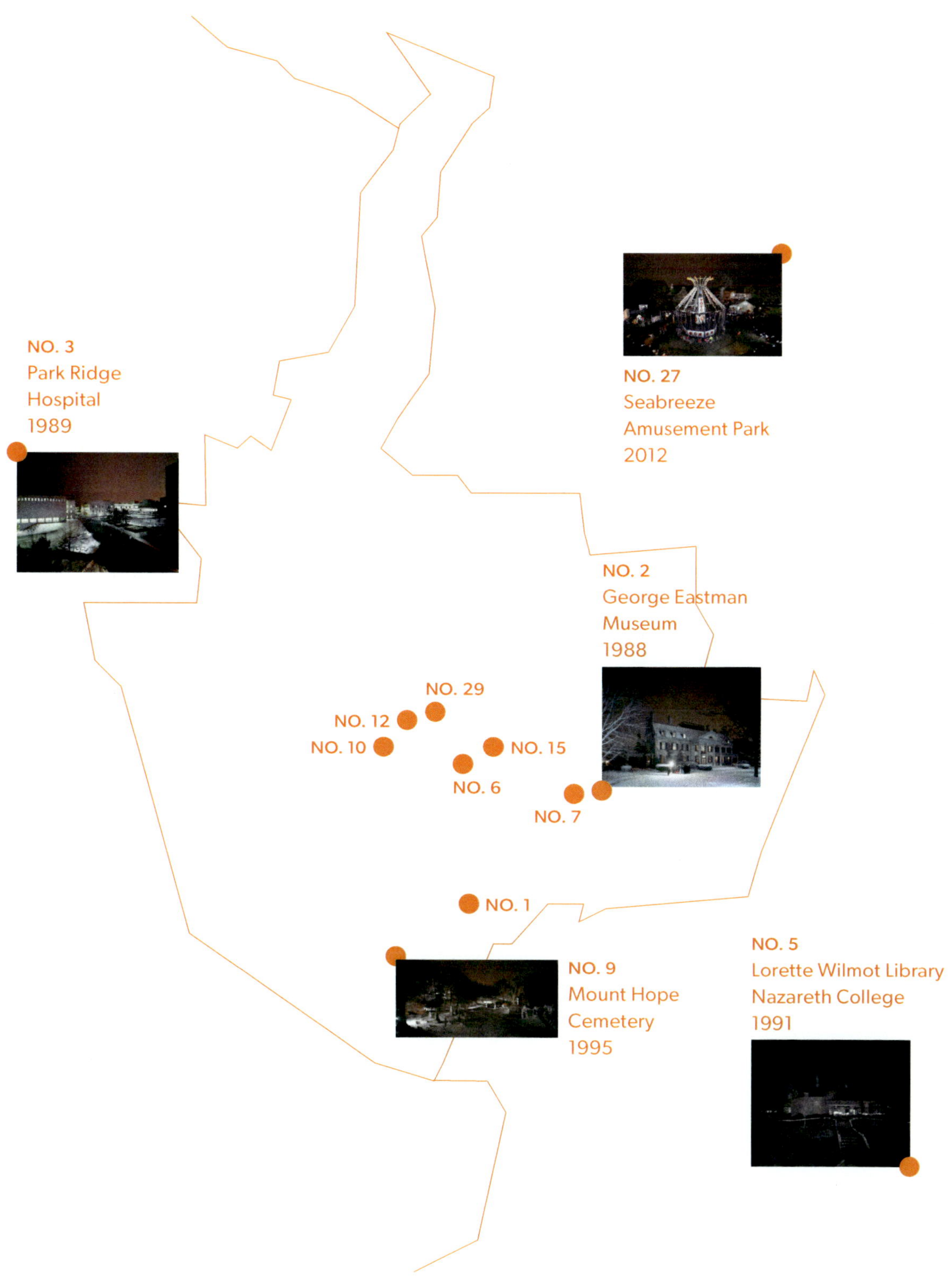
NO. 3
Park Ridge
Hospital
1989
NO. 27
Seabreeze
Amusement Park
2012
NO. 2
George Eastman
Museum
1988
NO. 29
NO. 12
NO. 10
NO. 15
NO. 6
NO. 7
NO. 1
NO. 9
Mount Hope
Cemetery
1995
NO. 5
Lorette Wilmot Library
Nazareth College
1991

Beyond New York

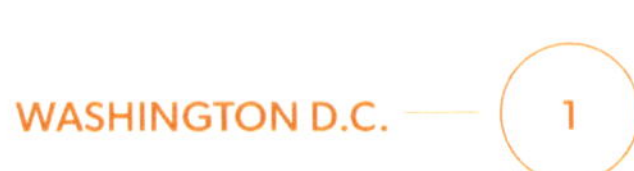

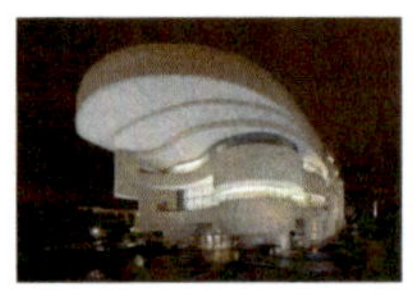

NO. 25
Smithsonian National Museum of the American Indian
2009

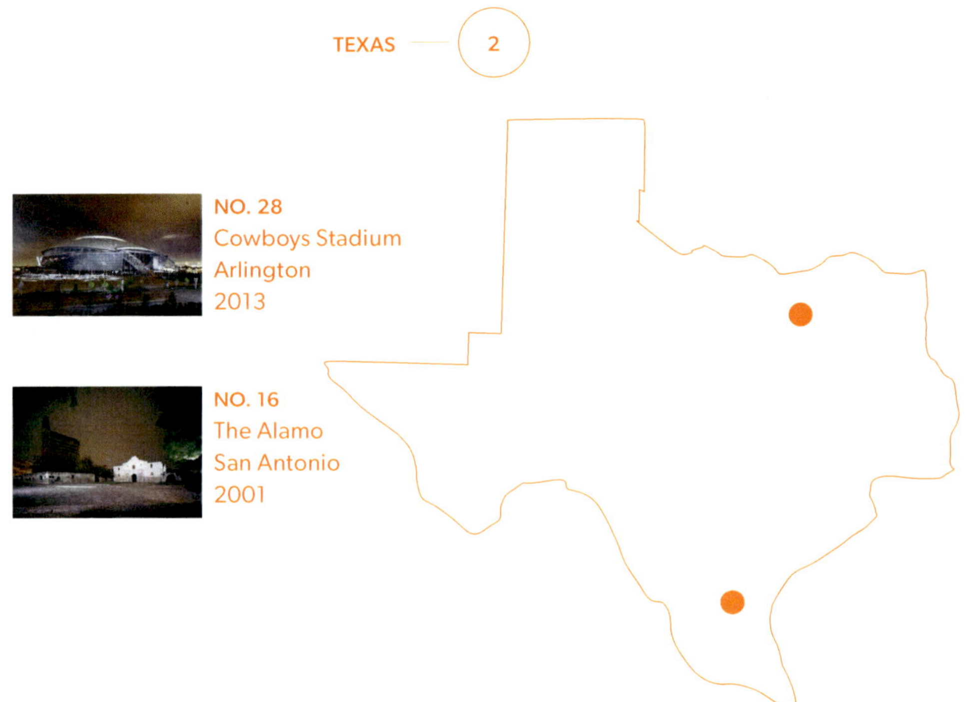

NO. 28
Cowboys Stadium
Arlington
2013

NO. 16
The Alamo
San Antonio
2001

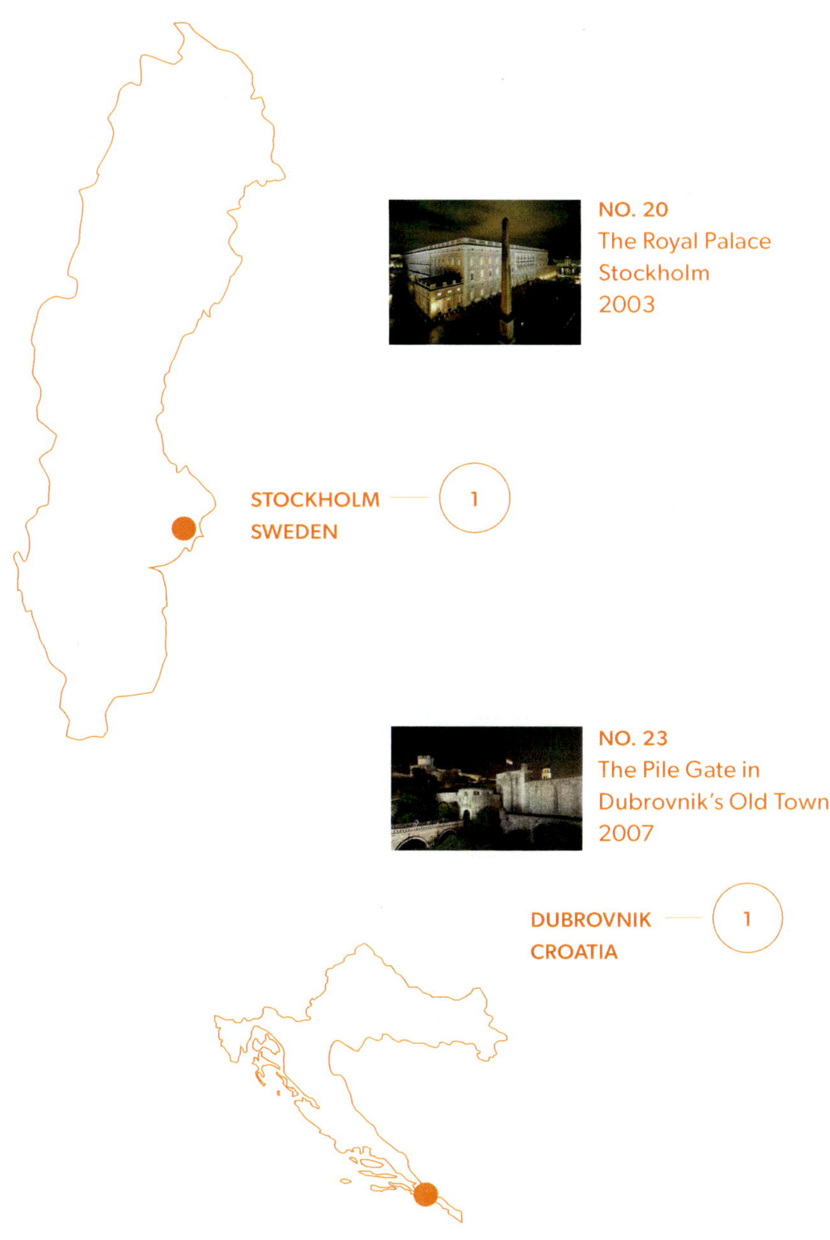
NO. 20
The Royal Palace
Stockholm
2003
STOCKHOLM
SWEDEN
1
NO. 23
The Pile Gate in
Dubrovnik's Old Town
2007
DUBROVNIK
CROATIA
1

Making a Big Shot

The making of Big Shot photographs entails a complex process requiring approvals, partners and much planning as to the proposed location. No detail is too small or too large to consider when trying do something of such magnitude as large-scale nighttime photography. Location conditions, including the number of volunteers needed to realize a photograph, play an important role in planning an appropriate considered view. Each Big Shot photograph requires more than a year of planning, with involvement of many groups to get a project off the ground. Gaining the trust and approval of location personnel, often including government or site managers, is the first step in the process as well as defining the pictorial scope and merit of the shoot. Separate from a technical vision, concerns for safety, weather on day of shoot, and creating a fun and family-friendly activity is paramount. Strategic partnerships are also critical to taking on new projects and creating larger and more ambitious events. In 2007, the Big Shot organizers began a strategic partnership with Nikon Professional Services, which provided camera hardware, financial help, and personnel assistance.

Once location permission is received, setting a date, finding the ideal vantage point of the architectural view and developing a lighting plan with placement of participants is the focus of organizers. This is followed by fund-raising, building community engagement, alerting media, and inviting students.

On the evening of a shoot, all ambient lighting that might obscure the extended exposure of the nighttime photograph are extinguished when possible. These might include street lamps, light through windows, etc. After a public countdown, the Big Shot photographers record an extended exposure of the architectural view while volunteers—who are dressed in dark clothing and strategically located in predetermined areas—"paint" the subject with handheld lights. At most, four exposures are made of the pictorial scene and, upon completion, the Big Shot team work to finalize the best image via image processing prior to dissemination to those who participated and news organizations.

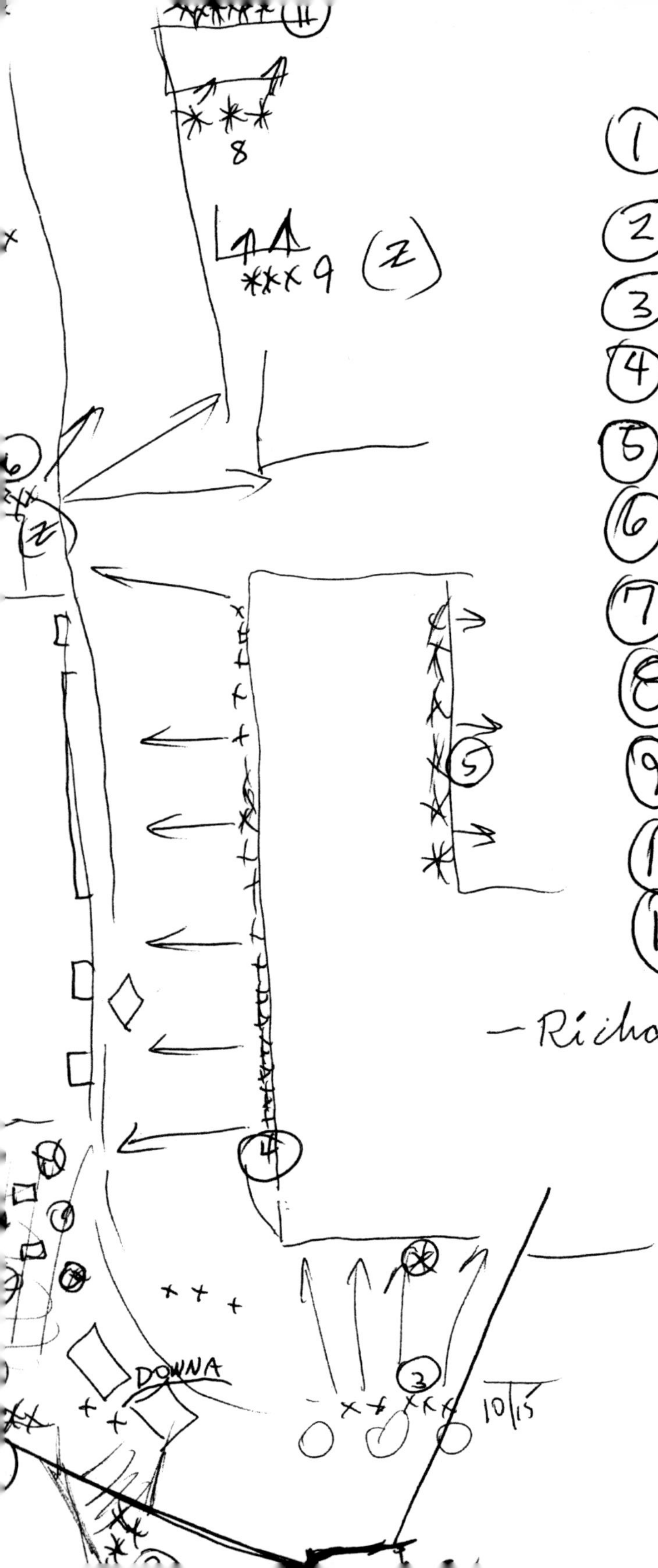

(11)

8

9 (Z)

(6)

(Z)

(5)

(4)

(3)

DONNA

10/15

(1) gunther 50/75

(2) Retallak 10

(3) Christye 10 — 100

(4) LeVant 50

(5) 10/15

(6) ZIGON 15 100

(7) white 10

(8) white 10/15

(9) 10 50

(10) Haven } 50/75 100

(11) Richardson

— Richardson

gunther

(1) 50

(2) 10

(3) 10

(4) 50 — 100

(5) 20

(6) 15

(7) 10 150

(8) 10

(9) 10

10 & 11 50

/200

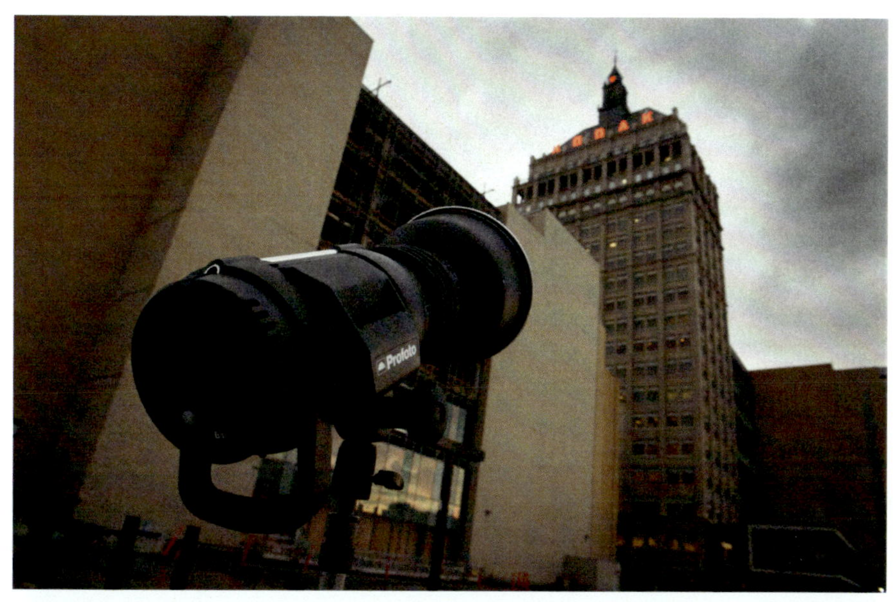

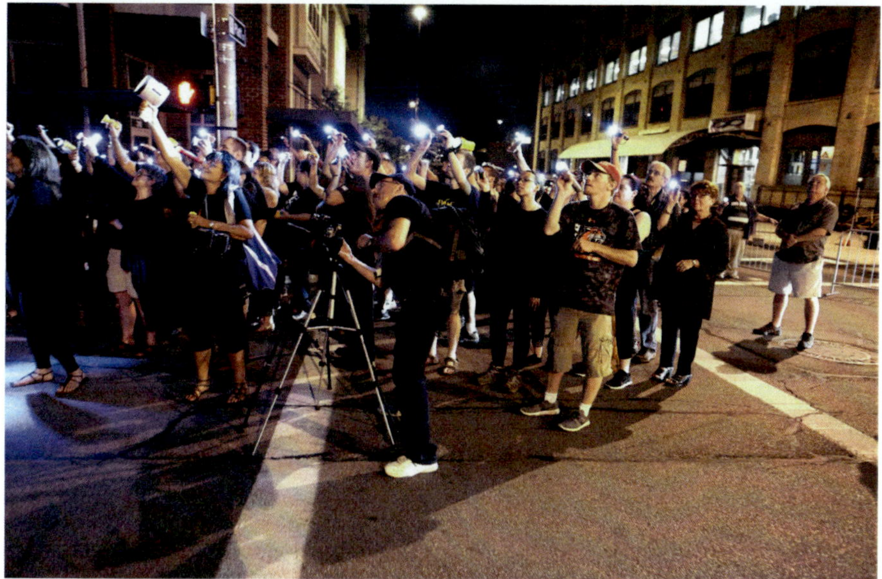

Above: Setting up Profoto lighting equipment for for Big Shot No. 32 at the base of the Kodak Tower. Bottom: Participants light Kodak Tower from State Street, Rochester, New York. Left: A drawing of the lighting plan for Big Shot No. 12 Brown's Race.

PHOTOGRAPHY

Setting up a big shot

BY MICHAEL BROWN

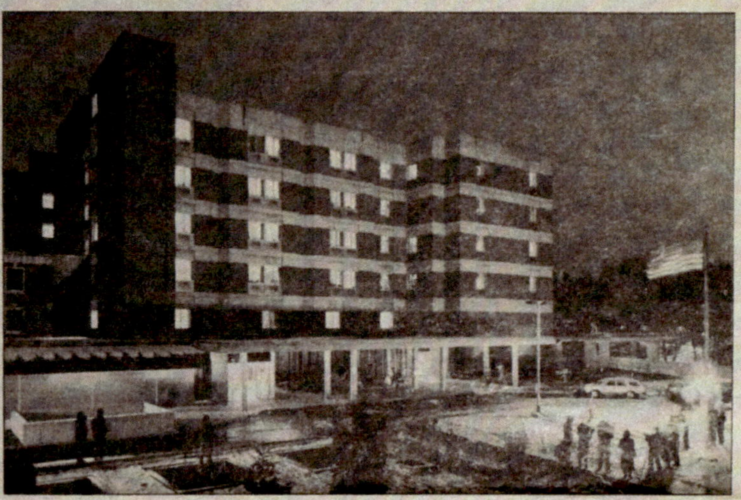

It was a Friday evening early last month. Night had fallen and the temperature was hovering at the freezing mark. Snow clouds, faintly illuminated by the city lights, were low in the sky. About 34 RIT photography students scrambled in front of Highland Hospital getting ready for the "Big Shot."

The "Big Shot" refers to a method of outdoor illumination used to photograph large buildings or other massive structures. It involves carefully placing flashes around the structure to create a collective and very powerful light source.

In the past, it has been done with hundreds, even thousands, of flash bulbs and generally sponsored by the flash bulb maker, Sylvania. These publicity events were most popular in the 1950s. Structures the size of the pyramids were photographed this way but the most impressive was Joseph Costa's photograph of the aircraft carrier *U.S.S. Antietam*. He lined the carrier with flash bulbs, and, from an airplane, he tripped the bulbs with radio remote control getting a single chance to make the photograph.

He got his picture.

Electronic flashes provided the illumination for the Highland Hospital photograph. Each flash was manned by a student with the instructions to aim high and fire it as many times as possible while the camera shutter was open. They were also instructed to keep the batteries warm for faster recycle time.

Organizer Michael Peres, an instructor in RIT's Biomedical Photographic Communications department, placed about half of the students in a line by the flagpole in front of the hospital. Other students were under the portico, some just wandered.

When asked why they did the photograph at all, Peres said, "We want to demonstrate that you can do nice photography with a minimum of equipment and how to paint with light from our flash equipment".

The hospital had agreed to participate by turning off all outside lights for about 15 minutes and asking all rooms on the west side to have the interior lights on.

Associate Professor and Chairman of the Biomedical Communications department, Bill Dubois, assisted with the official 4x5 camera mounted on the top floor of the parking garage. He also had what can only be described as a whoopie whistle to signal when the camera shutter was being opened and closed.

The final exposure was 30 seconds at f/11. It was hard to beleive but the first test exposure on 400 speed Polaroid film was grossly overexposed and Dubois had to cut the exposure time in half and add an f/stop. The final photograph was taken on Kodak black-and-white T-Max 4x5 inch sheet film.

To add some novelty to the scene student Corey Meitchik and Kodak employee Martin Scott used flashpowder in the traditional tray to add some light. As Peres called for everyone to take their positions, those near the flashpowder quickly scattered. A bright flash accompanied by a loud bang and what would be most easily described as a mini-pyrotechnics display stole everyone's attention. The flashpowder had a light output equivalent to about a dozen Vivitar 283 strobes going off simultaneously.

Dubois says the Highland Hospital picture-taking was also a good lesson in problem solving. He says biomedical photography is basically a problem-solving field because most of what you're asked to photograph hasn't been photographed before and it's your job to make the picture.

QUESTIONS?

Have a question about photography? Put it on paper and send it in. In my *Q&A* section I'll get the answers to your photography questions from local experts and publish them in this column. Include your name, address, day and evening phone numbers and any appropriate photo samples that would help describe your problem. Mail to:

Upstate Photography
Attn.: Michael Brown
55 Exchange Blvd.
Rochester, NY 14614

CALL FOR PRINTS

If you have a photograph you would like to share with *Upstate* readers, we would like to see it. Some will be published with this column. Include information about camera type, lens, film, shutter speed, f/stop and any other facts pertinent to the picture. Send black-and-white prints, color prints or color transparencies to:

Upstate Photography
Attn.: Michael Brown
55 Exchange Blvd.
Rochester, NY 14614

If you want your photos returned, enclose a self-addressed, stamped envelope large enough for the material. We'll make every effort to take care of your photographs, but we cannot be held responsible for loss or damage.

MICHAEL BROWN is photo editor for the Democrat and Chronicle *and* Times-Union.

Above: Article from the Rochester Times-Union Weekend Magazine featuring Big Shot No. 1 produced December 1987.

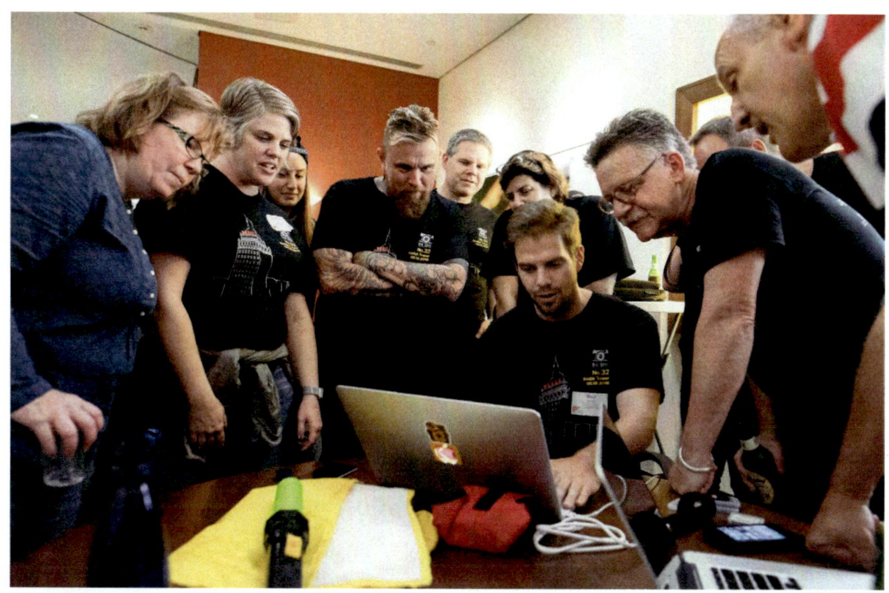

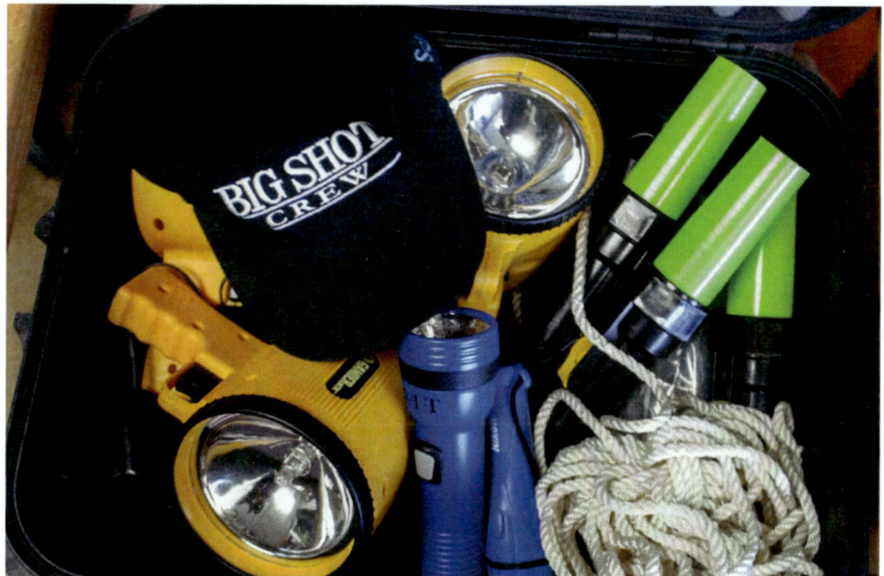

Above: Members of Big Shot team watch coordinator Dan Hughes prepare the Kodak picture file for publishing. Bottom: The Big Shot toolkit including handheld flashlights, hats, and the Big Shot good luck rope.

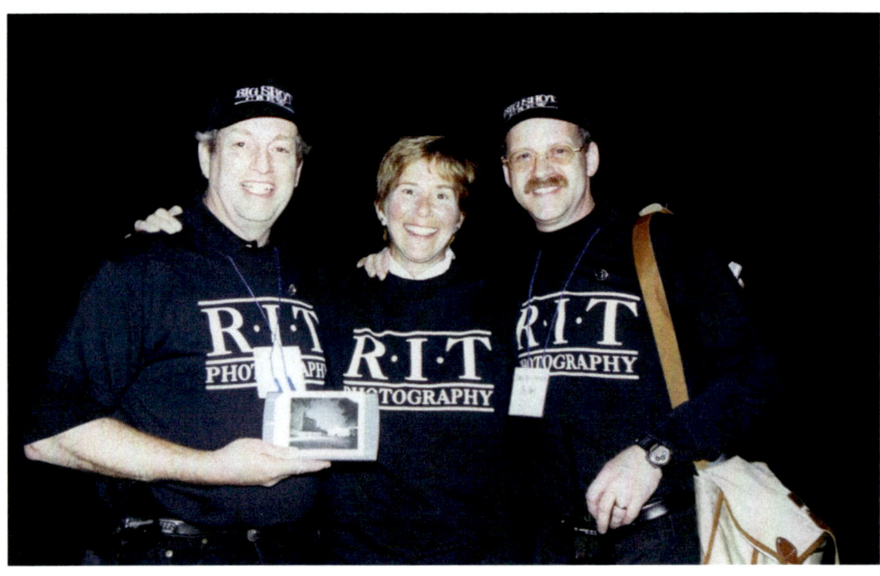

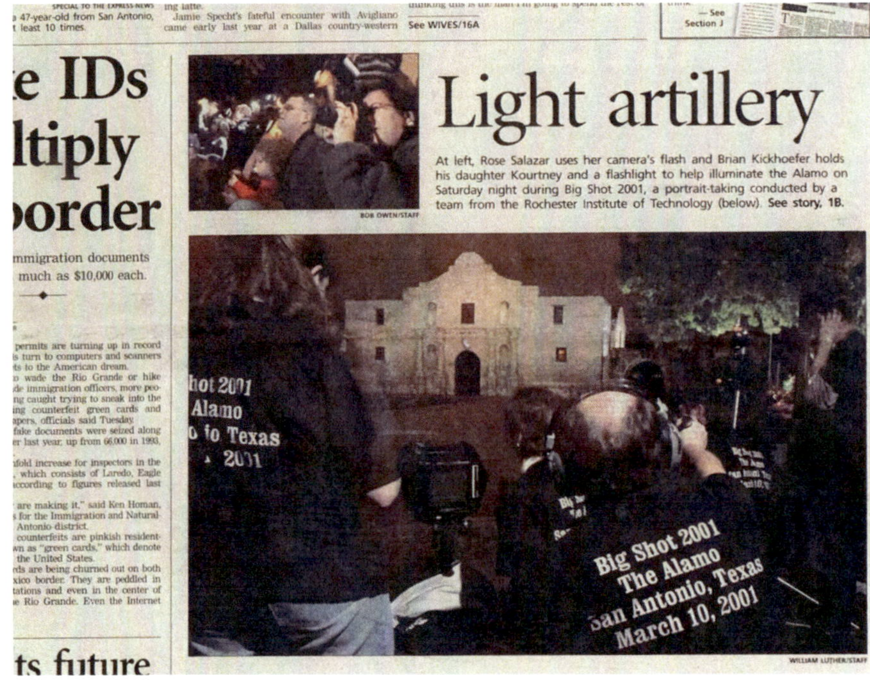

SPECIAL TO THE EXPRESS-NEWS
a 47-year-old from San Antonio,
t least 10 times.

ing latte.
Jamie Specht's fateful encounter with Avigliano came early last year at a Dallas country-western

See WIVES/16A

— See
Section J

e IDs ltiply border

mmigration documents much as $10,000 each.

permits are turning up in record s turn to computers and scanners ts to the American dream.
o wade the Rio Grande or hike de immigration officers, more peo- ng caught trying to sneak into the ing counterfeit green cards and apers, officials said Tuesday.
fake documents were seized along er last year, up from 66,000 in 1993,

fold increase for inspectors in the , which consists of Laredo, Eagle ccording to figures released last

are making it," said Ken Homan, s for the Immigration and Natural- Antonio district.
counterfeits are pinkish resident- wn as "green cards," which denote the United States.
ds are being churned out on both xico border. They are peddled in tations and even in the center of e Rio Grande. Even the Internet

ts future

Light artillery

At left, Rose Salazar uses her camera's flash and Brian Kickhoefer holds his daughter Kourtney and a flashlight to help illuminate the Alamo on Saturday night during Big Shot 2001, a portrait-taking conducted by a team from the Rochester Institute of Technology (below). **See story, 1B.**

BOB OWEN/STAFF

WILLIAM LUTHER/STAFF

Above: Big Shot founders Bill DuBois, Dawn Tower DuBois, and Michael Peres. Bottom: Front page coverage of Big Shot in the San Antonio Express. Right: article from 2001 in the San Antonio Express News promoting Big Shot No. 16 featuring the Alamo.

Alamo to get more exposure at Big Shot photography event

CONTINUED FROM 1D

Year after year, the project has grown larger and 14 years later, the Big Shot is leaving the Empire State for the Alamo City.

More than a year ago, Saldinger was in Austin for an alumni reception and approached the school's president about bringing the event to San Antonio.

RIT coordinators visited Alamo Plaza in September to study the problems and challenges of taking such an elaborate photo.

After green-lighting the project, organizers ran the plan by the Daughters of the Republic of Texas, the Alamo caretakers, who frown upon any commercial uses of the hallowed ground.

"Anything done on the Alamo complex is looked at closely. We don't jump into anything" says Mary Womack, Alamo committee chairman of the historical group.

After they learned more about the event, the Daughters gave the school their blessing. They even agreed to turn off the exterior lights.

"As far as I know, (the lights) have never been shut off. This might be the first," Womack says.

The usual hospitality of San Antonio has shined upon organizers. Not only are the Daughters cooperating, the City of San Antonio has agreed to turn off traffic lights in the area, and the nearby Emily Morgan Hotel will be asking hotel guests to close their curtains.

Of course, in addition to the canopy of trees, the historic hotel will be looming in the background — that's the way the shot is set up.

"It's merely a coincidence," says General Manager Stephen Robbins. "The real significance is the way they do this picture — it's unlike anything else."

To amateur eyes, a Big Shot photo looks like a typical nighttime photograph, but it's far from ordinary. The process makes it unique.

Participants are divided into teams and directed to strategic points, where they wave their light sources like sabers. The image is captured with two 4-by-5 cameras (one loaded with color film, one with black and white). Typical exposures last two minutes with ISO 400 at f/11. The shutter is opened, the cue is given, and the structure is awash in a stroboscopic light show, resulting in a smooth, even lighting on film.

Michael Peres, one of the Big Shot founders and coordinators, says there's a wave of excitement, laced with anxiety, as the two-minute climax approaches.

"You are totally emotionally spent when it's over," he says.

The Alamo film will be rushed to Alamo Photolabs and placed in the capable hands of owner Wilson Parish, also an RIT alum.

"It's planned to the nth degree once the film is exposed," he says. "It's kind of like the space shuttle lift-off. One thing goes wrong and it affects everything."

Although there is little room for error, the Big Shot continues to be a good educational experience for students, RIT's Peres says they learn something new about lighting and exposure every year. And it's a lot of fun for participants, who take part in a unique collective experience.

In the past, other Big Shot sites have included the Ontario County Courthouse and most recently, New York City's Intrepid Sea-Air-Space Museum. The Alamo shot will be the first Big Shot outside the state of New York.

Of course, it takes a lot of work to plan such an event, says Peres. RIT students and faculty have spent numerous hours figuring out the photographic challenges imposed by the Alamo. Not only is the Alamo a light-reflecting, chalky white, but also a surprisingly small structure.

"Our photograph has to make it look huge. It has to be the image that people think it is," Peres says.

The amount of time spent on this project has the team thinking only about the Alamo, and not the next Big Shot. Peres hopes to take a small break after the event.

"We've been planning a year and a half for 10 minutes," he adds.

"It's like a huge wedding party that you've planned, and now you hope people show up."

earadillas@express-news.net

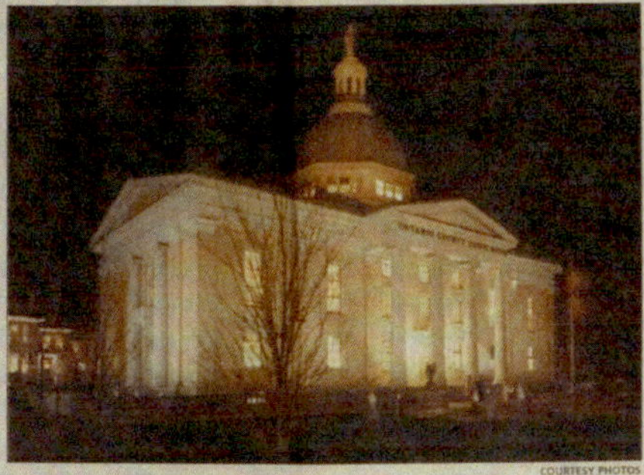

COURTESY PHOTOS

Majestic lines and columns made the George Eastman house (above left) in Rochester, N.Y., an appealing choice for this 1988 Big Shot photograph. The Ontario County Courthouse in New York is a dramatic sight at night, as illustrated by this 1998 Big Shot photo.

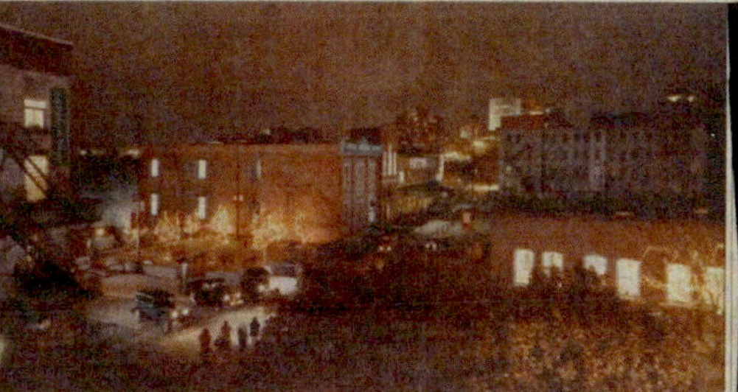

COURTESY PHOTO

External lighting was provided by many hand-held electronic flash units operated by about 200 people for this 1997 photo of the Browns Race auto event.

Big Shot 2001

What: An educational photography project organized by New York's Rochester Institute of Technology. Public is invited to help illuminate the Alamo — with camera flashes and flashlights — for a photograph with a two-minute exposure.

When: Participants gather at 6:30 p.m. Saturday; photo taken at 7:30 p.m.

Where: The Alamo

Etc: Wear dark clothing and bring a flashlight or camera flash.

"Not only are you a flasher, we teach you how to be a good flasher. . . .They (Big Shot events) are magical. You really bond with the people around you."

SCOTT SALDINGER, local project coordinator and RIT graduate

DAILY DIGEST

'Big Shot' does Alamo

Remember the Alamo?

You definitely will after it has been the subject tonight of a "Big Shot" — the periodic photography project of photo students at Rochester Institute of Technology's School of Photographic Arts and Sciences.

Under the Big Shot project, a subject is bathed in light from hundreds of sources and then photographed in a several-minute exposure.

The result is a visual effect in which the subject almost appears to glow, in stark contrast to the nighttime background.

The Big Shot started as an extracurricular photo exercise in 1987. Past targets of the Big Shot have included Mount Hope Cemetery, the High Falls business district and the aircraft carrier Intrepid, now a museum in New York City.

A group of RIT students has been in San Antonio, Texas, since earlier this week checking out the next Big Shot target — the Alamo. The results of the Big Shot will be posted on the Big Shot Web site.

A series of pictures will be posted throughout this afternoon into tonight.

Go to:
www.rit.edu-biomed/activities/bigshot.html

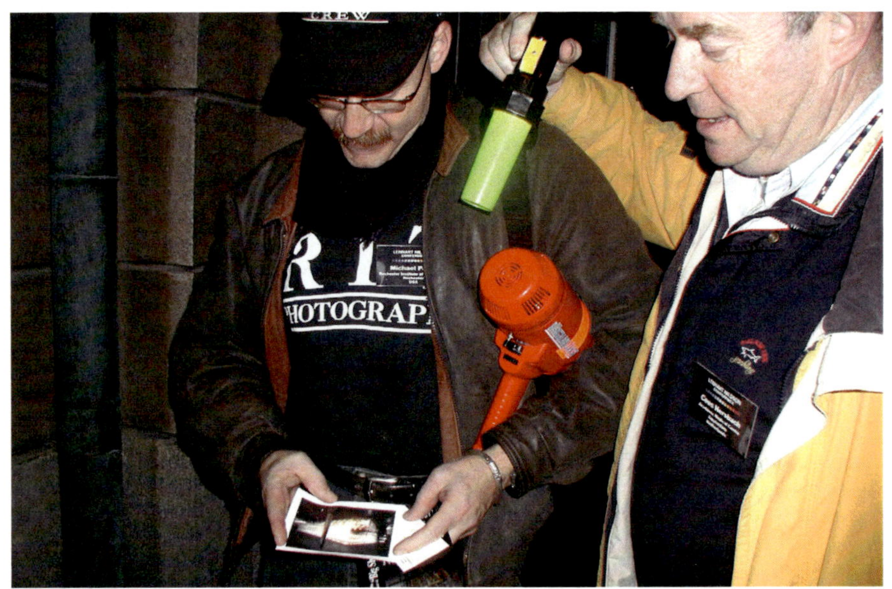

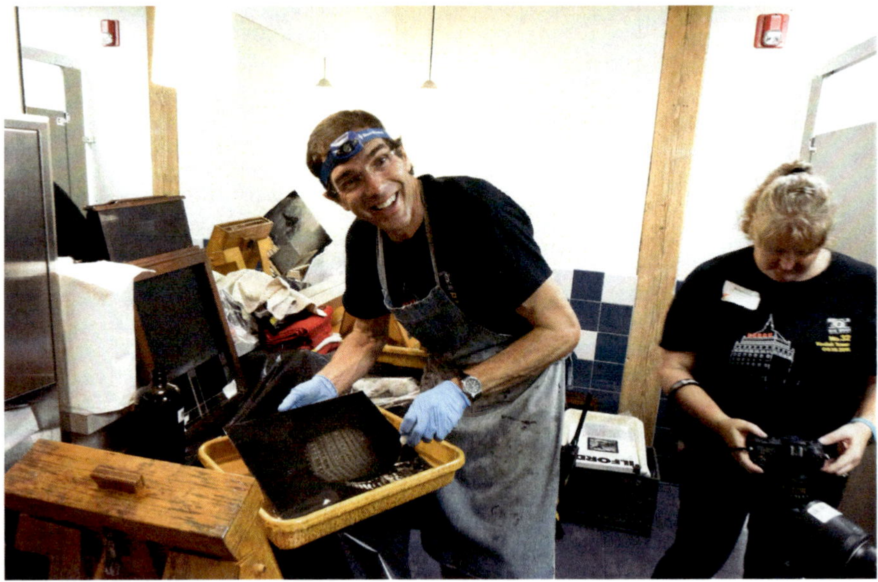

Above: Michael Peres reviews the Polaroid test shot with Dutch photographer Cees Hersbach featuring Royal Palace in Stockholm, Sweden in October 2003. Bottom: RIT professor Willie Osterman evaluates the 11 × 14 wet plate collodion image of the Eastman Kodak Building with Nikon Professional Services member Kristine Bosworth. Right, Above: RIT student Ben Lubin broadcasts the Cowboys Stadium Big Shot live on Google® Hangout. In the background is the camera platform. Bottom: A diagram of the lighting plan for Big Shot No. 28 Cowboys Stadium.

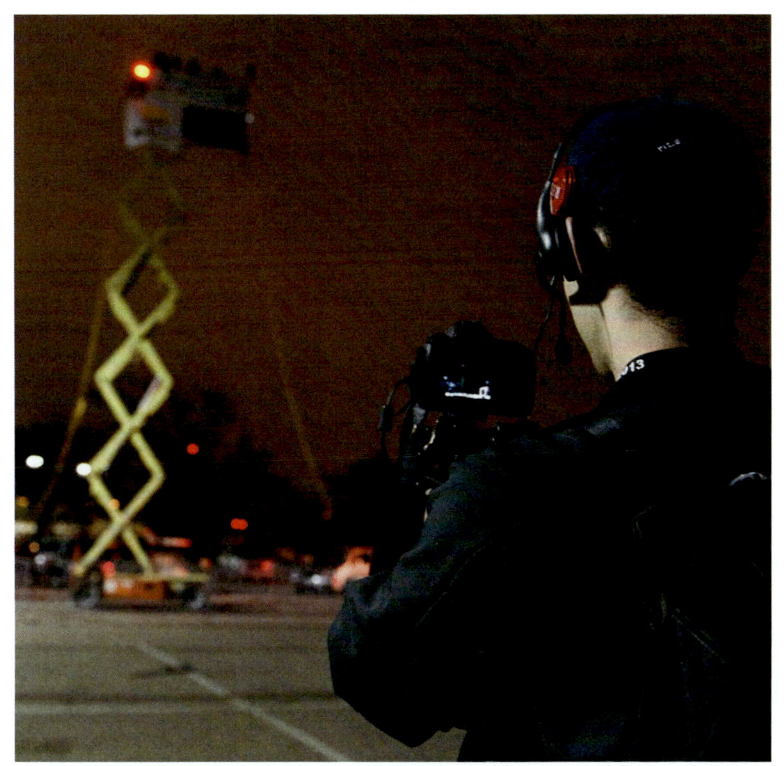

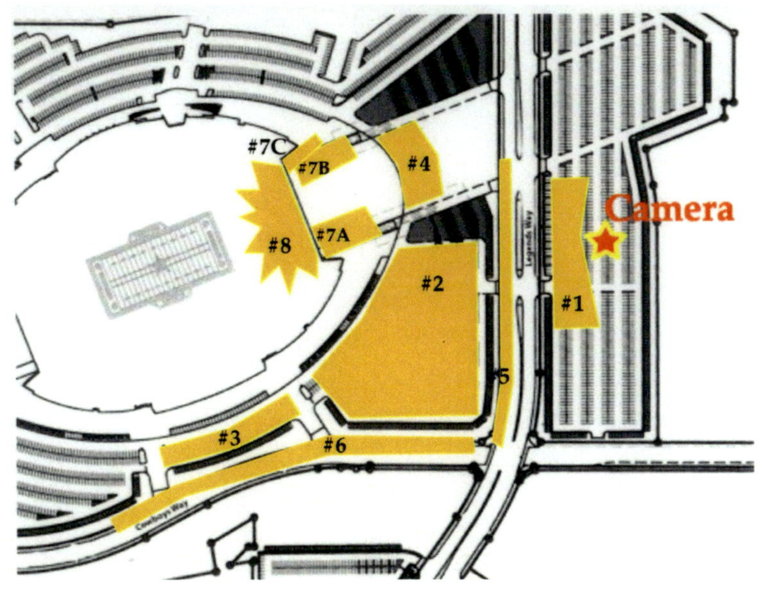
#7C
#7B
#4
Camera
#8
#7A
#2
#1
5
#3
#6

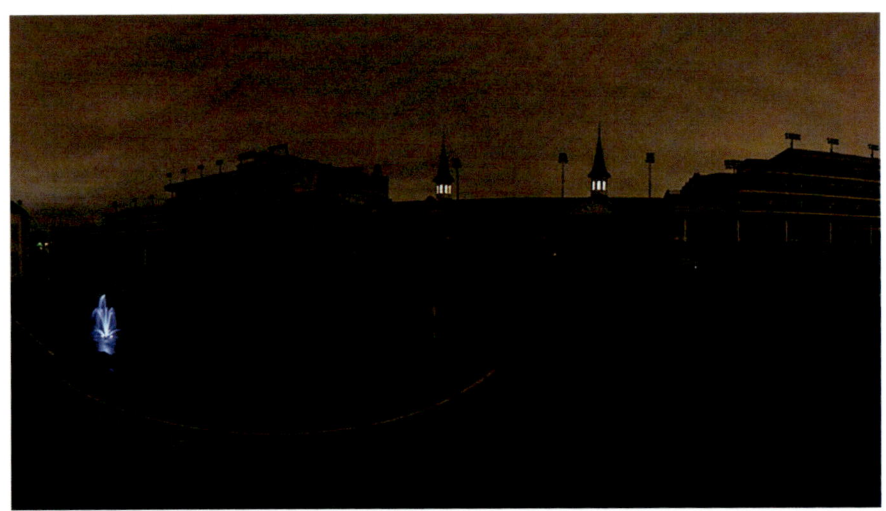

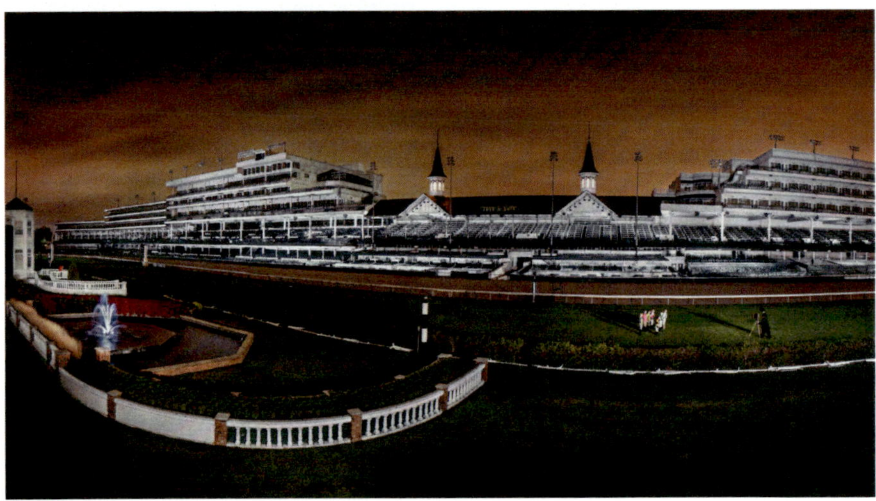

Above: The before and after painting with light photographs featuring Big Shot No. 31, Churchill Downs, October 3, 2015. Right: The promotional poster produced for Big Shot No. 14 featuring the Intrepid Air Sea & Space Museum, New York City, October 1999.

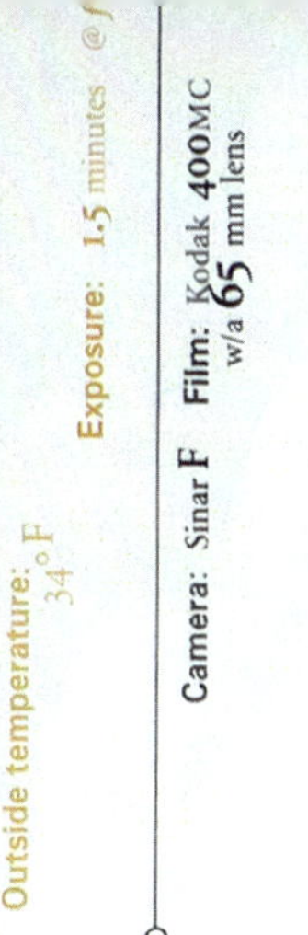

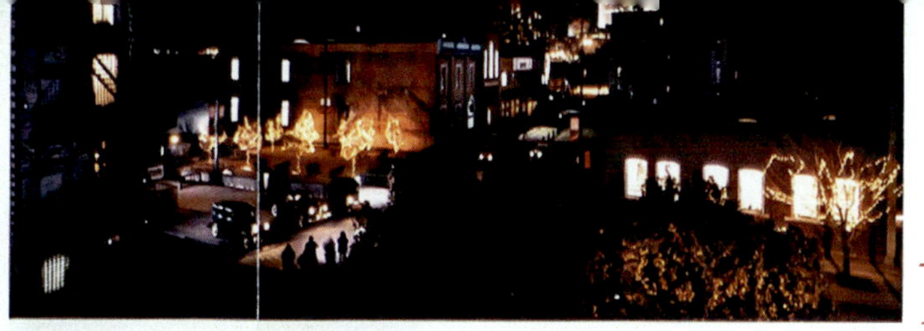

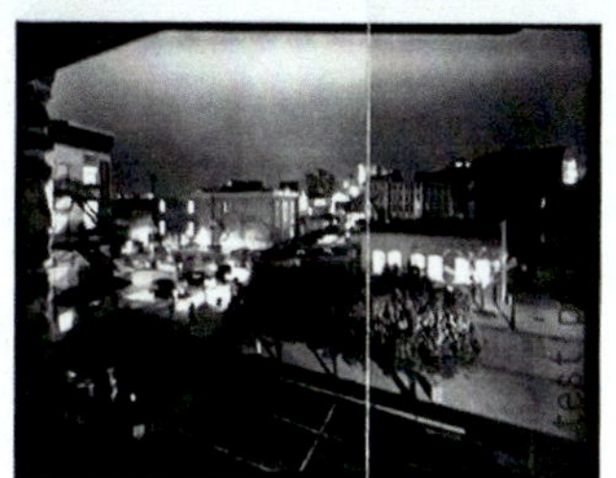

1997 Browns Race Rochester, NY

A Painting with Light Experience

All external lighting was provided by multiple hand held electronic flash units operated by approximately 200 people

sponsorship includes:

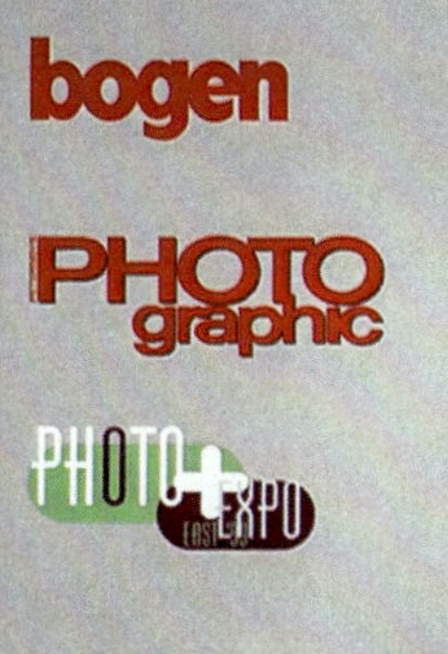

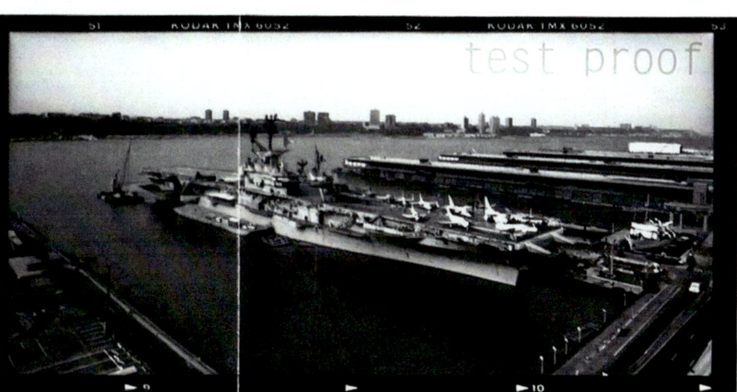

Kodak

SEKONIC

studio photography&design

The BIG SHOT

A major subject illuminated with hand held flash units by teams of volunteers

2000 volunteers needed

Sponsored by Rochester Institute of Technology
School of Photographic Arts & Sciences

October 28, 1999

6:10 pm - arrive at Pier 84
for team positioning and instruction

7:10 pm - shoot

*bring a business or 3x5 card with name and address to receive a free momento 8"x10" color print.

For further information:
Donna / 716.475.2863
DMS2334@rit.edu

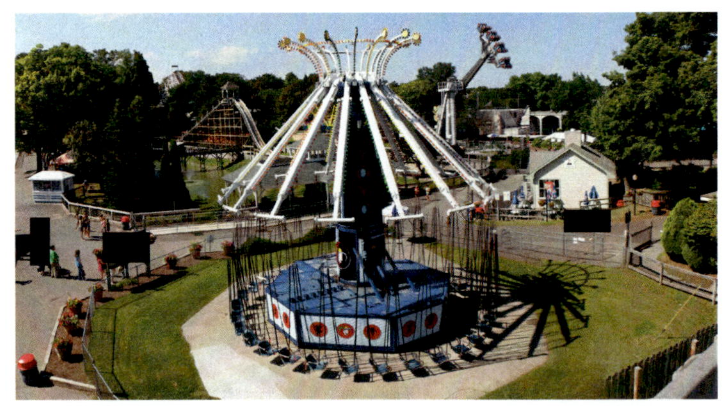

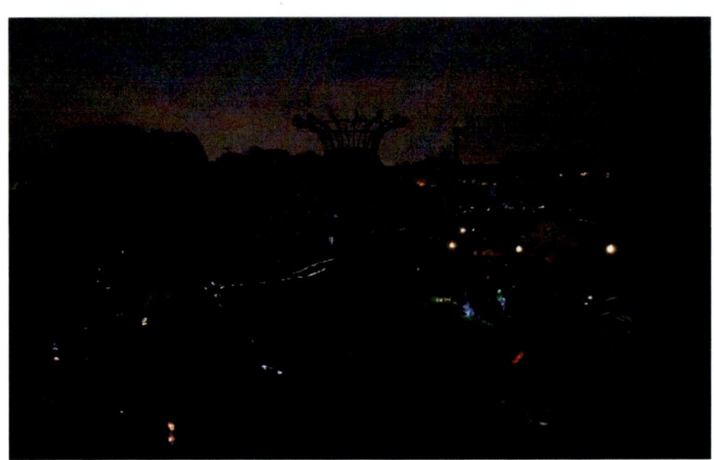

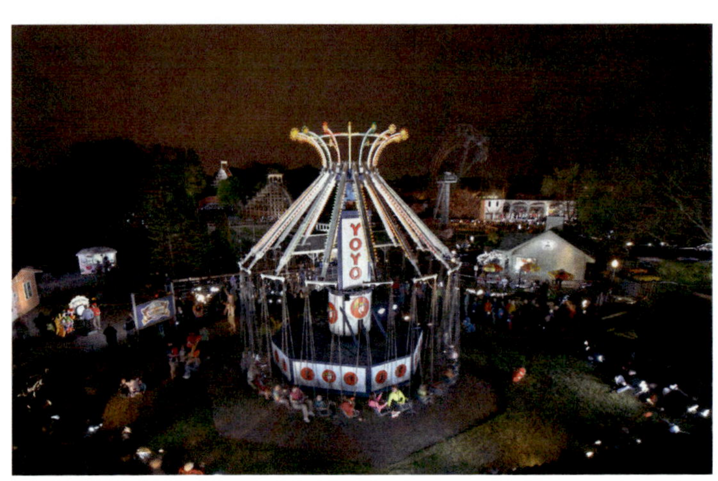
YOYO

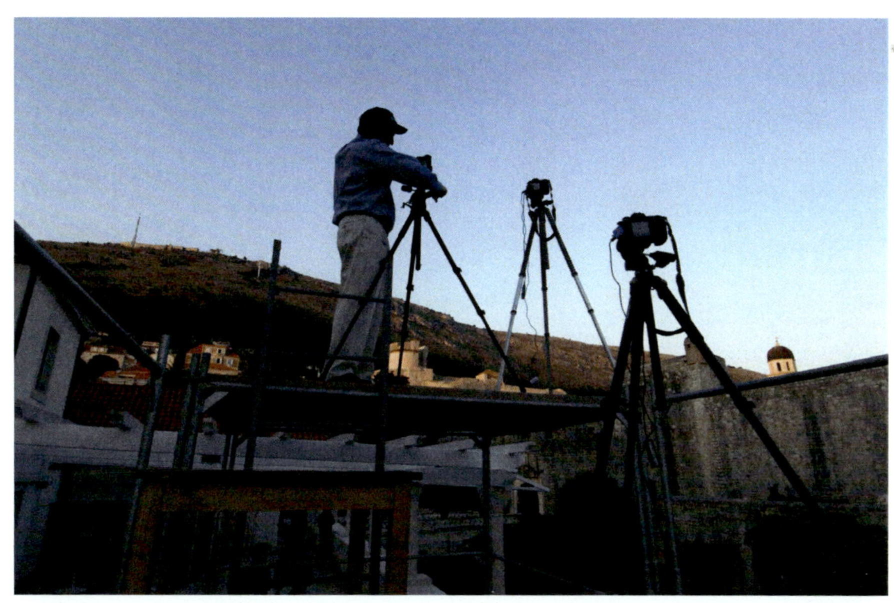

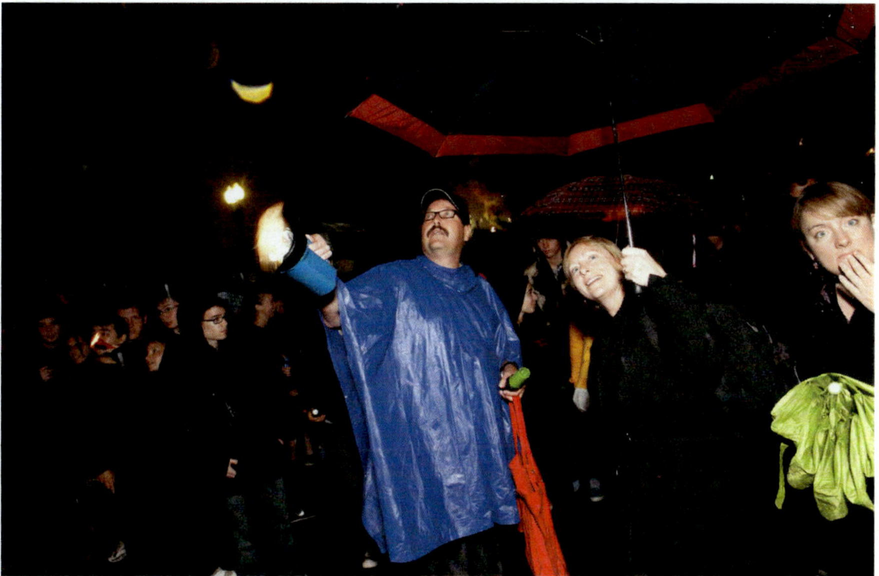

Above: Big Shot coordinator Bill DuBois readies the cameras on scaffolding to record the photograph of the Pile Gate in Dubrovnik, Croatia, April 2007. Below: Professor Denis Defibaugh paints with light during a driving rain storm when photographing Big Shot No. 25, National Museum of the American Indian, Washington, DC., September 2009. Left: The daytime, before and after painting with light photographs featuring Big Shot No. 26 at Seabreeze Amusement Park, Rochester, New York, May 2011.

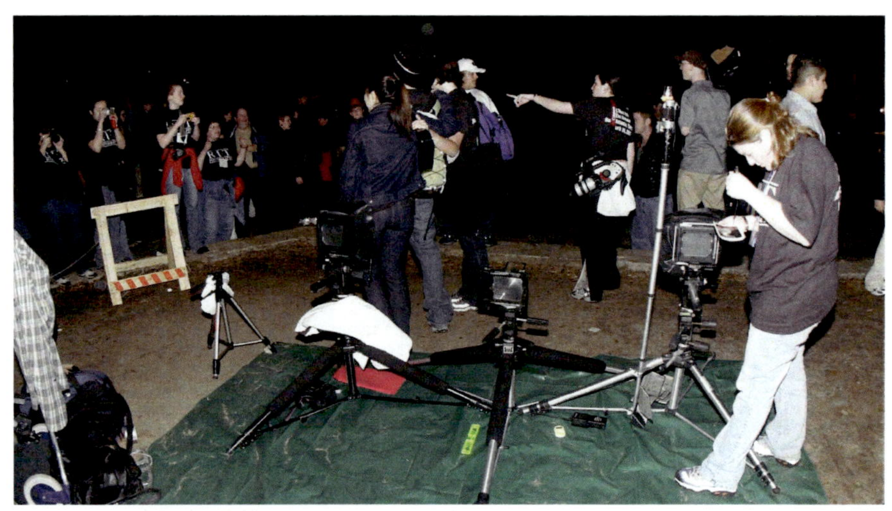

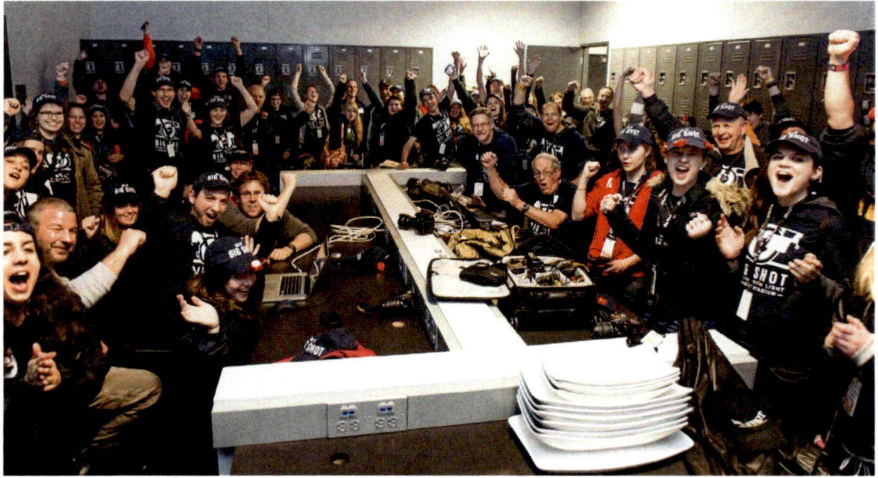

Above: Students and Big Shot photographers with 4 × 5 film cameras used for photograph the Alamo in San Antonio, Texas, March 2000 . Below: The RIT Big Shot team celebrates the publishing of the Cowboys Stadium Big Shot No. 28 in the media room March 2013. Right: Big Shot No. 20 was featured on the front page of the daily Stockholm City newspaper October 10, 2003.

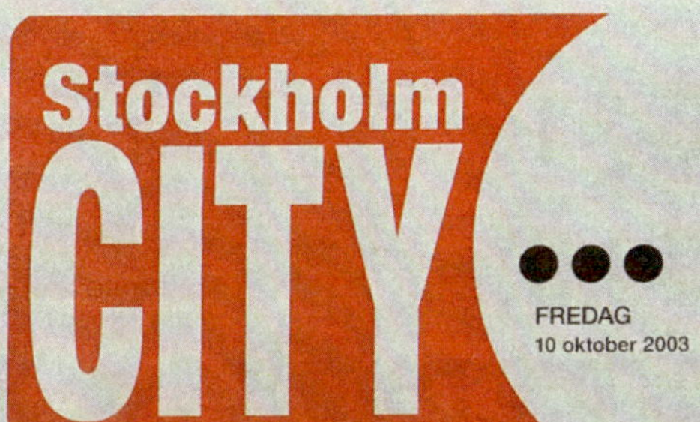

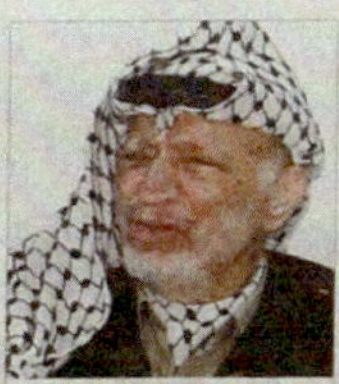

Arafats nya minister vill redan avgå

VÄRLDEN SIDAN 11

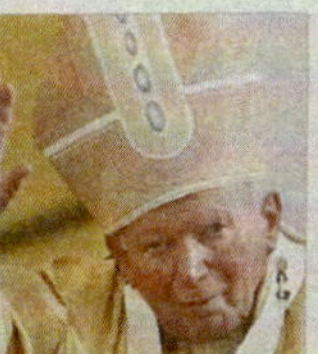

I dag kan han få Nobels fredspris

VÄRLDEN SIDAN 12

Så mycket dyrare kan ditt SL-kort bli

Politisk strid hotar om tjänstemännens förslag till landstinget

LÄNET. Landstingets tjänstemän vill höja priset på SL-kortet med en hundring eller mer. Det kan bli en politisk strid i landstinget. Socialdemokraterna är öppna för alla sätt att lösa landstingskrisen – men vänsterpartiet och miljöpartiet vill hellre höja skatten än SL-kortet.

Tillsammans lovade partierna att inte höja priset förrän 2005 när de fick makten. Även om priset nu skulle höjas krävs en rejäl skattehöjning för att fylla budgethålet på 3,2 miljarder. SIDAN 2

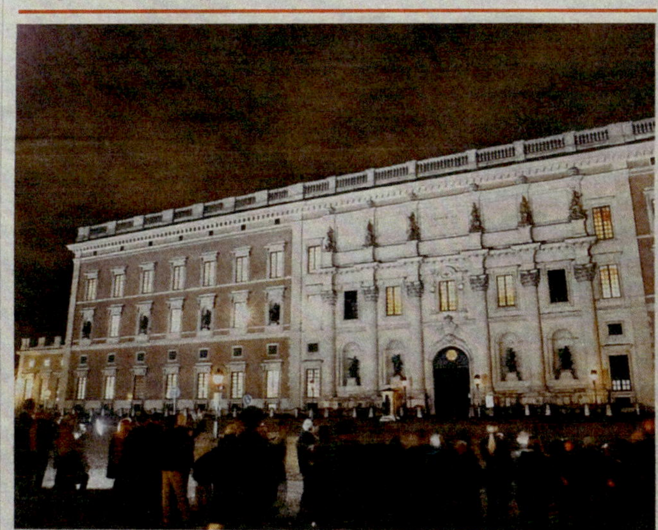

Cirka 400 personer ställde i går kväll upp för att sätta ljus på det Kungliga slottet. Belysningen, som var en del i fotoprojektet "Big shot", bestod av allt från pannlampor till spotlights. Foto: PRESSENS BILD

Stockholmarna hjälptes åt att lysa upp slottet

SLOTTSBACKEN. Pierre Almén från Järfälla kom till slottet i går med en orienteringslampa på huvudet. Pierre var en av de uppåt 400 frivilliga som såg till att tre amerikanska professorer kunde pläta vårt slott i the "Big shot". Idén går ut på att pläta olika byggnader i kvälls- eller nattmörker och poängen är att byggnaderna lyses upp av frivillig arbetskraft.

Gårdagens fotografering var unik. Hittills har bara amerikanska byggnader fotograferats. SIDAN 6

Lågprisjätten Lidl viker sig för facket

SKÄRHOLMEN. Tyska lågpriskedjan Lidl har gett efter för kraven från Handels. Företaget slopar en rad omdiskuterade formuleringar om bland annat tystnadsplikt i villkoren för de butiksanställda. SIDAN 3

Södertörns högskola kan bli universitet

SÖDERTÖRN. 12 stockholmspolitiker motionerar om att göra Södertörns högskola till universitet.

– Det skulle ge regionen en injektion. Det behövs, säger Niclas Lindberg (s), riksdagsledamot. SIDAN 7

Anders Milton ska rädda psykvården

SVERIGE. Anders Milton blir mannen som ska se över den svenska psykvården. I går utsågs han av regeringen – men några formella direktiv har han ännu inte fått. SIDAN 8

City kollar in Sveriges hjältar och hjältinnor

SPORT. Det råder fotbollsfeber i Sverige – av en like vi inte sett sedan 1994 då herrarna tog VM-brons i USA. City har jämfört de två mästerskapen. Se så lika de är. SIDAN 13

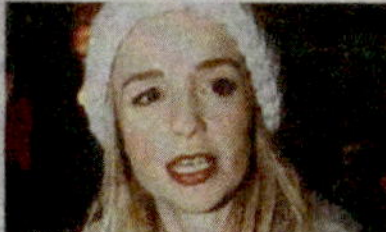

Lisa Ekdahl ger sig ut på vägarna.

Elva sidor om helgens Stockholmsnöjen

NÖJE. I kväll hålls en hyllningsfest till Bob Dylan på Kägelbanan. Och i morgon kommer rocklegenden själv att inta Globen. Rock'n'roll kör även Owe Thörnqvist på scenen på Tyrol alltmedan Lisa Ekdahl förbereder sig för en ny turné. SIDORNA 16–24

ANDERS CARLBERG:

Snålheten bedrar visheten

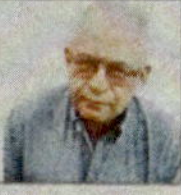

SIDAN 4

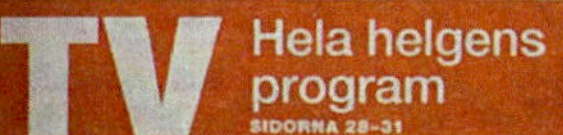

STOCKHOLMSVÄDRET I DAG

10°

SIDAN 4

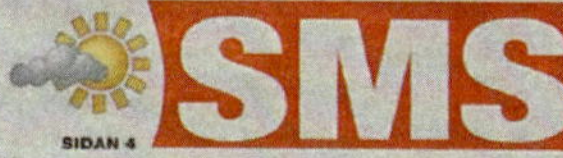

SIDAN 17

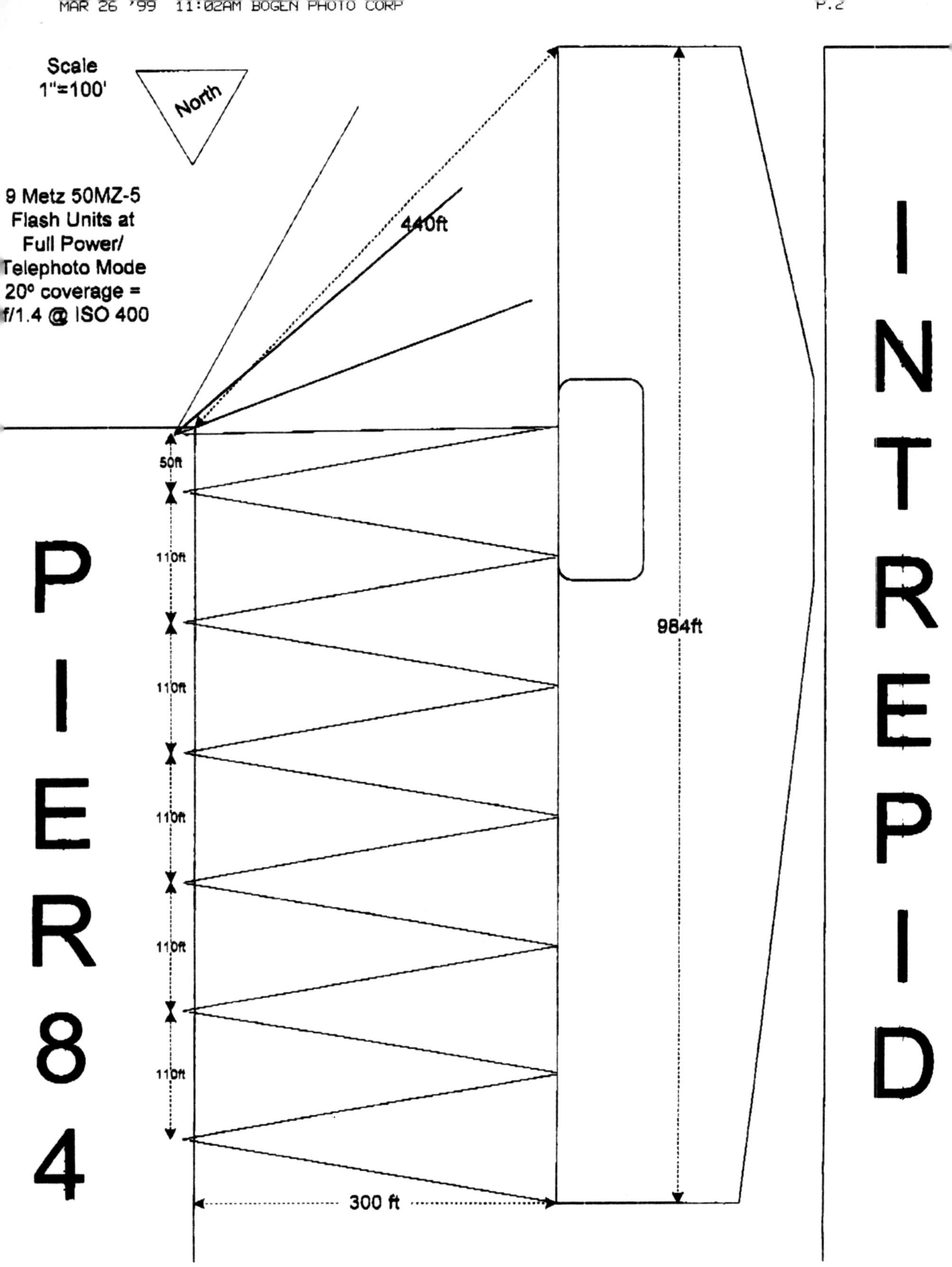
Scale
1"=100'
North
9 Metz 50MZ-5
Flash Units at
Full Power/
Telephoto Mode
20º coverage =
f/1.4 @ ISO 400
440ft
50ft
110ft
110ft
110ft
110ft
110ft
984ft
300 ft
PIER 84
INTREPID

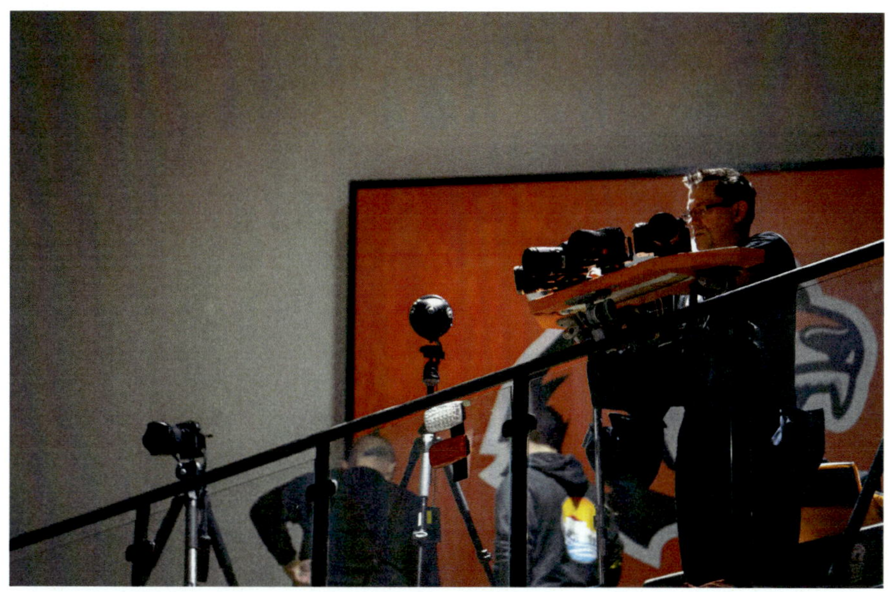

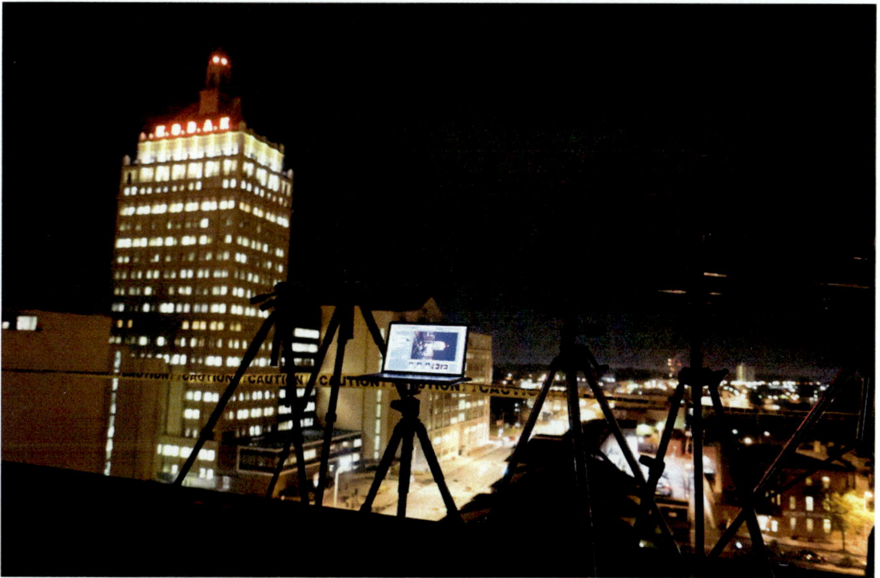

Above: Big Shot coordinator Eric Kunsman readies the cameras to be used for the first inside Big Shot No. 34, April 2022. Below: Some of the cameras positioned on the roof of the Rochester Button Factory used to photograph the Kodak world headquarters. Left: The lighting plan prepared for use of 16 Metz flashes to light Intrepid Air, Sea & Space Museum in New York City.

Big Shot Past and Future

Throughout its history, the Big Shot project has been featured by CNN, the Washington Post, the Dallas Morning News and countless other news sites, including the Chronicle of Higher Education. In 2009, Rochester's PBS station, WXXI, produced a nationally released 48-minute documentary on the unique history of the Big Shot.

No matter how complicated a project, the Big Shot always remained true to its mission of solving nighttime photographic problems using teamwork while building community for students and public alike. Dawn Tower DuBois, retired Professor from the National Technical Institute for the Deaf, and one of the original Big Shot organizers, shared the Big Shot always drew large crowds: "We were always appreciative of responses from the communities where the project went and it is really something special to have been a part of."

"Participant responses to the photographs, their experiences, and their excitement is what kept us coming back year after year," Professor Michael Peres, another one of the Big Shot co-founders commented when reflecting on the projects he helped produce along with his colleagues.

Emeritus Professor Bill DuBois also a co-founder shared "...we were initially drawn to subjects that had character and interesting details. We tried to light them in unusual and new ways."

Big Shot has realized outcomes no one could have imagined. The photographs are the direct result of the energy, ideas, creativity, support, and selfless contributions of countess members of the extended RIT and School of Photographic Arts and Sciences communities including faculty and staff, students, alums, and Big Shot aficionados. Over the decades, new members/ coordinators assumed leadership roles including Willie Osterman, Therese Mulligan, Christye Sisson, Mike Dear, Debbie Kingsbury, Donna Sterlace, Lisa DeRomanis, Mary Lavendar, Betsy Saxe, Ron Goldberg, David Turner and Clay Patrick McBride enabling the project to grow and explore more ambitious challenges. Today, Eric Kunsman and Dan Hughes are the project's primary coordinators and have their eye on new exciting things.

Recently, on April 2, 2022, Big Shot No. 34 was produced on the RIT campus with an interior view of Ritter Arena, the temporary home of the University's library collections. Students drawn from the Photography School and across campus contributed to the realization of the project. Thirty-four years in the making, the Big Shot continues in the hands of a new generation of organizers and participants, with new sites both near and far considered for future shoots, ensuring the lasting legacy of the project for years to come.

Acknowledgements

Spanning thirty-five years, the expression — it takes a village — describes the Big Shot project's essential constitution. It relies on students, volunteers and generous sponsors who have enabled the project to evolve while engaging evermore challenging photographic and location endeavors in places such as Dallas, Washington, New York and Dubrovnik. This exhibition celebrates all those who contributed to the making of Big Shot photographs. A special debt of gratitude is owed to Rochester Institute of Technology, College of Art and Design, National Technical Institute for the Deaf, and the School of Photographic Arts and Sciences for their support. Big Shot organizers also recognize the special contributions of Nikon Professional Services for its premier sponsorship and collaboration. The prints in this exhibition were expertly produced in the Imaging Systems Lab and the exhibition booklets were produced by the Visual Communications Studies department | NTID.

Big Shot Coordinators
Dan Hughes, Eric Kunsman

Committee Members
Michael Peres
Willie Osterman
Debbie Kingsbury
Clay Patrick McBride
David Turner
Therese Mulligan
Christye Sisson
Mike Dear
Ron Goldberg

Administrative Coordinator
Lisa DeRomanis

Emeritus Coordinators
Bill DuBois, 1987–2013
Dawn Tower DuBois,1987–2014

Supporters & Sponsors

BioCommunications Association (BCA)

Eastman Kodak Company

Laura Burroughs Zigarowicz, Kodak Branding Officer

McGowan Foundation

Nikon Inc. USA

Nikon Professional Services (NPS)

Bill Pekala, Retired Director, NPS

Kris Bosworth, NPS

Profoto USA

Bill Gratton, Prophoto

Joe Lavine, Prophoto

SanDisk

Shades of Paper

Studio Photographic Design Magazine

Sunpak Corporation

Ted Van Horne, Chief Operating Officer, Global Medical Response

Xerox Corporation

Rochester Institute of Technology

Albert Simone, President 1992–2007

William Destler, President 2007–2017

David Munson, President 2017–present

Bill Springer, Photo Lab Manager, College of Art and Design

Betsy Saxe, Budget Director, College of Imaging Arts and Science

David Walter, Operations Manager School of Photographic Arts & Sciences

Debbie Stendardi, Vice President of Community Relations, 1979–2020

Dr Linda Kuk, Vice President of Student Affairs, 1993–2002

Ed Lincoln, Assistant Vice President, Enrollment Marketing

Frank Cost, Interim Dean, College of Imaging Arts and Science, 1982–2022

Henry Navas '74, '77 (MBA, Accounting)

James Watters, Senior Vice President Finance and Administration

Jerry Hafner, Provost, 2008–2018

Kelly Sorensen, formerly RIT University News

Laurel Price Jones, Vice President Development and Alumni Relations, 2005

Lisa Vasaturo, College of Art and Design Advancement

Mary Beth Cooper, Vice President Student Affairs, 2001–2013

Melinda Ward, Associate Vice President Global Risk Management Services (GRMS)

Otto Vondrak '99 (BFA, Graphic Design)

Paul Stella, formerly RIT University News

Paul Meunzer, RIT Professional Advisor

J. Fernando Naveda, Department of Software Engineering, 1999–2019

Rich Kiley, RIT University News

Scott Saldinger, '91 (film and video), Big Shot Groupie

Students, Faculty & Friends of RIT Photography

Todd Jokl, Dean, College of Art and Design

Wendy Marks, University Gallery Director

National Technical Institute for the Deaf, Rochester Institute of Technology (NTID)

NTID Theater Costume Department

RIT Alumni Relations

RIT Amateur Radio Club

RIT Biomedical Photographic Communications Dept.

RIT Campus Safety

RIT Center for Imaging Science

RIT Dining Services

RIT Division of Student Affairs

RIT Electronic Pre-Press Lab, School of Printing

RIT Facilities Management Services

RIT Innovation Center

RIT Office the Provost

RIT Public Safety

RIT School of Photographic Arts and Sciences

RIT School of Art, Faculty & Students

RIT The Center for Orientation and Transition

Imaging Services Lab (ISL), College of Art and Design

The Center for Integrated Manufacturing Studies

Rochester, New York

City of Rochester Police Department, Special Events Unit

City of Rochester, Bureau of Water & Street Lighting

City of Rochester

City of Rochester, Office of Special Events

Cornhill Navigation

DiMarco Constructors

ESL Federal Credit Union

EnterCom Radio

Flaum Management

Frontier Field

George Eastman Museum

High Falls Business Association

Highland Hospital

Hugh Ives, Director of Special Projects, Rochester Gas and Electric

Industrial Communications

Infinity Radio stations

James McIntosh, City Engineer

John August, LLD Enterprises

Jim Cardella, Director of Special Projects, Seabreeze Amusement Park

Julia K. Caters

King Sales/Costume City

Lamar Advertising

M.L. Caccamise Electric

Memorial Art Gallery

Monroe Community

College Rochester

Monroe County Bureau of Traffic Lights

Mount Hope Cemetery

Nazareth College

Ned Kelly, Rochester City Lighting Engineer

Park Ridge Hospital

Democrat & Chronicle

Rochester Gas & Electric

Rochester Museum & Science Center

Rochester Red Wings Minor League Baseball Team
Rundel Memorial Library
Ryder Trucks, Inc.
S. R. Bacher Electric
Seabreeze Amusement Park
Stephanie Gradinger, Office of Special Projects, City of Rochester
The Asset One
Todd McCammon, Vice President WXXI Public Broadcasting
U-Haul of Henrietta
WHEC-TV / News10NBC
Wilmorite Corporation
WROC-TV

New York State

Genesee Country Village Museum, Mumford, NY
Genesee Valley Antique Car Society
M & T Bank, Buffalo, NY
Old Fort Niagara
Ontario County & Courthouse
Personnel, Canandaigua, NY
Schoen Place, LLC
Village of Pittsford

New York City

Bogen
Hasselblad
Intrepid Air, Sea, and Space Museum
Nextel
Petersen's Photographic Supply
Photo District News
Photo Plus East
Sekonic
United Parcel Service

Arlington, Texas

Art on the Green
Steve Moya, Art on the Greene
Association of Texas Photo Instructors
Decima Cooper, Director of Public
Relations and Communications, Experience Arlington
Brett Daniels, Director of Special
Projects Cowboys Football Stadium
Bill Porter, Arlington Camera
Amy Dodenhoff, Catering and Special Events Manager, Legends Hospitality
City of Arlington
Cowboys Stadium
Dallas Cowboys Football Organization
Jerry Jones Foundation
Manfrotto
Mark Murray, Coordinator, Technology Systems, Arlington ISD
Paul O'Brien, President & CEO, Tactical Impulse
Reginald Lewis, Communication Coordinator, Arlington Chamber of Commerce

San Antonio, Texas

Alamo Photo Labs
City of San Antonio
Coach USA Transportation
Emily Morgan Hotel
Daughters of the Republic of Texas, Custodians of the Alamo
IMAX Theaters
KMOL TV Channel 4

Dallas, Texas

American Medical Response
Carlos Nacarro, Sales Manager, BlueStar Graphics & Design
High School Photographers of Texas Association
National Ambulance
NBC 5 – KXAS
Southwest Airlines
Tactical Impulse
Telemundo Dallas

Louisville, Kentucky

Churchill Downs
Mark Stone, Director of Special Projects, Churchill Downs
Louisville Photo Biennial
Mohawk Paper
Murphy's Camera
Paul Paletti Gallery
Revelry Gallery
St. James Art Festival

Washington D.C.

National Museum of the American Indian, Smithsonian Institution

Florida

CSX Railroad, Jacksonville

Dubrovnik , Croatia

American College of Management & Technology, Dubrovnik
City of Dubrovnik
Don Hudspeth, President and Dean, RIT Croatia
Dubrovnik Tourism Bureau
Friends of the Wall, Dubrovnik

Stockholm, Sweden

Jakob Forsell
Lennart Nilsson Conference
Staffan Larsson, Karolinska Institute
Swedish Royal Palace

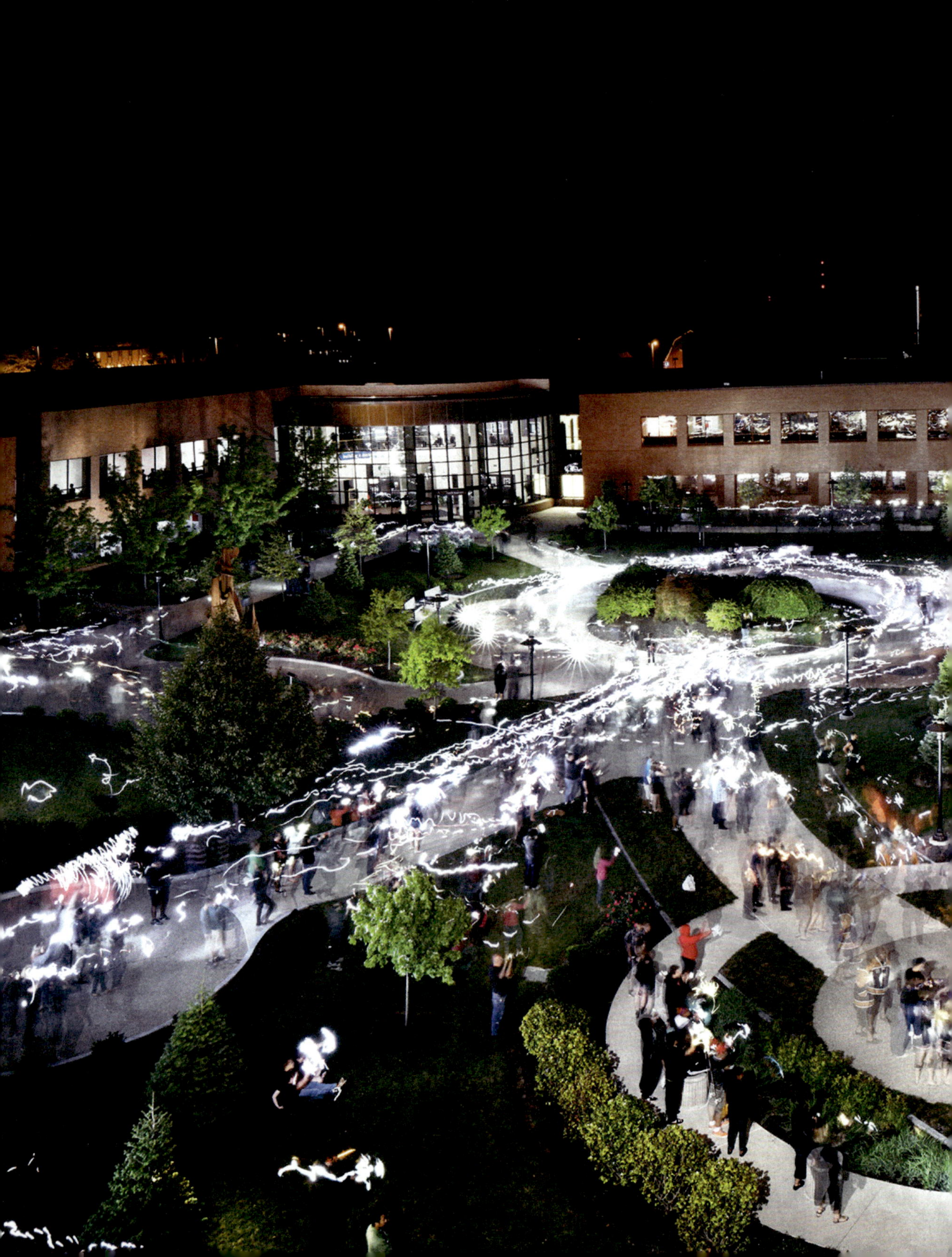

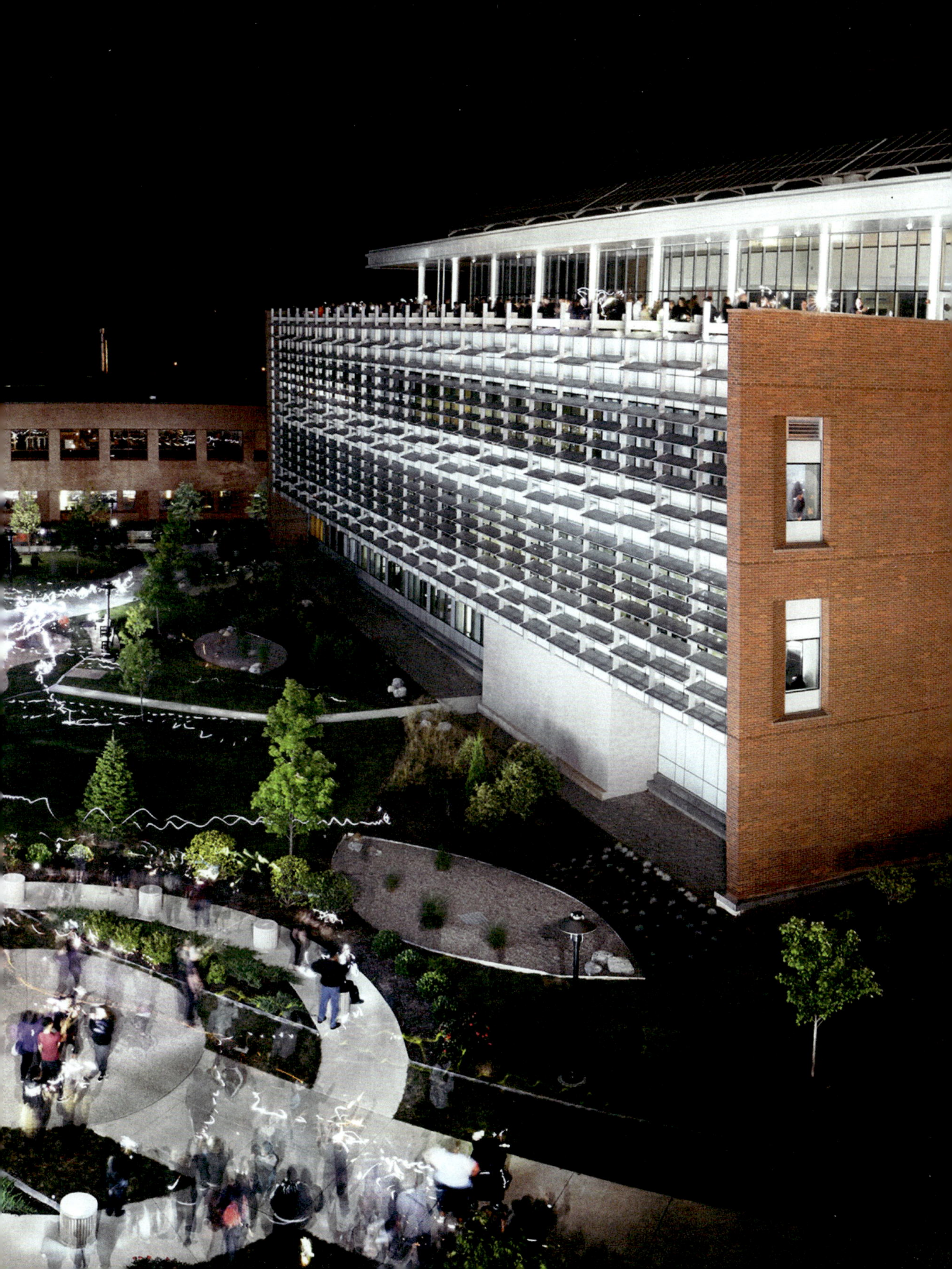

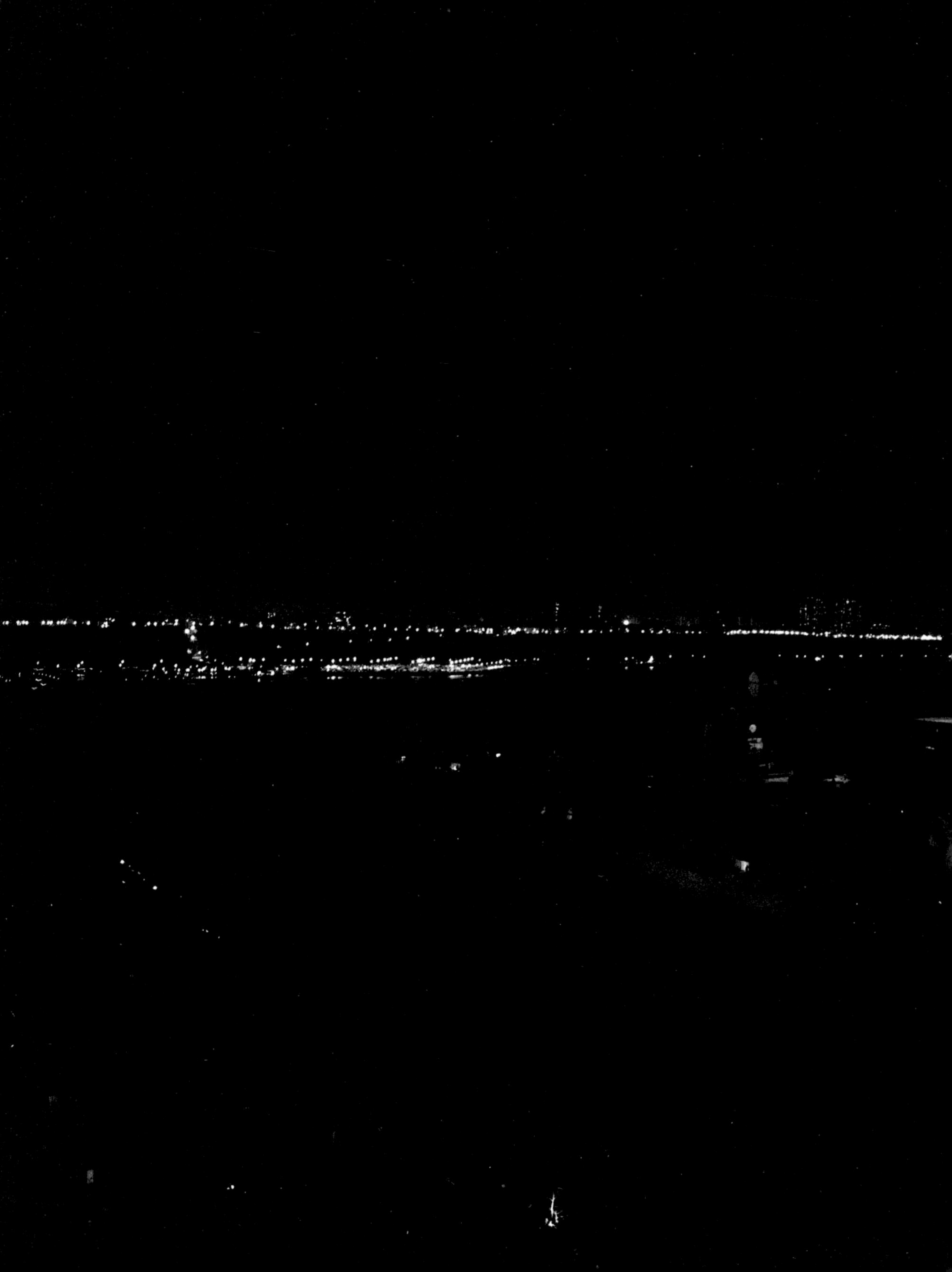